D1528778

# The Rainmakers

# The Rainmakers

AMERICAN "PLUVICULTURE" TO
WORLD WAR II

CLARK C. SPENCE

UNIVERSITY OF NEBRASKA PRESS
LINCOLN AND LONDON

Publishers on the Plains

UNP

**Library of Congress Cataloging in Publication Data**

Spence, Clark C
  The rainmakers.

  Includes bibliographical references and index.
  1. Rain-making—United States—History.
I. Title.
QC928.7.S69     551.6'8     79–26022
ISBN 0–8032–4117–8

Portions of Chapters 3 and 4 have previously been published, in somewhat different form, as "The Dyrenforth Rainmaking Experiment: A Government Venture in 'Pluviculture'," *Arizona and the West* 3 (Autumn 1961): 205–32, and "Melbourne, the Australian Rain Wizard," *Annals of Wyoming* 33, no. 1 (April 1961): 5–18.

*For Dorothy and Johnny*

# Contents

*A section of illustrations follows page 86.*

# Preface

It was many years ago that my interest was first aroused in the subject of rainmaking by a brief paragraph in Walter P. Webb's *The Great Plains*. In the course of time I gleaned much information from periodicals and newspapers, collecting material as an avocation while pursuing other research projects. Eventually, I spent a summer at the National Archives in Washington, where in "the old days" archivist Harold Pinkett turned me loose in the stacks to browse for myself among the records of the United States Weather Bureau—a freedom I have always appreciated. I am also indebted to the staffs of the U.S. Weather Bureau Library at Suitland, Maryland; the Los Angeles Public Library; the U.C.L.A. Library; the San Diego Historical Society; the Kansas Historical Society in Topeka; and the California Room of the San Diego Public Library. I have profited greatly from the aid of R. Sylvan Dunn of the Southwest Collections at Texas Tech University and from the sharp eye of Elizabeth M. Daniels, who called my attention to the Wilder D. Bancroft manuscripts in the John M. Olin Library at Cornell University. I also wish to thank Lee Scamehorn of the University of Colorado for making a number of early newspaper citations available to me. In their graduate school days, Claire Booth King, Joseph E. King, and Berry Hoffman showed perseverance and imagination is chasing down many of the details of the "pluviculture" story. Although a number of peope made positive contributions to this study, the results are my responsibility alone.

                                                            Clark C. Spence

# 1. As Intriguing as the Idea of Perpetual Motion: Setting the Stage

Sing a song of sixpence
A warehouse full of wheat
Of all the season's good things
This rain just can't be beat.[1]

On a cool day in mid-November 1946, General Electric scientist Vincent J. Schaefer flew over a cloud east of Schenectady and scattered three pounds of dry ice over it. Still in the air, he watched as it began to precipitate snow, then turned to his pilot and shook hands. "We did it," he said.[2] Schaefer was the brilliant laboratory assistant of Nobel laureate Irving Langmuir. Working together on problems related to cloud physics, the two had inaugurated a new era: Schaefer had just demonstrated the feasibility of man-made rain by seeding supercooled clouds. Soon silver iodide, dropped from above or generated from the ground, would become the magical ingredient, and science would realize an ambition rooted in antiquity—at least some measure of weather modification. To be sure, even scientific cloud seeding and the extent to which it might increase rainfall or snow mass would be controversial. Meteorologists accepted the idea only grudgingly—claims were sometimes grossly exaggerated—but by the 1960s and 1970s there was no doubt that some degree of success was a reality.

But that is another story. The one told here is pre-1946 and is less scientific, more emotional, and more human. It is concerned with the aspiration of earlier Americans to control the heavens and produce or prevent rain by artificial means. It focuses primarily on the century or

1

so before Schaefer's epic experiment, especially the age of "pluvi-culture," from roughly 1890 to 1930.

It was a natural-born skeptic, David Starr Jordan, former chancellor of Stanford University, who invented the word *pluviculture* in 1925 to describe the growing and marketing of rainmaking schemes—"a never-failing drought crop," according to the U.S. Weather Bureau's foremost expert on the subject. Like astrology and palmistry, Jordan's "pluviculture" was a branch of "sciosophy," as he called it; it stood in the "shadow of wisdom" and was the special domain of the sharp "quacktitioneer."[3]

Only the words Jordan coined were new, not the concepts behind them. The idea of the manipulation of the weather is seemingly as old as mankind and has continued to intrigue human beings down through the ages. In ancient and primitive society mortals had to deal with the gods, to wheedle and persuade or even to use subterfuge. Thus ancient Greeks solicited rain from Zeus by prayer and sacrifice, reinforced by the rite of dipping an oak bough into spring water. Roman women in bare feet and streaming hair went in procession up the slope to the Capitol, imploring showers from the great Jupiter, head of the Roman pantheon. Mandarins of China and Korea conducted special sacrifices to bring rain or to clear the skies and were rewarded for success and punished for failure. Primitive peoples in all parts of the world sought to invoke rain by imitating lightning, thunder, or rainfall or by mimicking aquatic birds or animals. Or they sacrificed animals, especially black ones. The Iroquois burned tobacco; the Omahas sprayed water into the air from the mouth; other tribes used juggling ceremonies or medicine sticks. The Dieris of central Australia believed that when used ritually the foreskins taken from lads at circumcision had great rain-producing power. The inhabitants of some Persian villages invited rain by parading in public without turbans and in mean garb; in parts of eastern Europe women walked to the edge of the village at night to pour water on the ground, clad in no garb at all. To prevent rain or hail, primitive people also used homeopathic magic: shunning water and emphasizing fire and warmth. Thus as late as 1850 people around Château-Thierry still celebrated the midsummer festival of Saint John, believing that lighted bonfires would bring rainfall to a halt.[4]

In recent years, the links between magic and early experimental science have been explored in considerable depth, with scholars noting superficial resemblances but drawing a distinction between the two. In its time, that "elaborate and systematic pseudo-science," magic, no doubt increased man's sense of power and gave him more confidence in solving his problems of living; but as applied science brought technical solutions, reliance on magic proportionately waned, lingering sometimes as explanatory trappings for the uninformed or among the cranks and charlatans.[5] By the early nineteenth century, vestiges of the old persisted, but the beginnings of the scientific revolution were at hand.

Both American science in general and meteorology in particular were in flux at the opening of the nineteenth century. Meteorology itself has been called "an interesting example of a field in transition from folklore to science" during the fifty years or so following 1800. Already by 1800 the study of weather and the atmosphere had become a major scientific concern; research on heat would soon give birth to thermodynamics, which would contribute much to meteorology; and an increasing number of physicists and astronomers were becoming interested in meteorological questions. As the century progressed, the scientific revolution in America tore technological knowledge loose from its traditional craft moorings and anchored it firmly to science—a science which gradually became more specialized, professionalized, and institutionalized. Although historians would not necessarily agree that nineteenth-century American scientists were indifferent to basic science, the entrepreneurial climate of the era was clearly more conducive to practical applications, with a growing appreciation by the public of the role played by science and technology in the idea of progress.[6]

While Jordan's "pluviculture" was set against this background of unfolding science, it was also cast against the "Golden Age of Quackery," as Stewart Holbrook calls it. The nineteenth century was the heyday of patent medicines—for man or for beast. Snake oils, painkillers, and elixirs of life cured every ailment, from cholera to piles, scrofula to catarrh. In this era of "pipe-and-wire therapy," special vacuum or galvanic gadgets relieved the gamut of disorders, from falling hair to neuralgia and male loss of vigor. Fancy medicine shows toured the land beating the drums for "sure fire" health combinations: Doc Bevan and his pine pinon cough cure; Doc Hammon and his tapeworm remedy; Healy and Bigalow's Kickapoo Indian shows and their line of native oils, syrups, and panaceas.[7]

All Americans, both urban and rural, were prey to quacks such as these, and a host of specialized others, but farmers were especially susceptible. While the anti-intellectualism that characterized much of American agriculture at the beginning of the nineteenth century was gradually eroding, folklore and superstition persisted. By the time of the Civil War, greater mobility and the impact of the new science and technology were challenging the old concepts. Thrown suddenly into the impersonal world of trade and industry, farmers were often over-receptive to innovation and vulnerable to humbuggery of all types. Slick "plug hat fellows" descended like locusts, hawking patented beehives, incubators, or new illuminating oils. Lightning rod sales-men became both common and stereotyped. The ubiquitous seed huckster and the tree peddler, with a "tongue as long as your arm, as oily as a piece of bacon, and as loose as a calf's tail in fly-time," promised watermelons big as bushel baskets and fantastic yield from exotic Hungarian corn or Bohemian oats. Traditionally, throughout the nineteenth century, the flimflam artist went out of his way to harvest the American farmer.[8]

David Starr Jordan was speaking of a new breed of rainmaker, one who fitted this new transitional world, one who relied less on magic or religious faith and more on practical psychology, science or pseudoscience, and Everyman's confidence in the brave new technical world that was nineteenth- and twentieth-century America. Like per-petual motion or aerial flight the possibilities of rainmaking had long been inviting, in terms of both fantastic, glowing futures and poten-tialities for more prosaic fraud. By the mid-1920s, the country had experienced the gamut of rainmaking proposals, from the absurd to the plausible, from the nonsensical to the scientific, and from the innocent to the criminally fraudulent. Some ideas came from wags or crackpots and some from sincere but ignorant folk hopelessly bound to ideas that were futile; others were serious proposals from reputable men of the business or scientific community; still others were the offspring of men who flagrantly and avidly exploited the drought mentality to line their own pockets. And in all too many cases, the lines were blurred between self-delusion, ignorance, and char-latanism.

Jordan's gaudy age of "pluviculture" reflects human frailties and foibles. At the same time, it involves the dreams of common folk, usually rural, struggling against the environment. It pits amateurs against professionals: in almost every one of the hundreds of schemes for rainmaking, hail prevention, or fog dispersal prior to the mid-twentieth century, the meteorological fraternity stood firm in its opposition. As one member put it in 1921, "talking to a meteorologist about rain-making is about on par with discussing Mother Goose with Professor Einstein. It is not ordinarily done."[9]

Only a small part of the story is concerned with the "rash paradoxers," as one scientist calls them—those impractical pipe dreamers whose schemes fell far beyond the realm of practical applications. One man, for example, proposed destroying blizzards with a line of coal stoves along the northern boundary from the Red River to the Continental Divide. Another suggested tanks atop a long row of towers, to which water might be pumped and then sprayed out to induce the air to give up its moisture; he also suggested that the Weather Bureau officer who scoffed at his idea "get something in the way of a nut meg grater to work on that section of your brain that takes so ingenious a view of my plan." Another was the discoverer of a "wonderful full Herb which when boiled for 2 hours will produce Rain," though to be effective it had to be picked before November 15.[10] Still another advocated a number of large concave glasses set on platforms along oceans or rivers to focus the sun's rays and draw up water vapor, which would then cool and condense. A Denverite offered for a million dollars "to sweep the sky with a certain ray and make it rain," while a more modestly-priced rain advocate urged the president: "Just send me $100,000 (one hundred thousand dollars in gold) and the country will have plenty of rainfall." More than one American in the 1930s attributed drought to radio broadcasting; others blamed pollution from automobiles and industry; one person even believed that "the intense vibrations of modern life completely abridge and render inert the natural vibrations and concussions that occur in nature and which are vital to production of rain and seasonable climate."[11]

Down to 1946 most of the weather modification proposals involved milking the clouds of their moisture; for convenience they may be classified in one of several categories. There were those proposals, first of all, based on the upward convection of warm, moist air, either through the use of ground fires, in the manner of James Espy, or by means of conduits or blower systems. Another popular approach was built on the "boom-boom" theory: that explosions in the air or on the ground somehow jarred rainfall out of the sky. An even more common approach was that of the "smell makers," the cloud milkers who performed their work by releasing some chemical or combination of chemicals (usually secret) into the atmosphere. With the airplane came the "salt-shaking school," the rainmakers who sowed the clouds with chemicals, electrified sand, or other substances to induce them to part with their moisture. And a small group of methods were electrically based, designed to produce rain either by removing electricity from the atmosphere or by putting it in. A number, of course, fit no category: either their proponents never divulged their method, or they were too far-fetched or fraudulent to be considered seriously.

During the nineteenth century it was a common belief that civilization modified the American climate, whether as a result of the clearing or cultivating of land, the growing of crops, shrubs, and trees, or even certain of the more mechanical trappings of the westward advance. For example, some Americans were convinced that the railroads acted as electrical conductors "partially equalizing the electrical states of the earth and air" and were responsible for the mild winter weather of 1848. Rail and telegraph lines pushing westward triggered violent thunderstorms and increased the amount of moisture across the plains, it was argued, even though meteorological experts in Washington saw no data to prove the theory. Rather, they pointed out, railroads brought more people to an area; more people kept more records of rainfall than before. Scientists had the same reaction in 1882, when financier Jay Gould stated that railroad and telegraph construction had been moving the rainy district westward at a rate of about twenty miles a year.[12] Eastern "perfessers" and roll-top bureaucrats to the contrary notwithstanding, it was not hard for westerners to see the relation between the advance of civilization and expanded rainfall, even if the smoking, belching iron horse or the singing wires could not be shown to be directly responsible.

There had long been the feeling that the clearing of land and cultivation of the soil modified climate. Trees were usually equated with moisture: cutting forests made an area more arid. Conversely, when settlement began to push out over the Great Plains, the tilling of the soil and the increase in plant life enhanced rainfall over the dry, brown midriff of America. Travelers frequently noted this phenomenon, and scientists commented that trees drew rain from the clouds "as the lightning rod attracts the electric fluid from the stormy sky."[13] The planting of trees was a boon and the breaking of the sod permitted the ground to absorb more moisture which would then evaporate, explained Samuel Aughey, professor of the natural sciences at the University of Nebraska in 1880. Fellow Nebraskan Charles Dana Wilber distilled it all into the catch phrase "rain follows the plow": cultivated soil and the growth of plant life reduced solar radiation and promoted cloud formation and precipitation. Such terms as *non-farming, non-irrigable,* and *pasturage lands,* appearing in John Wesley Powell's 1878 report on the arid lands, were artifically coined "by wiseacres, kid-gloved experts and closet philosophers," said Wilber, "but the farmer with his plow tears them asunder."[14]

> The myth grew and was widely accepted,
> And so, wherever the plow-shares run,
> The clouds run overhead.
> And the soil that works and lets in the sun
> With water is always fed.[15]

Thus in the last quarter of the nineteenth century, encouraged by the boomer literature of railroads and western states and territories, land-hungry farmers shoved out onto the unbroken prairies of the Great American Desert. The seventies and eighties brought thousands of tough-minded sodbusters swarming into Kansas, Nebraska, and the Dakotas. Others began the task of taming the great arid central valley of California, convinced that the agrarian visions of the Jeffersonians were being fulfilled.

But they came during an inordinately wet cycle; for eight years before 1887 the rainfall was bountiful and above normal in Colorado and western Kansas and Nebraska. Then came the bursting of the bubble. The late eighties and the nineties were not gay, but grim and dismal. They were years of hardship, low farm prices, depression, and mortgage foreclosures. They were also times of drought—nearly a decade of dryness, with only two crops, which gave the lie to Wilber's "rain follows the plow" concept, an idea that subsequent meteorological studies would finish demolishing.[16] In Kansas and Nebraska, many a farmer watched his crops curl and die in the wake of natural holocaust. Helpless, he looked on with anguish while his stricken corn waned—"like a sick child, growing paler and paler." Half the population moved out of western Kansas between 1888 and 1892, with heavy exoduses from comparable parts of Nebraska and the Dakotas. But in the central portions of these regions, where investments were larger and operations more firmly rooted, the farmer elected to ride out adversity. As he hung on, he was willing to listen to any argument, whether it was for Populism or a less political way out. Perhaps he met with neighbors in the little white country church to pray for rain, and not "just a drizzle drazzle, but a real gully washer."[17] Uncertain even of divine support, in desperation he hedged his bets and called in one of the flimflam men, one of the "professional" rainmakers who cropped up like weeds in the spring to make a profit out of hard luck.

To a large extent, though not completely, it would be an agricultural clientele to whom the "pluviculturists" catered. In small rural towns everywhere, businessmen prospered only if their farm customers flourished, and often they joined together to "buy water from the sky." The chamber of commerce is particularly prominent in the rainmaking story. And usually present, though well submerged, is a persistent scientific thread—a serious interest in creating artificial precipitation by a handful of theorists, not actuated by the profit motive.

# 2. A Very Distinguished and Scientific Man: James P. Espy and the Theory of Rainmaking by Convection

To check the flood you brewed, I've heard
All efforts were in vain;
Until the Bureau in Washington, stirred,
And stopped the flood with a single word,
By just *predicting* rain.[1]

Rarely, until well into the twentieth century, were reputable scientists proponents of rainmaking theories or experiments. Meteorologists, in particular, were among the most persistent of the scoffers and debunkers. A notable exception was James Pollard Espy, a brilliant and totally committed man of science whose work in the mid-nineteenth century caused some to regard him as "the father of the U.S. Weather Bureau." After graduating from Transylvania University in Kentucky in 1808, Espy studied law and taught in Ohio, Maryland, and Pennsylvania, where he came to be closely associated with the Franklin Institute. By the middle 1830s he had begun to devote full time to studying and lecturing on his all-consuming interest, meteorology. By 1842 he had a government appointment, the first of several that helped materially in furthering his scientific experiments and observations.

Espy made contributions in several areas. First of all, he was one of the early advocates of a national system of simultaneous meteorological observation, with the federal government underwriting the cost of salaries and equipment. With other interested scientists, he urged colleges and learned societies to petition Congress for the

9

establishment of one observer for each hundred square miles. "This is the only information now wanted to predict rain," he wrote in 1836.[2]

In addition, Espy early developed a theory of cloud and storm formation that won him the Magellanic Prize of the American Philosophical Society in 1836 and the general appellation of "Storm King." It brought him plaudits from a distinguished committee of the French Académie des Sciences and the reported comment from the distinguished meteorologist François Arago: "England had its Newton, France its Cuvier, and America its Espy." Espy devised a "nephelescope," with which to demonstrate cloud formation by expansion of moist air. The forerunner of modern expansion cloud chambers, it was "certainly one of the first pieces of laboratory equipment used in the history of cloud physics."[3] Espy's calculations were surprisingly accurate, and he was far ahead of his time in deducing the role of latent heat in cloud formation and rainfall—one of the fundamental principles in cloud thermodynamics. Briefly in scientific journals, then at greater length in his *Philosophy of Storms* (1841), he argued that heated air rises and, because of diminished pressure in rarer regions, expands. Expansion is accompanied by a fall in temperature, causing the vapor in an upward moving air column to condense. This condensation releases enough heat to bring about a further rise of the central column, more expansion, and the condensation of the vapor into clouds until rain ultimately falls. Although an Edinburgh professor called it "a peculiar physical theory of storms," Espy noted from observation that volcanoes and "great cities where very much fuel is burnt" and "even battles, and accidental fires, if they occur under favourable conditions, may sometimes be followed by rain."[4] Favorable circumstances meant a high dew point and relatively calm, sultry air. If a large body of air could be made to ascend artificially in a column, Espy contended, a large cloud would be generated, "and that could well contain in itself a self-sustaining power, which may move from the place over which it has formed, and cause the air over which it passes to rise up into it and thus form more cloud and rain, until rain may become general." The agent forcing convection, he believed, was a fire substantial enough to cause an updraft. Rain induced by humans through deliberate burning he thought highly likely—and, if successful, "highly beneficial to mankind."[5]

This was by no means a new idea, but Espy restructured it and gave it a scientific explanation. Men had long observed that large conflagrations were somehow connected with rainfall, but a theoretical base had been lacking. As far back as the Peloponnesian War, according to Thucydides, the two were sometimes linked togehter. Had not the Archbishop of Dublin in 1708 pointed out that burning "defiles the air, causes rain and wind"? Jesuits in 1784 had noted that Indians in Paraguay deliberately fired the prairies," having learnt that the thicker smoke turns into clouds which pour forth water"; North American natives were reputed to have done likewise. Traveling in America in the 1790s, the Frenchman C. F. Volney saw some correlation between the clearing and burning of timberland and turbulent weather; and the German scientist Alexander von Humboldt commented on volcanic eruption and its production of a column of ash and smoke that subsequently formed clouds, a thunderstorm, and eventually "a continued and violent rain." Others, including the illustrious Arago, from time to time made similar observations of what they believed were direct relationships between forest fires and rainfall,[6] and Espy was not unaware of these views.

As advanced through the press in the middle 1830s, in *The Philosophy of Storms*, in 1841, in the pamphlet *To the Friends of Science* in 1845 and 1846, and in several government reports in the 1850s, Espy's plan was simple but grandiose. First, he urged readers to keep a careful record of rainfall during the dry season and to send these records to the Franklin Institute. Noting that rains in the United States tended to travel from west to east, he proposed an experiment to embrace a vast area. Let forty acres of timber for every twenty miles be burned every week in the summer over a line stretching some six or seven hundred miles north and south. The probable results (and Espy was careful to qualify his predictions) would be "a rain of great length, north and south," that would travel eastward to the Atlantic without the adverse side effects of hail, tornadoes, or violent winds. Nor would there be destructive floods or oppressively hot or cold temperatures; only beneficial results. It was likely, he thought, "that the farmers and mariners would always know in advance when the rains would commence, or nearly so, and when they would terminate; that all epidemic diseases originating from floods and droughts, would cease; that the proceeds of agriculture would be greatly increased, and the health and happiness of the citizens much promoted . . . for a sum not amounting to half a cent a year to each individual in the United States."[7]

Realizing the impracticability of such a pretentious scheme, Espy also suggested more modest experiments, including the firing of forty acres each week throughout the summer in each of ten counties in Pennsylvania, Maryland, and Virginia. As an alternative, he proposed a coordinated burning action by all farmers with fallow or other large masses of combustibles to kindle, these to be fired on prescribed days at prescribed hours, according to a definite, preconceived plan.[8] To what extent Espy attempted to test his theory is unclear. Possibly he did conduct one trial near Washington, with scant success. What gave his ideas wide currency was the fact that he was a scientist and that he "showed remarkable power in explaining his ideas," according to a colleague. Newspapers gave him much coverage; he lectured widely in the towns and cities of America and was superb at it. A Maine newspaper called him "one of the best lecturers that ever appeared—living or dead."[9] His was an enthusiasm that was at once convincing and contagious. As one editor said of him: "He is enthusiastic but no quack—no pretender—and we have not a doubt would create a profound impression by his theory in any scientific circle of the world," a comment borne out by experience. Scientists criticized or supported his ideas, but either way they respected them. Even if they rejected his views, they believed them "ingenious" and the result of "great ability and research." Others might disagree but still accept his theoretical premise, as did Professor Denison Olmsted of Yale, who saw Espy's rainmaking principle as "correct" but, because of the magnitude of nature, doubted "the practicality of producing rain by artificial means,"[10] an argument that would be used by scientists down to the present.

Nonscientists were often less dubious and more enthusiastic. Espy was on the trail of fundamental laws that enabled storms to be charted like planets, a contemporary editor explained. If his thesis could be definitely established, "he will be deserving of the Homeric epithet of the cloud-compelling Jupiter."

When we get up in the morning, in our variable clime, instead of being compelled to doubt long and anxiously over a thick coat or thin one—a vest of woollen or silk—we have but to calculate scientifically the motion of the air, and we can sally forth independent of overcoats or an umbrella.

The farmer will know when to mow down, or to gather up his hay. Science will take hold of the sickle, and when the harvest comes, the farmer need not fear for every cloud that gathers over his wheat field.[11]

Numerous Americans came to accept the Espy idea. In 1839, for example, traveler Josiah Gregg experienced what he called "An Espy Shower." First came a sudden prairie fire, accidentally kindled, which "spread with wonderful rapidity" and "great violence for a few hours." Then an unexpected rain appeared—"a phenomenon often witnessed upon the Prairies after an extensive conflagration; and affording a practical exemplification of Professor Espy's celebrated theory of artificial showers."[12]

In his several meteorological reports of the 1850s, Espy himself buttressed his case with an array of testimonials from around the country. Six Pennsylvanians, one an Episcopal clergyman, described rainfall produced by burning six acres of fallow near Cowdersport in 1844. A medical doctor reported a similar phenomenon following an Indiana prairie fire in 1843, and others observed like results from a forest fire on Isle Royale in Lake Superior three years later. A Universalist minister described "a perfect and undeniable demonstration of the truth of the theory" in New Hampshire's Monadnock Mountains in the summer of 1856.[13] Espy also cited the report of a survey crew on the coast of Florida in 1845. One of the group, Captain Alexander Mackay, jokingly suggested testing Espy's theories and at the same time convincing superstitious members of his power to make rain. While the jovial Mackay went through a spontaneous ritual of mumbo jumbo, mostly in broken French, other crewmen fired grassy marshland to clear the ground for their surveying work. One of those present related what happened next:

At this juncture came a roll of distant thunder; every glance instantly turned upward; a cloud was spreading there; the thunders increased; the lightnings flashed more vividly; the knees of the negroes shook together with alarm; already was the rain descending and in torrents, though the clear sky could be seen in all directions under the cloud. The captain, meanwhile, maintained his mystical attitude, and continued his wild and extraordinary evolutions. Some of the whites who were in the secret of the hoax fell upon their knees, and were imitated by the negroes, whose fears augmenting as the storm grew fiercer, with clasped hands fastened upon the captain a stare of awe and deprecation.[14]

But even with a good press and with at least a portion of the public wanting to believe the examples set forth by Espy or observed independently, there were plenty of skeptics. An 1846 correspondent of an Illinois newspaper commented on the presence of the "Storm King" in Washington, "I suppose [Espy] would like an appropriation of a few thousands, by Congress, just to get up a little bit of a shower somewhere." "Pshaw!" he continued, "I am willing to trust the Almighty for rain. . . . Let the worthy Professor turn his attention to something of more practical utility."[15] Where Espy had been careful to point out that air must be moisture-laden and atmospheric conditions favorable, his critics just as carefully noted that in time of drought, when rain was most desperately needed, circumstances were precisely the opposite. After widespread forest fires in the eastern states in the spring of 1845, editors asked: "Ought we not to be well drenched in rain, in consequence of all this combustion, instead of being parched with drought as the whole country now is? Pray, if this is not fire enough to get up a single shower, how much would a good soaking artificial rain cost?" "If heat is the cause of rain," said an Illinois farm editor, "we would ask why then is not a constant fall of rain over the craters of volcanoes and large furnaces? According to this theory, Pittsburgh and other large manufacturing cities should be constantly inundated." Another agricultural expert, apparently willing to accept Espy's basic premises, raised an objection that would be reiterated wherever future rainmakers practiced: "that he cannot limit his showers to his own land, and all the public would never be ready for a shower on the same day." Good land drainage was even more beneficial than man's efforts to induce precipitation, even in helping to increase rainfall.[16]

Theory and practice were separate. Theory was cheap, but practice required financing—and when Espy sought funds, state legislators and United States senators were less than receptive. In 1839, in response to a petition asking a reward for Espy's discovery of a method of producing rain, the upper house of the Pennsylvania assembly appointed a committee to inquire and observe but contributed no money. The following spring, the Pennsylvania House of Representatives was asked to help verify "the truth of his Theory in relation to Storms," a request "of extraordinary character" to help "a very distinguished and scientific man, to substantiate a theory which has formed the subject of his deepest investigation and most anxious reflection for nearly twenty years past," a request which, furthermore, could only benefit the cause of science in general and the nation's maritime, mercantile, and agricultural interests in particular. After pondering the matter, a house committee brought forth a bill that with subsequent amendment would specially compensate Espy "for discovering certain natural laws regulating the fall of rain." When certified by three commissioners, Espy would receive five thousand dollars if he brought precipitation over a ten-square-mile area of Pennsylvania "when it would not have rained without his agency." For rain over one thousand square miles in the commonwealth, he was to be paid ten thousand dollars; for moisture over five thousand square miles, apparently not limited to Pennsylvania, twenty-five thousand dollars; and if he kept the Ohio River navigable for steamers up to 150 tons all summer between its juncture with the Mississippi and Pittsburgh, fifty thousand dollars. But the bill was lost by more than a two-to-one margin, although later the House voted Espy free use of the legislative hall for two lectures on his law of storms.[17]

Nor had Espy's supporters in Congress been idle. In mid-December 1838 James Buchanan of Pennsylvania brought what he called "rather a strange petition" before the United States Senate—a monetary proposal apparently similar to that brought before the legislature of the Keystone State. Admitting some skepticism but acknowledging that there remained "several things in nature that philosophy had not yet dreamed of," Buchanan pointed out that Espy was respected and learned and that "in the science of meteorology there was scarcely a man in the United States his Superior." Thomas Hart Benton of Missouri urged withdrawal of the petition "for reasons too obvious to require notice," and John J. Crittenden of Kentucky agreed. Even if Espy's ideas were feasible, he said, they ought not to be encouraged. No individual should have the power "to take the Ohio river under his especial protection. Why, sir, he might enshroud us in continual clouds, and indeed falsify the promise that the earth should be no more submerged. And if he possesses the power of causing rain, he may also possess the power of withholding it, and in his pleasure, instead of giving us a navigable river, may present us with rocks and shoals and sandbars." Besides, argued Crittenden, the scheme "had too much the appearance of a Sub-Treasury about it; a hoarding up of clouds and vapors to be dispensed at will by an individual." Fellow senator John M. Niles of Connecticut took a similar point of view, insisting that the Senate ought not to spend time debating such preposterous questions; but if it insisted, then the Espy rain bill should properly be referred to the Committee on Finance because like paper money it was "a sort of sublimated bubble . . . promising great things, magnifying credit, blowing it up, and making magnificent fortunes out of nothing, till in the end it is all blown away by the first breath of reality that touches it." Reality was close by: the Senate quickly tabled the question.[18]

But Espy kept at it. Early in 1842 the "Storm Breeder," as dour John Quincy Adams dubbed him, called on the former president, who then sat in the U.S. House of Representatives. Espy came with a three-point outline for congressional support of a meteorological program. These "three wishes," Adams grumbled, were "about as rational as those of Hans Carvel and his wife. The man is methodically monomaniac, and the dimensions of his organ of self esteem have been swollen to the size of a goitre by a report from a committee of the National Institute of France, endorsing all his crack brained discoveries in meteorology."[19] Espy's "three wishes" included a provision for simultaneous meteorological observations, a "fixed salary" for himself to oversee such an operation, and "a conditional appropriation to be made by Congress of ten thousand dollars provided he causes it to rain copiously over 10,000 square miles in time of drought, and so in proportion to the extent of the rain."[20]

In Washington, Espy failed to gain compensation for his "discovery," but in 1842 he did find himself a minor niche in the War Department—a "small interloping office which allowed him to pursue his study of storms," as Adams put it.[21] Six years later, he was conducting his meteorological work for the naval surgeon and after 1852 in conjunction with the Smithsonian Institution.

Time tended to be more kindly to James Espy than John Quincy Adams had been. It was not true that "he had in his possession the true secret of storms," as an admirer expressed it in 1860, but neither would he be regarded as a fraud or a crackbrained fanatic. He was never a man without honor or respect; and more than any other advocate of rainmaking before the mid-twentieth century, he added a scientific dimension. "His theory was probably more philosophical than any of his successors," one editor wrote in the 1890s, when the West was in the grip of a new wave of rainmaking fever.[22] But, he added with a touch of sadness, Espy was no more successful.

In the 1860s and 1870s there would be renewed interest in the general idea that rain followed major fires. During the Civil War, the sentiment was expressed that more rain and lower temperatures than usual in the South bore out Espy's theory that rainfall could result from the atmospheric disturbance due to great or continued fires, though in this instance it was not clear whether the rain was "attributable to the chemical effects of burning such an immense amount of 'villainous Saltpetre,' or to the tremendous concussions" of the artillery. It was claimed that the great Chicago fire of 1870 triggered off heavy rainfall, which in turn helped check the holocaust. Subsequent investigation indicated, however, that the moisture showered down upon Chicago was part of a much broader storm system over a wide part of the country.[23]

Important scientists continued to respect Espy's ideas in the abstract and to view the link between fire and rain with an open mind. Harvard physicist John Trowbridge found some evidence that fire might precipitate moisture by changing the electrical charge in the atmosphere but admitted that far too little was known about the subject to draw conclusions. Joseph Henry, the first secretary and director of the Smithsonian Institution, could accept the concept that large fires did sometimes "overturn the unstable equilibrium of the atmosphere" and "give rise to the beginning of a violent storm," but he balked at the idea of economical rain production. The Englishman J. K. Laughton saw some connection between fires and rainfall but had severe qualifications for their cause-and-effect relationship.[24] Thirty years after Espy's death, at a time when Lucian Blake's experiments on dust particles as nuclei for rain drops were drawing attention, writers gave new credit to the "Storm King." His observations on fire and rain, said one, had been "so striking that it is a wonder no more attention has been paid to them."[25]

As a matter of fact, some attention had been paid, but the theory was more attractive than its practical application. In the early 1880s the Australian government had taken a hard look. The official astronomer in New South Wales studied the matter carefully and estimated that to increase the rainfall by 60 percent, it would be necessary to burn at least 8.8 million tons of coal daily at a cost of £4.5 million.[26] In 1891, at a time "pluviculture" was kindling the public's imagination, a dreamy-eyed pamphleteer believed he had found the reason for the Egyptian pyramids. They were to make rain, contended Joseph G. Konvalinka, a versatile thinker who also had ideas for aerial navigation, a personal telegraph system, and a means of suspending humans in sleep for as long as two centuries. Using the knowledge of the ancients, Konvalinka would combine colonization and the modification of climate. His colony would be established in an arid region, with an uncultivated square, four thousand feet across, in the center. Within this was to be a smaller black square one thousand feet across, which would be darkened by soot, coal, or lampblack and in the middle of which would be constructed a hundred-foot-high pyramid, also black. Absorbing the rays of the sun, the black square and pyramid would become hot and push air up into the atmosphere, where it would expand, cool, and condense to fall as rain.[27]

Nothing came of this proposal. But even official U.S. Weather Bureau meteorologists by 1919 were willing to accept the idea of strong convection and cloud formation over forest fires, although they could see no practical use for it. Their response was the same in 1937 when two Hungarian scientists advocated burning a film of petroleum spread over water to produce rainfall. In the 1960s scientists proposed coating the ground with asphalt to produce rising warm air and—hopefully—precipitation; and the Frenchman Dr. Henri Dessens, working in tropical Africa, developed his "meteotron," a system of a hundred oil burners deployed in a large circle, designed to provide convection.[28] But no breakthrough came: the problem was basically one of scale, of the immensity and openness of nature.

Ingenious inventors and dreamers would improve on Espy's approach by suggesting mechanisms to channel or force warm air upward. To this end, why not use conduit or even deflecting planes? As early as the 1850s an unnamed Virginian had constructed a novel "rain tower," with large flues extending sixty feet into the air. Pine wood burned at the base was supposed to create convection, and precipitation was to result. But although the persistent inventor spent one thousand dollars in building the apparatus and consumed "hundreds of cords of wood" in repeated trials, his efforts to break a drought proved futile. In 1880 an inspired New Yorker designed but never erected "a charming little structure of stone," to stand a thousand feet high and to be topped with a wooden or iron tower extending another five hundred feet. The entire tower was to be hollow, with a reversible blower pushing warm air into the atmosphere to cause rain. A similar scheme was contemplated by John Jacob Astor IV in the early 1890s; and the versatile James M. Pitkin of Kansas City would use large canvas tubes of different lengths, with their upper ends attached to balloons, and with blowers to draw cool air down one conduit and force moist, warm air up a second. A Texan sought to interest both the public and Weather Bureau personnel in his "Rainolette" machine, which was designed to blow a column of air upward, but he found no takers, despite his offer of paid-up stock to those officials who would help get his company started.[29]

In 1925 a Nashville editor suggested modernizing Espy's plan, the government to build furnaces with tall smokestacks, with air forced through them and heated by electricity from Muscle Shoals power plant. A French scientist, Bernard J. Dubos, thought a two-thousand-foot steel and concrete "meteorological tube," tapered like a telescope, could be used to pull up air and create rain, and he visited the United States in 1935 to gain support for this ten-million-dollar vision. Another man would blow refrigerated air through a patented "cold air elevator stack"; still another would push air through seventeen thousand feet of corrugated iron tubing, twenty feet in diameter, up the side of Mount Whitney in California. Willis Gregg, then head of the Weather Bureau and a man of much restraint, responded to the latter. "Your schemes are ingenious," said he, "but Nature does not fit them."[30]

Occasionally it was suggested that powerful fans alone—without conduits—could be used to bring down rain. Why not set up two rows of fans, each one thousand feet in diameter, to deflect air upward into the cooler regions? asked an Oregonian in 1934. The French were known to be experimenting with such ideas in the Sahara Desert. Ten or a dozen large windmills in the mountains, it was insisted as late as 1954, would not only relieve the smog problem of Los Angeles but would also greatly increase the rainfall as far east as New Mexico.[31]

A few of the would-be "cloud compellers" believed that moist air could be drawn laterally from humid regions. Possibly one of the most ambitious such suggestions was made in 1940 by an Indianan who urged the U.S. Department of Agriculture to build one thousand steel towers, 528 feet apart, beginning at Muscatine, Iowa, and running in a straight line west and slightly south. When each tower was equipped with an airplane propeller, operated by a thousand-horsepower engine, this combined one million horsepower was literally supposed to pull moist air currents onto the plains from the Gulf of Mexico.[32]

Other visionaries proposed gigantic deflecting planes to take advantage of the fact that moist air cooled and condensed as it rose. James Pitkin in 1892 had suggested a modest piece of canvas (two hundred by four hundred feet) supported by balloons at right angles to the air current. Another had in mind a huge rooflike structure one hundred miles long and sloping up from the ground nearly a mile high, a structure that one government official pointed out would require fifty billion carloads of dirt—enough to fill a single train of freight cars circling the globe about twenty-five thousand times.[33]

With the exception of the anonymous Virginia inventor of the 1850s, few of the advocates of blower or deflecting plane schemes even went beyond paper or made serious efforts to induce public support. One other exception came after World War I, when concerted attempts were made in the Southwest and in Washington, D.C., to find financial backing for an invention called the Cyclorain, the brainchild of Ira N. Terrill, an early Oklahoma boomer turned Texas oilman. The Cyclorain was a blower-conduit arrangement, designed to be built of reinforced concrete 220 feet high and, according to its backers, capable of moving 3.5 million cubic feet of air per minute. With one large unit in each county of a belt eight counties wide running from the mouth of the Rio Grande as far north as the southern boundary of Wyoming, said Terrill, "enough of the humid air of the return trade winds can be diverted westward and northward and give abundance of rain over the great plains country of the U.S." In addition, all destructive gulf storms could be eliminated by distributing a number of the machines in a belt along the Gulf Coast and reversing them to draw the air downward at a total cost of eighty million dollars.[34].

In 1918, when he issued his first Cyclorain brochure, Terrill called for "ten big hearted, broad minded men" to join in promoting the invention. Two years later, he was appealing for 150 men, but still "big hearted" and "broad minded." With money scarce, in 1920 or 1921, Terrill organized the I. N. Terrill Trust, holding 98 percent of the shares himself. In addition to trying to sell fifty thousand shares at ten dollars per value—some to federal officials in the nation's capital—he actively sought the aid of the Department of Agriculture to obtain a congressional appropriation on behalf of his scheme. Secretary of Agriculture E. T. Meredith, however, passed the question on to Chief Marvin of the Weather Bureau, who condemned the Cyclorain in blunt and unequivocal terms. Indeed, Marvin had already been instrumental in blocking Terrill's application for a patent and would soon call in the Post Office Department to investigate the Cyclorain trust on charges of soliciting funds under false pretenses.[35]

No doubt Espy, the scientist, would have been aghast at some of the suggestions that stemmed from the idea of rainmaking by warming air columns moving upward. As for himself, he became convinced of the rightness of his storm theory and so enthusiastic and dogmatic in pushing it that he refused to examine his premises and soon became locked into his own ideas. But he was no crank, no faker in the traditional "pluviculture" sense: his approach was in its day a scientific one in keeping with the serious work then being done in the developing meteorological field. His grand proposal for making rain could only have been made at a time of the lavish exploitation of resources, a time when America's magnificent forests were being ruthlessly decimated. "As an expression of the American character," writes a modern observer, "the proposal deserves to be remembered."[36]

# 3. We Do Not Desire to Cannonade the Clouds Any Longer at Government Expense: Rainmaking by Concussion

I can take a pound of rackarock and tie it to a kite
And make a thunder shower on a clear and starry night.[1]

One of the most persistent and readily accepted theories of rainmaking came to be linked with war and eventually with concussion. Did not rainfall invariably accompany battle? Even the ancients noted the connection. Writing of Marius and his clash with the Teutons in 102 B.C., Plutarch had commented that "extraordinary rains pretty generally fall after great battles; whether it be that some divine power thus washes and cleanses the polluted earth with showers from above, or that moist and heavy evaporations, steaming forth from the blood and corruption, thicken the air, which naturally is subject to alteration from the smallest causes."[2] Even as late as the 1890s, a few Americans still subscribed to the idea: in the course of twelve hours fighting, according to a Boston newspaper, one soldier gave off six gallons of perspiration, which, multiplied thousands of times, charged the atmosphere with moisture and in nine cases out of ten brought rain. Meteorologists scoffed at the theory, pointing out that if soldiers "were nothing but blood and sweat" and ten thousand of them "were wholly evaporated and then all condensed back," the resulting rain would be only half an inch over a field of thirteen acres.[3]

With time the rainfall-warfare correlation came to be associated with the explosion of gunpowder and the impact of concussion. The

22

idea was an old one, well worn by tradition and with only a vague scientific base. Early observers could not help but see a relation between thunder and rain, and by the eighteenth and nineteenth centuries some came to accept this natural concussion as an explanation for precipitation. Some believed they discerned a direct cause-and-effect association between the rumblings of earthquakes or volcanic eruptions and heavy showers.[4] Heavy gun and artillery fire during battle gave an easily acceptable theory to buttress what soldiers learned by experience—the concussion of gunpowder explosions brought down rain, an idea carried to popular heights in the late nineteenth century.

At the same time concussion came to be seen as a means of breaking up storms to avoid hail damage to crops. As early as the seventeenth century Italians and Frenchmen, especially, believed that the ringing of church bells would dissipate dangerous storms. Originally the bell represented the voice and prayers of the Church, but eventually it was the bell's concussion in the air that was thought to release precipitation prematurely. Europeans also subscribed to the idea that artillery fire might cause storms to disintegrate. In the 1530s, according to his autobiography, Benvenuto Cellini used this approach to milk the clouds of their moisture so that the Duchess Ottavio might carry on a celebration in Rome. Faced with a great tempest, with "darting Lightning, and follow'd with terrible Claps of Thunder," a knowledgeable French admiral on the coast of South America in 1680 "found a Way to disperse them by the Firing of Cannon," a feat that left local citizens "both surprised and terrified." Some believed that the smoke and vapor of burning gunpowder produced a chemical reaction favorable to the formation of raindrops in the atmosphere; most attributed the results to concussion, but without a more explicit explanation. Whatever the theory, hail shooting with cannon, handguns, and rockets was common in the Beaujolais wine districts almost to the twentieth century. In France and Italy as many as ten thousand shots were sometimes fired at a single storm, and special mortars fitted with long sheet-iron funnels hurled smoke rings at ominous clouds. Science, however, remained skeptical. Even the gigantic salute fired in unison by massed French soldiers in 1831 failed to break up an approaching thunderstorm. European meteorologists like Arago viewed it all with some doubt but were usually less explicit than the twentieth-century U.S. Weather Bureau critic, William Humphreys, who believed this mode of "saluting" a hailstorm "about as effective as booing a blizzard!"[5]

If many were convinced that concussion might deprive a cloud of its hail prematurely, others were persuaded that it jostled minute cloud particles together and caused them to fall as rain. Many Europeans, including Napoleon, believed there was a definite relationship between gunfire and rainfall, but one of the first to formulate a positive statement of causation was the American J. C. Lewis of Washington. Lewis pointed out that the firing of artillery in 1825 to celebrate the completion of the Erie Canal had been followed by a deluge; careful study convinced him as early as 1841 that rain could be produced artificially by concussion.[6]

One John Evarts wrote a series of articles on the subject for a New York newspaper in the late 1850s—a time, he later reported, "when it was thought very unpopular and impious to make the reference." The Civil War did much to popularize the idea. Hundreds of thousands of soldiers, Yankee and Rebel alike, were convinced by firsthand experience in mud and slush that gunfire inevitably brought down torrents of rain. Supporters of the concussion theory strongly urged that careful investigation be made, on the assemption that artificial battles could be devised to revolutionize agriculture in dry areas. Whether or not the unusually cool and wet weather of the South in 1863 had any connection with heavy artillery concussions or with "the chemical effects of burning such an immense amount of 'villanous Saltpetre'" was not clear but was a matter for serious enquiry.[7]

About the same time European writers were preaching the same doctrine. The Frenchman Charles Le Maout of Saint-Brieuc had already published two of his five pamphlets on the subject; and in 1863 a slim volume entitled *Cannons and Tempests* formalized the theory in England. Four years later another Briton, Andrew Steinmetz, published his *Sunshine and Showers*, in which he described a number of major battles that had been accompanied by rain. The British government might well test the hypothesis with "a hundred or two" cannon, suggested Steinmetz, and at the same time provide occasion for artillery practice.[8]

More important for its impact on American thinking was the book *War and the Weather; or, The Artificial Production of Rain*, first published in 1871 by Edward Powers, a Chicago civil engineer. A subscriber to the old Huttonian theory of the precipitation of rain from two intermixed and saturated air masses of unequal temperature, Powers was more observer than scientist. As early as 1841, according to his own account, he had publicized his contention that heavy gunfire precipitated rainfall. In *War and the Weather* he listed some two hundred battles that had been fought in rain. If certain engagements had not caused precipitation, he argued, it was because the guns had not been properly deployed, the firing had been too sporadic, or the wind currents had carried the moisture away to fall elsewhere.[9]

In *War and the Weather*; in a letter to General Albert Myer, chief signal officer of the army; and in at least two memorials to Congress (one presented by Representative Charles B. Farwell of Illinois in 1874), Powers urged the federal government to set aside funds for experiments near a number of arsenals throughout the country. Three hundred cannon would suffice, he said, and they should be positioned in such a way as to create opposing shocks in order to mix warm and cold air currents. Artillery should be set in two lines facing each other, or arranged in a circle a mile or so in diameter with the muzzles pointing inward and upward. Firing should be rapid and simultaneous by electrical detonation, and a second, heavier barrage should follow the first by a few hours. "A well-defined method of causing rain to fall at will"—formerly thought to be a divine prerogative—might well be within reach, predicted Powers, if the government would make "an earnest inquiry into the truth."[10]

Powers received considerable support, especially from laymen who caught hold of his ideas as carried in the newspapers. Amateurs frequently cited examples to support the concussion theory and added their voices to the call for careful "scientific" investigations. A Brooklynite urged the army to fire fifty rounds of heavy ammunition from every fort in the arid part of the country to break the drought, which in 1874, he said, threatened to cause the nation "an untold daily loss, and prospective high prices and thereby want of food, want of clothing and want of comforts, to many thousands during the coming winter."[11] But skepticism was not dead. Rainmaking by concussion was a topic of discussion at the fictional Sazerac Lying Club. Operating in Nevada, its proponent, "the Philadelphian," had seriously misjudged his explosives: as a result, he lifted a mountain fourteen feet off its base and brought a cloudburst that "came down with a thud." Scientific editors adopted a wait-and-see attitude. If they worked, said one, Powers's proposals promised "a far better use of cannon than to devote them to the slaughtering of human beings." Another commented dryly that vast amounts of powder was "burnt in missing Indians" on the plains without appreciable impact on the rainfall, then launched into a tongue-in-cheek assessment of the implications of artificial rainmaking. He saw endless wrangling by farmers over plebiscites to determine if they wanted rain; the price of ordnance would rise precipitously; and he predicted lawsuits for damages "from excitable tea-drinkers and nervous chickens without end." But discussion in the 1870s was lively, and the very dry winter of 1877–78 on the Pacific Coast kept it animated, with due attention given to the observation that rain usually followed Fourth of July celebrations.[12]

Edward Powers was encouraged in his efforts by Daniel Ruggles of Virginia, whom some have called "the real inventor of the rain-producing process." A veteran of the Mexican campaigns, former brigadier general in the Confederate army, and owner of a ranch along the Rio Bravo in Texas, Ruggles in 1880 had patented "a new and useful Mode of Producing Rain or Precipitating Rain-Falls from Rain-Clouds." Ruggles's idea—which some charged he had appropriated from the real inventor, a German farmer in New Zealand—concerned the use of small, cheap balloons capable of carrying aloft explosives to be detonated by a time fuse or by electricity from the ground. The aerial concussion thus created, contended Ruggles, would condense vapor in the air, "thereby precipitating rain to sustain vegetation, prevent drought, and also to purify and renovate the atmosphere during periods of pestilence and epidemics."[13]

Like Powers, Ruggles appealed to the press and to the federal government. In the spring of 1879 the *Austin* (Texas) *Statesman* alluded to a visit by Ruggles in favorable and optimistic terms. "We have Jove's chosen successor on earth, even in this modest capital," said the *Statesman*. "He used to make it thunder at the head of his legions on battlefields, but now he devotes genius and toil to draining down from the skies, even when these are mailed in brass, genial showers and refreshing rainstorms." While the Austin editor was not convinced that Ruggles would necessarily succeed, he thought he saw the "beginning of the end": "We may yet learn to ride the storm and guide the tempests and milk the juicy atmosphere, even as Jove gathered clouds when the blind old bard sang in a tropical sea three thousand years ago."[14]

Ruggles approached both the secretary of war and the secretary of the navy in 1879, advocating experimentation with his invention and pointing out that "as an industrial and philanthropic scheme it stands unrivalled." He memorialized Congress, asking an appropriation of ten thousand dollars for tests under the commissioner of agriculture. Ruggles would deal with the clouds "in conformity with the Darwinian theory, by selection," he said. With the increasing need for more food in the world, he was convinced that mankind's salvation lay in the application of his concussionist ideas. But Congress failed to respond; and Ruggles's subsequent attempts to interest the chief signal officer of the U.S. Army were rebuffed, largely because of the opposition of trained meteorologists.[15]

Ruggles's scheme received wide ventilation in the newspapers but probably was not tested on any scale by its inventor. In March 1886 he authorized Henry Pomeroy of Saint Louis to conduct experiments under his patent rights. Pomeroy, a former banker who had unwisely invested and lost his money in the Wabash Railroad, had previously invented an exploding rocket for producing rain. Although Pomeroy made limited experiments, he had no success in using his own or Ruggles's ideas.[16]

Meanwhile it was becoming more and more apparent to western farmers that the plains were not the salubrious, luxurious Garden of Eden so graphically represented by the promotors of the land and railway companies. Drought struck with monotonous regularity, and more than one sodbuster looked anxiously elsewhere for relief. Desperation, plus reports of foreign inventions designed to produce rain by concussion, prompted growing interest and made it possible for enthusiasts like the Reverend L. B. Woolfolk to lecture in Montana on how weather might be controlled "by the firing of cannon balls" and seasons turned "into one perpetual summer." Fireworks manufacturers sought to sell their products to state government for use in rainmaking experiments, citing previous successful experience in Europe.[17]

Washington received an increasing number of pleas for federal action. A Californian, for example, suggested the use of naval artillery at Mare Island; a Texan believed that with surplus cannon and powder and with thousands of idle soldiers, the government had nothing to lose by conducting rain tests; an Ohio editor urged experiments near Dayton, where the old soldiers' home could supply experienced ordnance men at nominal cost. In response to such requests, both the secretary of war and the commissioner of agriculture asked the signal Office—then handling the Weather Bureau functions—for a scientific statement on the feasibility of the concussionist approach. Captain F. B. Jones, acting signal officer, prepared a carefully researched and worded reply. He doubted that gunpowder explosions could bring rain and suggested that if experiments were made they be conducted in some reasonably moist region like Kentucky when a low-pressure area was traversing the section but when no rain was falling nor expected to fall.[18]

This was the extent of government action at the time. In 1890, however, Edward Powers added renewed weight to the theory with a reissue of his *War and the Weather*. Plates of the 1871 edition had been lost in the Chicago fire, and the author had no time to push his artificial rain scheme from the platform or from his desk. With recurring drought in the eighties and with the popularization of what he called "hopeless" irrigation projects, he now felt compelled to publish a new edition of the book. Casting aside earlier criticisms, particularly from Godkin's *Nation*, Powers specifically asked that field or siege guns from the federal arsenal at Rock Island, Illinois, be made available for experiments under the jurisdiction of the secretary of agriculture. He set forth detailed estimates for the cost of such tests as follows, calculating that with permanent stations three good rains per month could be produced at a cost of $20,897 each.

| | |
|---|---:|
| Mounting 200 siege guns at $10 each | $   2,000 |
| Rail transport for 200 siege guns at $40 each | 8,000 |
| 40,000 blank cartridges at $2.50 each | 100,000 |
| 50 tons of hay for wadding at $12 a ton | 600 |
| 10,000 electric primers at $150 per M | 1,500 |
| Electrical battery and insulation wire | 500 |
| Services of 10 men, 26 days at $2.50 per day | 650 |
| Services of 600 men, 26 days at $1.50 per day | 23,400 |
| Rent of ground for the experiment | 250 |
| Return transportation of guns to arsenal | 8,000 |
| Dismounting and handling guns | 2,000 |
| TOTAL | 146,900 |
| Add 10% "for contingencies" | 14,690 |
| Total for two experiments | 161,590 |
| Total for one experiment | 80,795[19] |

One station for each state would be adequate. If the Department of Agriculture moved rapidly, Powers said, it might be able to perfect its system in time to impress visitors to the Columbian Exposition scheduled for Chicago in 1893.[20]

Powers was widely read and often quoted; after all, his writings merely drew together what the average person already knew. The scientific world, however remained unimpressed with his "so-called facts and cranky arguments." Powers seemed unacquainted with twenty years of meteorological advance and unaware of the body of European literature on weather as the result of war. No weather maps were available for the Civil War, and Powers's questionnaires to former officers in 1870 could not be regarded as scientific evidence. Nor was coincidence discounted. Most battles were fought in temperate zones—where rain normally fell about once every three days—and were usually commenced in good weather, said his critics; hence, in many cases rainfall did follow battles by virtue of the law of averages.[21]

But the uninformed were convinced, among them at least one important public figure—Charles B. Farwell, by then a senator, who had introduced his 1874 memorial into the House and who owned extensive ranch lands in Texas. It was Farwell who almost single-handedly, so he later boasted, carried through Congress in 1890 a bill appropriating two thousand dollars "for experiments in the production of rain fall" to be conducted by the Department of Agriculture through its Division of Forestry. It was ironic that the chief of the division, Bernhard E. Fernow, a German-born pioneer in North American forestry, had little sympathy for the project he was to supervise. In the annual *Report of the Secretary of Agriculture* in 1890 Fernow declared tersely that he had neither men nor means to execute explosive tests and that any effort to use the appropriation as proposed by Congress "would hardly fail to be barren of results."[22]

On all sides Fernow was pelted with advice and queries from both scoffers and believers—including Farwell—many of whom presented pet rainmaking theories of their own. Veteran meteorologist Henry Hazen suggested that to save money experimental explosions be made on a high mountain where observations could be easily recorded. Others, including Mark Harrington, soon to become chief of the new Weather Bureau, were "somewhat amused" that Fernow should have fallen heir to the project and emphasized the necessity of laboratory experimentation first, Congress permitting. Fernow agreed: he wished to conduct controlled tests on a small scale and desired the cooperation of the War Department and the Weather Bureau. He privately doubted that the scientific method would prevail, for "the inaugurators of the idea want to hear it thunder without any preliminaries or experiments." The manner in which testing is conducted, said Fernow, "may lead either to the most desirable advances in meteorological knowledge or to eternal ridicule."[23] Although Fernow made preliminary inquiries concerning explosives and their detonation, once his attitude was made clear he was "excused from planning or conducting the experiments," an accomplishment on which one editor warmly congratulated him. These were "absurd experiments . . . in which a self-respecting man of science can scarcely engage without a blush."[24]

With Fernow out of the way, the project was delegated to Assistant Secretary of Agriculture Edwin Willets, who in turn appointed a special agent, giving him virtually a free hand to direct the rainmaking experiments within the bounds of the appropriation bill.

The man selected in 1891 as special agent was a Washington patent attorney, Robert St. George Dyrenforth. A person of varied background and experience, Dyrenforth by his own account had a Ph.D. from the University of Heidelberg and an M.D. from Columbian University—now George Washington University. He had enlisted in the Union armies at the age of sixteen, was twice wounded in campaigns under McClellan and Rosencrans, and had served as a correspondent in the Austro-Prussian War. From 1871 to 1885, when he entered private law practice, he was connected with the Patent Office in Washington and served as interim commissioner for ten days when Grover Cleveland became president. Described in 1891 as a "tall, well proportioned, and vigorous man, with a strikingly strong face—the face of a thinker, of a diplomat, of a man of the world, and also of a good fellow," Dyrenforth seems to have received his rainmaking appointment largely through the efforts of Senator Farwell, with whom he had repeatedly discussed "pluviculture" by concussion.[25] Dyrenforth also was strongly in sympathy with Powers and others of the same school. Fernow sarcastically called him "a patent lawyer in Washington, who knows more about explosives and the manner of exploding them than any other man. . . . I strongly advise everybody to have his ark ready for the deluge." Henry Hazen, a bachelor and a man of strong convictions, thought the choice particularly ill advised: "I am inclined to think that Dyrenforth has an idea that if he can only get men heartily in sympathy with his work, the clouds or clear sky or dry air or anything else will be more likely to sympathize with his serious efforts. I give him credit for a great deal of zeal but, oh! my! with very little knowledge in this connection."[26]

Dyrenforth set to work immediately, researching in the Library of Congress and in the Patent Office. At an early date, possibly because of Ruggles's patent rights, he discarded the idea of detonating explosives attached to balloons in favor of the idea of exploding balloons filled with a highly combustible mixture of one part oxygen and two of hydrogen. He believed that explosions in the atmosphere would reduce the danger to humans and would perhaps create "something in the nature of a vortex or of a momentary cavern, into which the condensed moisture is drawn from afar, or falls." The condensation of such an explosion, he said, "may squeeze the water out of the air like a sponge."[27]

After lengthy consultation with Carl Myers, expert and manufacturer of equipment at his "Balloon Farm" in Frankfort, New York, Dyrenforth ordered a number of ten-foot balloons made of varnished muslin, as well as some large kites designed to carry explosives. Originally he had hoped to use ballons made of special paper—reprocessed pulp from old greenbacks—but these proved unsatisfactory. With the help of several chemists, including Claude A. O. Roselle of the Patent Office and John Ellis of Oberlin College, he decided upon the processes to be used for manufacturing oxygen and hydrogen. Water, sulphuric acid, and iron would be used for the hydrogen; chlorate of potash and black oxide of manganese for the oxygen. A relatively new blasting powder, "rackarock," a mixture of potassium chlorate and petroleum, was selected primarily for its great power and its safety features.[28]

Late in June 1891 Dyrenforth detonated one oxyhydrogen balloon in the air near his Piney Branch home at the edge of the nation's capital. Daniel Ruggles and some fifty "scientific and practical observers" were present, but this and other preliminary explosions were designed more to test the balloon apparatus than to bring down rain. As it was, they produced a shower of complaints from nearby residents, including the chief clerk of the Smithsonian Institution, who lamented that the firing not only shook his house and frightened his family but in addition "was calculated to cause abortion" among his fine Jersey cattle.[29]

Next came the question of a site for the major tests. Ranch owners through the West offered their facilities. Dyrenforth finally accepted the invitation of Nelson Morris, wealthy Illinois meat packer, to use his "Chicago" ranch, twenty-three miles from Midland in west Texas. Midland was served by the Texas and Pacific Railroad, which provided transportation gratis between there and Fort Worth, and Morris promised not only free housing and subsistence for the experimenters but also labor and the payment of local expenses.[30]

As preparations and prefatory testing proceeded, the nation's press watched expectantly. Some newspapers, especially those in drought areas, urged haste. "Try it now, Uncle Jerry; try it now," said the *Wichita Daily Eagle*, imploring Secretary of Agriculture Jeremiah Rusk to hurry. But the *New York Tribune* contemplated the forthcoming experiments with skepticism. Its readers were reminded of the English scientific-farming enthusiast who remarked to his hired hand that he expected someday to be able to carry the fertilizer for twenty acres in one waistcoat pocket. "Ay," said the hand, "and I doubt not yer honor can carry the crop in the other." The *Chicago Tribune* believed that accounts of rainfall following battles in the pregunpowder era were in themselves evidence of the fallacy of the concussion theory and that the expenditure of public funds on such experiments was unwarranted. However, the use of private capital might be acceptable. Despite the lukewarm attitude of Fernow and of the scientific world in general, Congress, in March 1891, appropriated an additional seven thousand dollars for rainmaking experiments. This made a total of nine thousand dollars. Farwell was instrumental in expediting this action, and Dyrenforth's appointment was extended into 1892.[31]

In July and August 1891 the "cloud-compelling" expedition began to assemble for the trip to Midland, Texas. George E. Curtis of Washington was employed as meteorologist, although he could not be away from the capital for more than three weeks. Curtis was conservative in his scientific views and not inclined to see eye to eye with the concussionists. "One thing is certain," Henry Hazen wrote Fernow, "if Curtis admits anything in his favor it will be a big thing for Dyrenforth."[32] Among others who would join the expedition were John Ellis, who had much to do with procuring supplies; Rosell of the

Patent Office; balloonist Myers; Edward Powers; and an aide named
Keefer from Dyrenforth's law office.

Equipment and supplies came from many sources. Myers furnished the balloons and kindred apparatus; a limited number of
weather instruments were provided by the Weather Bureau, now under
the Department of Agriculture. The Navy Department contributed two
tons of iron turnings (from projectiles) to be used in the production of
hydrogen; the Smith Electrical Works of New Jersey loaned a number
of dynamos to be used in detonation. Ellis purchased most of the
chemicals in St. Louis, and several railroads offered free transportation west of that city. Dyrenforth was unsuccessful in acquiring surplus
powder stored by the government at Fort Warren, Wyoming, but a
Texas coal mine owner presented him with six free kegs of ordinary
blasting powder. "The programme is elaborate and the material abundant, and the science involved exhaustive," said the *Washington Post*.
"Success means the regeneration of the country."[33]

By August 7 the equipment was being unloaded at Midland, and
soon Dyrenforth was deploying his forces for the coming battle against
the clouds. He established three parallel lines, less than half a mile
apart. In the front line, at intervals of about fifty yards and set into the
ground at an angle of forty-five degrees, were sixty makeshift guns—
"something like mortars"—improvised from "bell-mouthed wagon-
axle boxes" and from six-inch well tubing sawed into two-and-one-
half foot lengths. In addition, the front line was bolstered by explosives tamped into prairie-dog holes. On the second line were the large
kites, some of them twelve feet high. To the rear on the third line,
which was shorter than the other two, were located the balloons to be
raised and exploded aloft. Scientists later complained that Dyrenforth
did not understand his problem and merely tried to imitate a battle.
"The general and his lieutenant even wore cavalry boots," said one
disgusted critic.[34]

On August 9 the expedition was joined by Edward Powers, a
distinguished-looking old man with a fine, flowing beard, and in the
evening a number of ground charges of "rackarock" were detonated in
order to improve the firing techniques. More than twelve hours later,
on the following day, rain fell, and one unidentified member of the
party immediately telegraphed Farwell: "Preliminary. Fired some
explosives yesterday. Raining hard today." Without hesitation newspapers in various parts of the country delightedly picked up the story.

"They Made Rain," said the Denver *Rocky Mountain News*; "Made the Heavens Leak," reported the *New York Sun*. "Heavy rain fell, extending many miles," announced the *Washington Post*. The *Chicago Times* gave full credit to Farwell: "His patent detonating rain machine has been exploded in Texas and copious showers descended within a measurable short space of time. . . . He has outdone Moses."[35]

Small-scale firing was conducted on the ground from August 12 through August 15 in the presence of meteorologist Curtis, who arrived on the eleventh. As ordinary blasting powder failed to create much concussion in the homemade mortars and the "rackarock" blew them to bits, the mortars were abandoned in favor of dynamite and "rackarock" exploded in holes, atop of rocks, or tied to brush. Technical problems prevented the inflation of any balloons until August 16, when the first one was sent aloft and detonated. Firing continued intermittently for several days, and on August 18 a rainfall of .02 inches was recorded. Then followed a momentary lull for repairs on oxygen equipment and on personnel, the latter suffering from the effects of alkaline water. Further skirmishing coincided with a slight sprinkle on August 20 and a heavy dew three days later.[36]

The newspaper reports of these operations generally stemmed from highly optimistic specials issued from the expedition. The .02 inches of August 18 was described by the *Washington Post* as a "Hard Rain" that commenced immediately after the explosion of "rendrock" and continued for four hours and twenty minutes. According to the *New York Sun*, the experiment had been a "great success," producing a six-hour rain that covered one thousand square miles. The *Chicago Tribune* ran the headlines: "Rackarock Made Rain Come. Apparent Success of the Dyrenforth Experiments in Arid Regions of Texas." Four times, said the *Tribune*, the sky skirmishers had brought down a "drenching shower."[37]

Curtis left the expedition on August 24, and on the following day there was a heavy ground and aerial bombardment until 11:00 P.M. When the explosions ceased, Dyrenforth said the atmosphere became "very clear, and as dry as I have ever observed it." Early on the morning of August 26, however, a heavy thunderstorm passed along the north edge of the ranch. Most of its moisture fell elsewhere, but with each renewed detonation "the quantity of rainfall increased."[38]

Ignoring the fact that local showers had been predicted by the

Weather Bureau and that barographic records showed the passage of a low-pressure area over much of the Middle West and Southwest, the proud rainmakers claimed full responsibility and were supported by flowing press releases. The *Rocky Mountain News* noted that rain had fallen almost daily since the beginning of the experiments. The *Washington Post* referred to the storm of August 26 as the "grand finale of the operations at this point of Uncle Jerry Rusk's sky-stormers, and a fitting victory." A reporter for the *New York Sun* predicted that political success would reward "General Jupiter Pluvius Dyrenforth" and that "more than one Congressman will go to Washington this winter with a rain-making bill in his pocket." In the same metropolitan journal an aspiring bard hacked out some verse for the occasion:

> I am Cloud-compelling Dyrenforth, a mighty able wight;
> I can call the clouds together with a load of dynamite;
> I can dally with the cyclone, I can monkey with the gale.
> I can fertilize the prairie where another man must fail;
> I can swell the gentle brooklet to a roaring mountain stream,
> I tell you, Me and Jerry are a pretty brilliant team![39]

Dyrenforth, Powers, and most of the other members left Midland on August 27. The gear was entrusted to John Ellis, who would make one more test if clear weather prevailed, then ship the equipment to El Paso to continue the experiments. Dyrenforth arrived in Washington tired but exuberant. Systematically berating the "scientific wizeacres" who scoffed, he insisted that his group had brought rain at least a dozen times, "always when the meteorologist announced as his opinion that the atmospheric conditions for a storm were most unfavorable." He would report to his superior, he said, that the appropriation "was a very wise move." The *New York World* interviewed former senator Farwell, who predicted that when Dyrenforth submitted his official report, Secretary Rusk would request at least five hundred thousand dollars and possibly one million dollars from Congress for rainmaking. "The Department of Agriculture has its inspectors and employees in the West," said Farwell, "and when an inspector reports that rain will be needed at a certain time in a certain region, the secretary will send on his men and appliances and make the rain." Rusk himself was quoted as saying that the press descriptions of the experiments were "underestimated" rather than overdrawn.[40]

Meanwhile at El Paso the tests entered another phase. Under the

supervision of Ellis, aided by Eugene Fairchild, a colleague from
Oberlin, the appartus was moved from Midland to the border city.
With the assistance of Lieutenant Shubiel A. Dyer and twenty-two
enlisted men from Fort Bliss, firing was resumed in mid-September,
aerial bombs shot from mortars now augmenting the oxyhydrogen
balloons. Ellis claimed to have brought showers, but his claims were
dubious. Once when rain fell twenty-five miles away in almost every
direction, but none at El Paso, a contributor to *Puck* observed:

> These are very funny fellers,
> Uncle Jerry's cloud-compellers.
> They mount the air to heights stupendous,
> Burst bombs with force and noise tremendous;
> And while they watch for drops of water,
> It falls just where it hadn't orter,
> By tons, in every other quarter.

After a few days the expedition moved southeast to Corpus Christi,
newspapers generally agreeing that Ellis had failed at El Paso and that
the city had poorly invested the $767 it contributed to buy explosives,
oxygen, and other gear.[41]

Robert J. Kleberg, of the King Ranch, and a few others sub-
sidized the tests in southern Texas. Lieutenant Dyer and ten enlisted
men accompanied the group from El Paso, arriving at Corpus Christi
on September 23 in a rainstorm. The "rain squeezers" postponed their
activity for a few days, then took credit for the rain that followed their
limited bombardment. "It was a complete success," reported the
*Minneapolis Tribune* of the effort.[42]

Wet weather continued, and the party moved some fifty miles
west to San Diego, a small station on the Mexican National Railroad.
Here firings in mid-October brought hundreds of spectators to view the
pyrotechnics at Camp Edward Powers, as Ellis dubbed the site. All
were rewarded with steady rainfall. "The water was pouring down in
torrents," said Ellis. Kleberg and others had furnished $1,636 for
salaries and supplies, while the government expended $633 at Camp
Powers. By October 19, when it disbanded, the expedition had incur-
red since leaving Midland an expense of $6,384, all but $1,450 having
come from private sources.[43]

Dyrenforth's official report, published by Congress early in
1892, presented the experiments as successful. It contained sym-

pathetic comments from Ellis and Lieutenant Dyer, not to mention a number of letters from onlookers who were convinced that the experimenters had "got a cinch on Old Pluvius," as one said. Eugene Fairchild of Oberlin, whose statement was included, believed that the tests were "entirely successful" and the scheme practicable. "A tax of a few cents an acre would cover the expense of operations extending over the entire dry season," he said. "Without a doubt it will soon be a thing of the past for the Texas cotton-grower to lose two-thirds of his crop for lack of rain at the right time."[44]

Dyrenforth was optimistic but more restrained than his subordinates. The tests were only preliminary, he reported, but from them came the inference that under favorable conditions concussion would bring down moisture from the clouds. Further experiments were needed before more definite conclusions might be drawn. Dyrenforth also went out of his way to repudiate statements attributed to him by the press and to discredit all "unauthorized, premature and undigested statements" made by any member of the party.[45]

Dyrenforth was undoubtedly reacting to the wildly colored and distorted accounts circulated by one segment of the press. For other newspapers, however, the Dyrenforth tests opened new vistas for sly humor or more critical jabs. They might describe the project's rainmaking technique as too costly and inconvenient for small families and suggest that expenses be reduced by "utilizing some of Theodore Roosevelt's numerous explosions." Or, like the *New York Tribune*, they might propose that since explosions brought rain, would not a serene atmosphere prevent rain? Why not send aloft string orchestras in balloons and music boxes attached to kites to soothe the clouds and halt impending rainstorms?[46]

The cartoonists missed few opportunities. One showed a jilted lover drenching the faithless damsel and his rival by means of a pocket rainmaking kit; another depicted a farmer threatening legal action if his neighbor did not keep his rain on his own side of the fence—"Don't you see my clothes are hung out to dry?" Another had a flashily dressed city dude petitioning a rainmaking farmer to call off his shower until he could get by with the lady in his buggy.[47]

A delightfully perceptive poem published in the humor magazine *Life* late in 1891 under the title "A Tale of the Rain Machine" poked fun at the Dyrenforth experiment and satirized man's puny efforts to control the elements. The poem read in part:

Said Jeremy Jonathan Joseph Jones,
　"The weather is far too dry.
So I reckon I'll have to stir my bones,
And try the effect of concussive tones
　Upon the lazy sky."

So Jeremy Jonathan Joseph went
　Away to the nearest town;
And there his money was quickly spent
For queer contraptions, all intent
　To make the rain come down.

There were cannon, and mortars, and lots of shells
　And dynamite by the ton;
With a gas balloon, and a chime of bells,
And various other mystic spells
　To overcloud the sun.

The day was fair and the sky was bright
　And never a cloud was seen;
When Jeremy Jonathan set alight
His biggest fuse, and screwed up tight
　The joints of his rain machine.

He fired a shot, and barely two,
　When the sky began to pale;
But the third one brought a heavy dew,
And the fourth a hurricane or two,
　The fifth, a storm of hail.

It rained all night and another day,
　And then for a year or more;
It flooded the farm and it spoiled the hay,
And drowned poor Jeremy right away,
　Who couldn't stop the pour.[48]

In addition to inviting droll or barbed comments, the experiments also generated severe and outspoken criticism from editors who could see little humor in the expenditure of public funds on rainmaking schemes. An article by Dyrenforth, "Can We Make It Rain?," had appeared in the October 1891 *North American Review*, accompanied by a mild rebuttal by scientist Simon Newcomb, who rejected the basic premises of producing rain by concussion. This exchange touched off a savage commentary by the editor of the *Nation*, who believed that in Europe a man like Dyrenforth "would never survive the shame of these ridiculous experiments." In fact, insisted the *Nation* in a subsequent editorial, "if Mr. Secretary Tracy should send out the North Atlantic Squadron to melt the icebergs on the Banks by bombarding the Gulf Stream off New York, his act would not be a whit more absurd than that of his colleague in sending his rain-making expedition to Texas."[49]

One of the most telling critics, however, was the *Chicago Farm Implement News*, one of the few papers that had a reporter at Midland to cover the experiments. Stories released by the *Farm Implement News* and by the *Dallas Farm and Ranch*, which also had had a man on the scene, were at such variance with the "specials" released by the expedition that it was soon obvious to discriminating readers the public was being misled, deliberately or otherwise, by unidentified members of the group at Midland. In describing the party, the *News* was casual. With Dyrenforth were half a dozen scientists, "some of them having become bald-headed in their earnest search for theoretical knowledge" but lacking in practical ability: their kites would not fly properly, their balloons leaked gas, and on all sides was a noticeable lack of discipline and system. There was "too much ballast"— too many young men along for "a pleasant summer excursion at government expense." Worse yet, the *Farm Implement News* cast serious doubt as to the origin of rain that did fall, pointing out that the period from mid-June to mid-September was normally the rainy season for the Midland area. The self-styled rainmakers merely took credit for moisture due to natural causes, the journal charged. Indeed, it was sometimes raining before the firing commenced, and in practically all cases the rain had been previously predicted by the Weather Bureau. A cynical cartoon in the *Farm Implement News* showed Dyrenforth in his cork helmet, rallying his "professors": "Hurry up the inflation, touch off the bombs, send up the kites, let go the rackarock; here's a telegram announcing a storm. If we don't hurry, it will be on us before we raise our racket."[50]

Meteorologist George Curtis, whose formal report was never printed, substantiated these criticisms not only in a series of published articles but also in a blunt letter to Fernow of the Division of Forestry in February 1892. He pointed out that the general public had been misled and that the federal government was partly responsible. How

could the public know that the appropriations had been largely the
work of one man and that the resulting experiments had not been part
of a closely calculated program worked out in detail by scientists in the
Department of Agriculture? The fact that these were government
experiments and were reported as successful by many newspapers
gave people confidence in them and left the way open for charlatans to
prey upon public gullibility, said Curtis. Already, he informed Fernow, companies had been formed to capitalize on rain production, and
the subject was "assuming serious and even disastrous importance
among the farmers of the northwest." Curtis believed that the federal
government should correct the popular impression of the Texas tests;
in fact, he volunteered to tour the plains states lecturing and explaining
that the Department of Agriculture was not responsible for the "un-
fortunate matter" but that it had been "imposed by Congress." Fernow passed these comments along to Mark Harrington, the versatile
and brilliant chief of the Weather Bureau—an agency only recently
transferred from the Army Signal Service to civilian control—with
the suggestion that the department issue a circular "disavowing any
conclusions to be arrived at from the experiments," this to be widely
publicized through the press. Even Secretary Rusk evidenced a growing skepticism. His *Report* for 1891 merely stated that "so far as the
production of explosions is concerned, these experiments were emi-
nently successful. As regards the object thereof, namely, the production of rain, I have no data yet on hand which would justify me in
expressing any conclusions on the subject."[51] Thus high officials of
agencies within the Department of Agriculture were either noncom-
mittal or were displaying concern over public reaction to the experiments. That the matter was suddenly dropped and no warning circular
issued was probably due to the decision of Congress to continue the
tests for another year.

The first appropriations of nine thousand dollars had been expended by the end of 1891. In the following spring Congress considered the matter of further funds. The House Committee on Agriculture
read Dyrenforth's formal report and listened to "complete and
exhaustive" statements by the rainmaker, by Secretary Rusk, and by
Assistant Secretary Willets, then recommended continuance of the
"pluviculture" project. According to Representative Hatch, Dyrenforth made a "strong impression" on the committee by his candor,
being "perfectly positive in his statement that every experiment that he

had made with these explosives had produced rainfall in greater or less degree."[52]

Some opposition was voiced in the House. The government should not meddle with the ways of Providence, said some. What would prevent the government from using the rainmaking power to aid its friends and punish its enemies? asked Representative Enloe of Tennessee. Kilgore of Texas called the experiment "a dead failure" and suggested prayer meetings instead. Even if artificial rainmaking were feasible and desirable, said Kilgore, it was a matter for the individual states, not the national government. Others feared bureaucracy; some complained of no provision in the law to halt the rain. Several asked why the Weather Bureau, which since July 1891 had been under the Department of Agriculture, was not handling the project instead of the Division of Forestry. It was argued that the Secretary of Agriculture himself was lukewarm on the matter. When someone complained that all farmers would not wish rain at the same time, it was suggested that the Signal Service might give all farmers two weeks notice before rain was produced. In the end, however, after a lengthy discussion embracing such diverse topics as the importance of religion and the effect of the Suez Canal on the vegetation of Africa, Congress passed an agricultural appropriations bill that provided ten thousand dollars for additional rainmaking experiments in 1892.[53]

The end of October 1892 found Dyrenforth's scientists busy at Fort Meyer (across the Potomac from Washington), experimenting with several new explosives, including "rosellite," invented by Claude Roselle. Henry Hazen, professor of meteorology for the Weather Bureau, and John Ellis were in charge of these nocturnal explosions. Their work brought "profanity in seventeen different languages drizzling down from chamber windows, accompanied by an electric display, all the way from the Chinese legation to the Italian quarter," as Washingtonians protested their disturbed slumber. "Raised a Storm at Last," smirked one local paper; "He Bombarded the Clouds," said another, "and Brought Down a Storm of Public Indignation." Both Ellis and Hazen, the latter now apparently an advocate of the concussionist theory, gave unauthorized news interviews, blithely taking credit for rain that fell, ignoring the fact that rain had been forecast for several days and had extended over an area one thousand miles wide.[54]

After the Fort Meyer preliminaries, the "drought busters" moved to San Antonio, Texas, where it was predicted they would do much better. There they could "do their own counting and their own certification." The government weather observer, who also received twice-daily weather maps, had been alerted to make careful but unobtrusive notes on what transpired. With Dyrenforth supervising, the 1892 expedition established Camp Farwell at Alamo Heights, four miles north of San Antonio, and prepared again to "wring or coax or startle water from the skies." Alexander Macfarlane, a physicist from the University of Texas, visited the camp on November 20 and found federal troops unpacking equipment and helping to mix "rosellite" under the personal direction of Rosell. As half of the ten thousand dollar appropriation was being held back for later trials in South Dakota, several large western landholders, including Charles Farwell and John H. P. King, contributed a total of eight thousand dollars for the San Antonio tests.[55]

At Camp Farwell a festive spirit prevailed. On Thanksgiving Day a number of shells were fired for the enjoyment of officers and ladies who visited from nearby Fort Sam Houston; on the following day, under overcast skies, the volleys commenced in earnest and continued until rain spattered down on the morning of November 26—officially .04 inches. For Macfarlane this "mere sprinkling" only demonstrated the impossibility of the concussionist approach. In newspaper accounts he castigated Dyrenforth and his supporters, earning as a result the wrath of Edward Peters, who now admitted Dyrenforth's incompetence but staunchly upheld the principle of the theory. Governor Hogg visited the camp. Then, Reverend King of the First Baptist Church in San Antonio, viewing the rainmakers as instruments of divine power, preached a sermon, taking as his text Leviticus 26:4— "Then I will give you rain in due season"—and Ezekiel 34:26—"and I will cause the shower to come down in his season; there shall be showers of blessing."[56]

By early December, with little or no rain forthcoming, Dyrenforth was under attack from all sides. The annual *Report of the Secretary of Agriculture*, issued about this time, stated that the facts did not justify the anticipations of the concussionists and that budget estimates for the next fiscal year did not include any sum for further experiments. A number of newspapers went out of their way to laud Rusk for this action, at the same time expressing a caustic disapproval of the "far-reaching and iridescent failure" already produced at public expense. "The scheme has gone up like a rocket and come down like a stick," reported the *San Antonio Evening Star* in an editorial entitled "Fakes and Fakirs"; "now let the rainfaking department of the agricultural bureau betake itself to greener fields and pastures new." The editor of the *San Antonio Daily Express* injected more color and less bitterness into his comments:

> General Dyrenforth assaulted the atmosphere all along the line. He attacked front and rear, by the right and left flank, in the open field and by Indian ambuscades. He shot high up and low down, striving to catch it "between wind and water." He exploded rosellite that tore great holes in the bosom of Mother Earth, and balloons that ripped the circumambient ether to ribbons. Great guns belched, shells screeched and cracked and enthusiastic spectors yelled "fer Jim Hogg an' the Kermishun," but not a drop of rain leaked through the shattered empyrean. . . . The sky remained clear as the complexion of a Saxon maid.[57]

According to the *Washington Post*, in one night 12 balloons, 175 shells, and 1,200 charges of "rosellite" were exploded, "and yet the whole hullabaloo did not lead to any more water than would furnish a canary bird with its morning bath." The only real dampness resulting, said the *Post*, was that which fell on the enthusiasm of Dyrenforth's backers. The *Chicago Times* believed that the money expended would have been "less ridiculously employed if it were devoted to the attempted manufacture of whistles out of pig's tails."[58]

This uninspiring San Antonio climax brought to an end the government's rainmaking experiments in the nineteenth century. In May 1893 Dyrenforth, now dubbed "Dryhenceforth" by the wags, wrote the new secretary of agriculture, J. Sterling Morton, concerning the disposition of the unexpended five thousand dollars of the 1892 appropriation. Morton requested Harrington of the Weather Bureau to prepare a tactful reply to the effect "that we do not desire to cannonade the clouds any longer at Government expense." Harrington's letter, which went to Dyrenforth over the signature of Morton, instructed that the unspent balance revert to the Treasury, inasmuch as "the present state of our national finances" did not warrant its use. Because the appropriation was not for the large-scale production of rain, but to devise equipment and methods to demonstrate the feasibility of the concussion theory, and because Dyrenforth had reported that suitable apparatus and techniques had been developed, Morton assumed that the purpose had been fulfilled. State and private funds should now replace federal support, he suggested. The letter ended on a less sympathetic note, one that reflected the attitude of the Weather Bureau: " . . . quite independent of the question whether light rains have been produced by dynamite explosions, yet, in my opinion, there can be no doubt that this method is too noisy, uncertain, expensive and dangerous to have any commercial value and I cannot consider it as an economical expenditure of Government moneys."[59]

Dyrenforth returned to the practice of law and relative obscurity, his name flashing across the headlines only at his death in 1910, when his will made provision for a strange, impossible supereducation for his grandson, combining Harvard, Oxford, and West Point.[60]

But "Uncle Jerry Rusk's cloud jugglers," as one editor called them, were not soon forgotten, though federal officials tried to do so. If Dyrenforth, the "head conjuror," submitted a final report, it is not extant; probably it was destroyed with many of the old records of the Department of Agriculture. Unfortunately, however, in 1899 at Dyrenforth's suggestion and without consultation with either the Weather Bureau or the Department of Agriculture, Congress authorized the reprinting of the first report (*Senate Executive Document* no. 45, 52d Congress, 1st session), thus keeping alive the fiction of successful concussion experiments. Weather Bureau Chief Willis Moore complained to the secretary of agriculture that the publication "does injury to the good name of the Department, for the reason that there is little or no scientific basis for the theory that rain, in copious quantities, can be produced by artificial means." The number of misleading newspaper accounts based on the report caused no little embarrassment and prompted the issue of a memorandum disclaiming it. The secretary composed a form letter answering all queries regarding the experiments, pointing out carefully that they were preliminary only and that results did not justify further tests.[61]

Most of the inquiries were passed on to the Weather Bureau, which down to the mid-twentieth century sought, not always with success, to minimize the Dyrenforth episode, an aspect of American meteorological history responsible men would like to forget. When the "Texas cloud puncher" sought to explain his concussionist theory, he was most unscientific. A series of explosions over a long period, he said, "causes the atmosphere to take a spiral or cyclonic action round an axis, and this produces a separation of the rain from the air. The water is sucked into the center of the whirl, as pieces of wood into the center of a whirlpool."[62] Knowledgeable men scoffed; and meteorologists in retrospect saw the affair as "a most humiliating experience," "a national disgrace," and "a monument to the credulity of arm-chair scientists" which for a time did much to discredit American science in European eyes.[63]

Following the Texas fiasco, the government was urged to send observers to the great naval review to be held in New York Harbor in April 1893, that they might determine whether or not the salutes from the forty or so participating ships brought down rainfall. More important was the rash of independent efforts by amateur concussionists. During the summer tobacco growers in Connecticut, for example, attempted to explode dynamite attached to balloons but panicked and abandoned their plans when the equipment caught fire. By preconcerted agreement in May of the same year, citizens of seven small Kansas towns simultaneously bombarded the heavens in an effort to break the drought. An onlooker noted: "Cannon and every explosive within reach were brought into requisition, and hundreds of men and boys with guns blasted away at the skies until 2 P.M., when the clouds opened their reservoirs and drenched the earth." But, as the Weather Bureau had earlier predicted and as responsible editors subsequently pointed out, the same clouds also drenched the earth in the greater part of five states.[64] Kansans had also taken up a subscription to experiment with a state-owned cannon but cancelled the tests in June, after Israel Markley and four others fired of 250 pounds of dynamite near the hamlet of Minneapolis and stirred up "the heaviest rain in months." Nebraskans were less successful. There in 1894 the "Rain God Association" was formed to raise one thousand dollars for gunpowder. Then, under a broiling July sun, from points designated as "Rain God Stations," Panhandle citizens commenced multiple cannonading which extended from Harrison to Lone Pine—but without avail. Another Nebraskan, W. F. Wright, described as "a man of moderate education," explained his rainmaking theories in a book in 1898. A "vortex spiral vibrational action" split molecules of water into gaseous elements. The firing of mortars, with special funnels attached to induce a spiral current, would produce a chemical reunion of hydrogen and oxygen to form rain. One problem was that firing blew the funnels off; another was that he was unable to obtain funds to continue his experiments, although he claimed showers as a result of a barrage of twenty-four mortars in the summer of 1901.[65]

But any bombardment of the clouds was expensive; and if local subscriptions were not always forthcoming, the national government was asked to provide artillery or other equipment that would-be rainmakers might substitute for their makeshift apparatus. A Coloradan, for example, requested a cannon in 1899, only to be advised by Weather Bureau officials that concussion did not work. The Coloradan knew better, Dyrenforth to the contrary notwithstanding: "We had good success in Kansas," he argued, "using only gaspipe which was loaded heavier and heavier till it exploded. . . . Now I don't care what Uncle Sam or his Grand Father think about that, but I want a shooting iron with a 2 in. bore at least 36 in. long that I can place in a perpendicular position which can be discharged with safety."[66]

Despite Weather Bureau discouragement and newspaper editorials branding rainmakers as charlatans, public faith was hard to shake. In 1903, when forest fires swept through the Adirondacks, Carl Myers, Dyrenforth's original balloonist, prepared a number of oxyhydrogen balloons to bring rain and quench the flames, but Nature provided a rainstorm before he could go into action.[67] Five years later, faced with the same problem, mill owners in Watertown, New York, tried to convince the State Forest, Fish, and Game Commission to help pay for concussionist rainmakers, only to be dissuaded by Weather Bureau spokesmen who cited artificial production of rain as "one of the worst forms of charlatanism that has been practised in this country in a long time." The ghost of Robert Dyrenforth was again invoked during the terrible forest fire that swept the Idaho-Montana border in August 1910, with a death toll estimated at 160. It was seriously proposed that army and naval artillery along Puget Sound and the mouth of the Columbia be fired off to bring showers and extinguish the flames. But the War Department, having already committed thirty-two companies of troops as fire fighters, refused, arguing that the cost would run around one hundred thousand dollars without real hope of success.[68]

The same period pushed to the fore one who was a believer and who also had the wherewithal to actively push his beliefs. He was Charles W. Post, the Michigan cereal king, who shot off thousands of dollars worth of explosives in at least eighteen spectacular "rain battles" mainly on the Staked Plains of Texas. Exuberant, energetic,

and optimistic, "Postum" Post, as he was popularly known, owned
some two hundred thousand acres of ranch land near Post City, Texas,
of which he was both founder and colonizer. He was a dedicated
subscriber to the concussionist theory; and his biographer calls his
rainmaking experiments "the last and greatest experiment of his life
and the most famous of its kind in history"[69]—a dubious assessment,
considering Dyrenforth and one of the later smell makers, Charles
Hatfield.

Noting that precipitation of rain by explosion "has been demonstrated many times," Post in 1910 made preliminary trials in detonating dynamite attached to kites in the air but was thwarted when Mother
Nature provided moisture just as the real tests were about to commence. In the drought of the following spring, he abandoned the kites
and instructed his managers at Post City to conduct rain battles, with
firing stations spaced regularly one-eighth mile apart over a two-mile
line along the Cap Rock. By the end of the summer, the Post sky
stormers were firing off three thousand tons of dynamite per battle,
and Post was apparently able to persuade the Du Pont de Nemours
Powder Company to share the expense of the 1912 war.[70]

Early in 1912 Post published an article, "Making Rain While the
Sun Shines," in *Harper's Weekly*, a piece that was copied and quoted
as far away as London. In it he paid homage to the success of
Dyrenforth's Midland experiments and several of his own, one of
which produced rain over four hundred thousand acres at a cost of
one-fourth cent per acre. Through the summer of 1912 his men continued their battles, refining their techniques and rattling the dishes in the
Post City hotel. Sometimes they lost; sometimes they won. Rain fell
on August 5, for example, and A. L. Marhoff, Post's moisture manager, took the credit. Firing had "created a storm center," he said, "as
we changed the direction of the wind," even though showers had
commenced twenty-five miles away before the dynamiting began.
According to Marhoff's records, of the thirteen attempts made in 1912,
seven were followed by "an appreciable amount of rain" and three by
"veritable cloudbursts." Post's last Texas rain battle—the twenty-
first—came in August 1913, nine months before he sent a bullet
through his brain. His commitment to the idea of rainmaking by
concussion was indicated not only in his patient response to the press
and to those who showed an interest in his work but also by the fact that
he had expended some fifty thousand dollars of his own money.[71]

In addition to this atmospheric warfare in the Southwest, Post was also responsible for a Michigan experiment that proved embarrassing to the United States Weather Bureau in the summer of 1912. Through the Battle Creek Industrial Association, he announced one of his battles, scheduled for the cereal capital on July 23, and invited the Weather Bureau to send an observer. The bureau's chief, Willis Moore, accepted and instructed the agent in Grand Rapids to make a full report. Moore was already perturbed at the favorable publicity attending Post's activities in Texas. Believing that the Du Pont Powder Company was partially responsible, he feared that such publicity fostered a revival of grasping cloud milkers. For release on July 21, he had prepared a leaflet condemning what seemed to be an epidemic of rainmaking and pointing out that in each case for which Post had claimed success, rain had already been forecast and had extended over a broad area. Moreover, he noted that, as in other instances, the advertised rain battle could not fail to bring an influx of visitors into the community, a factor certainly not unnoticed by the Battle Creek Industrial Association.[72]

When the association asked him to predict Battle Creek's weather for July 23, Moore first forecast clear skies; then, as conditions changed, he telegraphed that a five-hundred-mile-wide storm was moving eastward and that rain would fall. Local preparations proceeded: lapel tags were printed, reading "This rain was made in Battle Creek"; and two movie camera crews moved in to record the historic details of the appointed day. With appropriate ceremony and fanfare, forty-five hundred pounds of dynamite were exploded in approved Post battle fashion, and on the following day the Battle Creek Industrial Association telegraphed Moore in Washington: "Four hour dynamiting beginning nine yesterday morning brought half inch rainfall beginning three thirty afternoon. Sky clear at beginning and humidity twenty degrees less than this morning. People here satisfied Post system rain making successful not-withstanding department's prognostication."[73] Another Battle Creek group, the Central Fruit-Growers Association, issued a circular lauding Post's accomplishment, much to the Weather Bureau's consternation. Moore protested loudly that the claims were unfounded, that his second and revised forecast had indicated a large storm moving into the area. In addition, his Grand Rapids observer pointed out, and had affidavits to support his point, that it had rained even before the explosions were set off.[74]

Responsible newspapers had carried Moore's revised forecast and got the story straight, but the local *Battle Creek Enquirer* and the *Evening News*, both owned by Post, showed no mercy. "A Heavy Rainfall Follows Dynamite," said the *Enquirer*; "Chief Moore's Prediction of Fair Weather Is Knocked into a Cocked Hat." "Villains! You Have Me Rainstorm," the *Evening News* had Moore saying to his detractors.[75] Rival editors admitted that Battle Creek was "a live burg" with a "large corps of hustlers" and wondered if the rain test had not been primarily designed "to make a noise that would shake down a lot of type in the newspapers." If so, it succeeded. Numerous papers throughout the country picked up the stories from the *Enquirer* and the *Evening News*, reprinting them verbatim, or garbling the facts even more. An irate Willis Moore wrote countless letters attempting to offset this negative publicity and salvage the prestige of the Weather Bureau. Reputable national periodicals sometimes came to his rescue: witness the *Scientific American*, whose editor called "the rain-making hallucination . . . one of the incurable forms of mental disease."[76] But a good deal of damage had been done by what was fundamentally an excellent publicity stunt.

Post and Dyrenforth were the two most flamboyant examples of the "boom boom" rainmakers combated by the Weather Bureau. Others were low-keyed, their proposals ranging from the use of balloons in California, to box kites in Oklahoma, to dynamite on poles in Ohio. Washington meteorologists received some aid from abroad. In 1907 concussion experiments in Southern New Zealand drew a negative report from scientists there. In the British House of Commons five years later, when Viscount Dalrymple asked the fleet to refrain from heavy gun practice off the coast during harvest time, when rain might hurt the crops, he was told bluntly by the first lord of the admiralty that there was no evidence that firing brought precipitation.[77]

But popular beliefs persisted, and World War I reopened the question. Late in 1914 an English writer gave serious treatment to rain as the result of battle, citing the example of the Spanish Armada as one piece of proof and indicating to more responsible editors that "the myth is fixed—chrystallized—and probably imperishable." Once the United States entered the conflict, what doughboy could ever forget the muddy trenches of France, even though careful British and French studies both debunked the cause-and-effect idea, noting that the "amount of gun fire varies inversely as the amount of rain that is falling," rather than vice versa.[78]

Even in the twenties and thirties, American meteorologists were still explaining away the Dyrenforth and Post experiments, parrying proposals from those who would use explosives to bring down water for North Carolina power plants or possibly to create a "rain war," in which one man could "deluge a section of land of from 50 to 75 miles in diameter & he can do this 10 times in one day." In the depths of the depression, Amarillo oil-fire troubleshooter Tex Thornton, who noticed that showers followed his blasting, shot aerial torpedoes into the sky at Dalhart, vainly trying to capitalize on the idea. About the· same time—1935—an imaginative Denverite suggested that Wyoming, Colorado, and New Mexico all fire off dynamite simultaneously along the eastern slope of the Rockies to break the drought.[79] A Texan urged President Franklin Roosevelt to declare a national "Explosion Day," at which time each county in the United States would fire explosives to bring rain. An Ohioan suggested a "New Deal Radio Rainmaker," a recording of a severe thunderstorm played at right angles to the wind over a powerful amplified in order to cause concussion and atmospheric turmoil—and precipitation. And in the same year—1936—a Kansas City attorney pleaded with Secretary of Agriculture Henry A. Wallace to put a hundred pieces of field artillery under his direction so that he might produce showers in any part of the country within twenty-four hours. The writer, who suggested that this might be done as "army exercises," was Benjamin M. Powers, son of the author of *War and the Weather*. In 1939, when war again came to Europe, the new generation of soldiers, European and ultimately American, saw for themselves the coupling of gunfire and rainfall.[80] As persistent as Bermuda grass, the venerable concussionist theory was slow to die; indeed, not until after World War II was it finally displaced and then only because scientific cloud seeders finally presented a viable substitute.

It was ironic that at the same time one arm of the federal government was condemning the concussionists, another, through the Dyrenforth experiments, was doing much to fix the theory in the public mind. In public opinion the national government had put its imprint on artificial rainmaking. Dyrenforth's tests were termed *scientific*; yet they were conducted by a man who was already convinced, who sought to prove, not merely to test. The Weather Bureau was hardly consulted, probably because Dyrenforth was aware of its disapproval and wished as little interference as possible. The War Department, which might have provided artillery and technical aid, contributed a handful of men—mostly for routine tasks—and gave little professional advice. Thus the experiments were conducted by men of definite bias, amateurs as it were—chemists, electricians, balloonists, and lawyers—not by trained experts in ordnance and meteorology.

Meanwhile, knowledgeable and reputable scientists like Macfarlane, Fernando Sanford of Stanford, Simon Newcomb of Johns Hopkins, and Robert De C. Ward and William Morris Davis, both of Harvard, were not stinting in their criticism;[81] but the concussionists had the better press. Despite contemporary publicity to the contrary, there is no doubt that Dyrenforth, and Post after him, failed. If rain fell, it was coincident with detonations in storm areas already existing and predicted on the weather charts. The government tests should have done much to dispel popular belief in rainmaking by concussion; but because of misleading accounts in the popular media, the idea may even have been strengthened for the reading public. And those who would accept one theory of artificial precipitation would be susceptible to others.

# 4. Renew Every Hour and Stir Every Thirty Minutes Day and Night Until Rain Comes: The Kansas Smell Makers

After one intonation
  The rain came pouring down
    And Melbourne claimed the credit.
There was a celebration,
  And great grew his renown,
    And Kansas spread it.[1]

In 1891, when Dyrenforth "was pumping water from the ethereal blue" in Texas, according to the Denver *Rocky Mountain News*, "a pale-faced young fellow was at work in Ohio and Wyoming squeezing rain from cloudless skies as one would squeeze water from a sponge, and as much at will."[2] The young man referred to was the "Australian rain doctor," Frank Melbourne, one of the best-known and most spectacular of the smell makers, or chemical rainmakers, of the nineties.[3] Described as "a kind of barnyard Barnum,"[4] Melbourne was typical of the shrewd professionals who preyed on the desperate drought-smitten farmers of the Midwest. He was a confidence man, a calculating and ambitious gambler who took what profit he could from natural adversity and public gullibility.

Often referred to in his day as the "Rain King" or the "Rain Wizard," Melbourne was born in Ireland and had lived in Australia and New Zealand for a dozen years before joining his brothers in the United States. He had dabbled in real estate and in cattle ranching, and it was in New South Wales that he worked out his rainmaking techniques. Indeed, he later claimed to have been forced to flee the Australia–New Zealand region to avoid possible retribution for having produced rains of flood proportion.[5]

In 1891 a tall, dark-haired, bearded man of about forty-five, Frank Melbourne, appeared in Canton, Ohio, where his brother John, a wealthy contractor, refused to permit him to establish an observatory and laboratory atop his luxurious home. A brother-in-law in the same city, however, allowed him to conduct experiments from a shed on the edge of his property; and Melbourne, though first considered by some to be "teched in the head," soon built up an enthusiastic following, not to mention a bank account, by means of a series of "successful" rainmaking demonstrations. In July, for example, when he announced that he would produce rain on an appointed day, another brother, William, took bets from all comers; and when rain did fall, the Melbourne purses were fatter by several thousand dollars. Half a dozen times, said the press, he "has plucked the guileless gamblers of Canton, and now the rain wizard can offer odds of a thousand to one without takers."[6]

Frank Melbourne was never modest in his pretensions before the public. In the summer of 1891 he claimed to have induced rain in eight consecutive tests. To prove his ability, he promised showers every Sunday until September 1; but being a sports enthusiast, he scheduled them only in the evenings. Not only had he flooded the cellars of Canton and tied up its traffic, he boasted; if given the opportunity, he could produce rain in Death Valley. In fact, according to Melbourne, his invention could haul down moisture over an area "of upwards of 250,000 square miles at any time that I desire, and this without regard to climate." He was also at work on a "Cold Wave Machine"—a gigantic air-conditioning apparatus designed to provide a cool climate for a large section of the country.[7]

His rainmaking equipment was mysterious indeed. It was carried in several ordinary-looking black gripsacks, from which Melbourne was seldom parted. He once left a restaurant rather than check his precious bags. His machine had cost fifteen thousand dollars, and each operation of it required four hundred dollars, he said. It was small—"no larger than a dinner pail," said a reporter for the Denver *Rocky Mountain News*—and operated by a crank, with gases being liberated through a pipe protruding more than a dozen feet above the roof. Newsmen who watched outside his shed reported hearing a "rumbling, fluttering sound," a noise like the buzzing of a bee. Melbourne never made public his process, although once he hinted that his apparatus produced chemicals then unknown to science.[8] Other than that, he said nothing.

He did admit his machine was so simple that if the secret were known, everyone would imitate it and bring down rain at will. Such a situation would be unendurable, commented the editor of a Dodge City newspaper, because "there could never be a political barbecue without all the rain machines of the opposition being set in motion," and "the infidels would spoil all the camp-meetings and the church people ruin the horse races"; nothing but conflict and ill will would result.[9]

Melbourne came to the attention of the editor of the *New York Tribune* in August 1891, and the newsman stated his belief that such "would-be rainmakers" should be treated with respect so long as they appeared to act in good faith but that the evidence should be weighed very carefully. Why not draw a board of inquiry from a neutral agency—for instance, the Ohio Sate Board of Agriculture or the faculty of Oberlin College—to observe Melbourne and his work? Only then, if reputable organizations sanctioned his process and its results, could financial aid be expected from scientists or capitalists.[10]

No such impartial review was ever conducted, however, and Melbourne turned his eyes westward. Several times he had mentioned that the flatness of the plains and the thinness of mountain air would increase the efficiency of his rainmaking apparatus. In mid-June 1891 he had addressed a letter to the governor of Wyoming, outlining his talents and proclaiming a willingness to go anywhere. Late in August the Cheyenne press announced that negotiations had been completed and that Melbourne, "the Australian and New Zealand rain doctor," would soon be there. He was to receive $150 if he produced rain, and nothing if he failed. However, the *Chicago Tribune* insisted that if he did succeed, "a mammoth stock company with practically unlimited capital" would probably be formed to operate in the West.[11]

Melbourne arrived in Cheyenne on August 27 accompanied by his brother Will and was escorted by a local arrangements committee to the home of Frank H. Jones, a civil engineer who had been instrumental in persuading some twenty-three subscribers to contribute the $150. The "Rain King" would have made his Wyoming appearance earlier had he not been negotiating with farmers near Fort Scott, Kansas.[12]

The Melbourne brothers took a room at the Inter Ocean in

Cheyenne, but their work was conducted from a coachman's room on the upper floor of a stable on the grounds of the Jones home, the old Moreton Frewen house at Twenty-fifth and Van Lennen streets. The Frewen property was ideal: it occupied an elevated position, and its two and a half acres were enclosed to assure privacy. In the workroom itself shingles were removed from the apex of a dormer window to give Melbourne access to the open air.[13]

The press was sympathetic, if sometimes reserved. The *Cheyenne Daily Sun* described Melbourne as "a man in the prime of life, open, intelligent face, frank, a trifle nervous and intensely sanguine. He is confident as a new millionaire, and the brother has a sack of money to wager on their game." If successful, said the *Sun*, Melbourne could in effect name his own price: "If success attends the efforts of this remarkable man in a marvelous business, he can get a steady job right here at wages that, from a monetary standpoint, will make the president envious."[14]

John Carroll, editor of the *Cheyenne Leader*, evidenced more skepticism but would eventually become a firm supporter of the "Rain Wizard":

> It will be a great day when each granger can anchor a cloud over his own little eighty-acre farm and by pulling a string like an aeronaut in a balloon or sending up a few inexpensive whiffs of gas precipitate upon his parched land a copious downpour of rain. . . . The umbrella and gum coat dealer will have a perpetual picnic: people may develop web feet and the individual who can't swim may wish he had never been born.
>
> There's a great day coming when each man will be his own rain doctor, but with all due respect to Mr. Melbourne, it is yet a good ways off.[15]

Melbourne did not commence work immediately, probably because Andrew Gilchrist, one of the waiting committee, did not wish to risk having his haying interrupted, although Frank Jones, already being called "Rainwater Jones," was eager for the experiment to proceed. On August 30, however, the *Sun* announced that "Prof. Melbourne's Rain Mill Started Up at 5 O'clock This Morning." Captain Ravenscraft, the local signal officer, had predicted fair weather, and the committee had given the go-ahead signal. Melbourne had promised to produce at least one-half inch of rain within three days.[16]

The self-styled cloud compeller worked in secrecy. He entered the stable with his mysterious gripsacks and a "big revolver to discourage too curious spectators." The entire stable was kept locked, windows were covered with blankets, and all cracks were stuffed to keep out prying eyes. "Like a voter of the Australian ballot Melbourne was alone with his God and his lead pencil or whatever it was," reported Editor Carroll. Brother Will was ill at the Inter Ocean, but he pulled himself together long enough to cover bets. By all reasoning the odds should have been in Melbourne's favor. As the newspapers pointed out, the region was experiencing a dry spell of three weeks duration; besides, were not the state fair, a miners' convention, a teachers' institute, and the shooting tournament of the Rocky Mountain Sportsmen's Association all scheduled to meet in Cheyenne during the first two weeks of September?[17]

Early on the following day Signal Officer Ravenscraft noted the possibility of rain; and in the afternoon two brisk showers fell, the heaviest rain of the season. These were violent thundershowers that ranged out some twenty miles on all sides of town, depositing one-half inch of moisture and incidently killing two cows and two calves belonging to C. P. Organ, one of the members of the committee responsible for bringing Melbourne to Wyoming. It was "Melbourne's rain"; snow that fell at Casper, over a hundred miles to the north, was also attributed to his miraculous machine.[18]

Ravenscraft announced that he believed the rain was the result of "supernatural agencies"; and Melbourne was voted his $150, the committee calling his experiment "an unqualified success." Newspapers carried the story far and wide and made Melbourne a hero. "The Wizard," ran headlines in the Denver *Rocky Mountain News*, "Melbourne Astonished Cheyenne by Bringing a Heavy Downpour of Rain." "The Rain Doctor Did It," said the *Salt Lake Tribune*. "A Successful Attempt Is Made in Cheyenne," reported the *Minneapolis Tribune*.[19] The *Casper Derrick* probably gave as graphic a description of Melbourne's "success" as anyone: "Late Monday night he returned to his den, hung the monkey wrench on the safety valve, re-adjusted the water gauge and turned on the crank when lo! the heavens were suddenly overcast . . . and in the beaufitul language of the wooly West there was a devil of a rain and the Lord wasn't in it."[20]

The editor of the *Salt Lake Tribune*, admitting that he had previously considered the whole affair "as a sort of dismal fake on the part of the most improbable crank in the world," now was much more receptive of Melbourne: "He is a famine breaker, he is a dust disperser, he is a disease-germ exterminator, he is a daisy, and we need him very much indeed." The *Washington Evening Star* got the name wrong but carried the story with enthusiasm; the *Chicago Tribune*, in an account stemming from Lester Kabris of Cheyenne, pictured Melbourne as "a miracle performer" of great importance because of his "cloud squeezing experiments." The *Rocky Mountain News*, which published a cartoon showing "Melbourne as Jupiter Pluvius" pouring water down on Cheyenne, drew comparisons between Melbourne and the federal concussionist experimenter "General" Dyrenforth. Dyrenforth's system of detonating explosives in the air and on the ground was expensive and "inconvenient . . . for small families," said the *News*, predicting that in the end Melbourne's process would prevail.[21]

In Cheyenne, Melbourne was the man of the hour. Many of the ladies were impressed, said the *Daily Leader*. "Men of the faith are patting themselves on their breeches pocket," and "Col. Rainwater Jones walks on moist air." "It begins to look like gondolas would become necessary equipages in Cheyenne unless the committee should immediately call off the mysterious and puissant Mr. Melbourne," said the editor. "The irrigation ditch can go," commented the *Daily Sun*. "It might be well, however, to have another trial of the rain wizzard's [sic] skill before filling up the water trenches." No trouble or expense should be spared to demonstrate the practicability of Melbourne's invention: scientists and representatives of the Department of Agriculture should be invited to observe further tests. Unhappy were betting scoffers and a number of ranchmen whose haying had been disrupted by rain. The latter threatened legal action to collect damages from Melbourne; but as the papers pointed out, a successful suit of this type brought against the "cloud tapper" would establish him as a bona fide rainmaker and be worth millions to him.[22]

Meanwhile Melbourne promised to bring more rain. However, just as he "was preparing to collect and crack more rain clouds," the local committee persuaded him to postpone his work to permit clear weather for haying. A new date, September 7, was set, with Melbourne to receive a hundred dollars if he produced one-half inch of moisture on schedule. When he retired to his "laboratory" again on September 4, his secrecy was beginning to irritate newsmen a little. Reporters described him as being "artistically evasive"; he "would break the heart of the best lawyer in the state if put on the witness stand."[23]

Again there was a brisk wagering, with the odds seeming to favor

Melbourne, who had told the skeptics, jokingly perhaps, that if they continued to scoff he would flood the town. Interest ran high, but the appointed day passed without rain. On September 8, twelve hours after the expiration of the time limit, one-eighth inch fell. This was "only a scrawny little unassertive bilgewater instead of a deluge," but Melbourne claimed it as his own, insisting that high winds had hampered his work and blown his rain away.[24]

This second Cheyenne experiment was with some charity "catalogued as doubtful." Signal Officer Ravenscraft pointed out that the belated sprinkle was actually part of a major storm that had covered the region extending from Portland, Oregon, to Omaha, Nebraska. Furthermore, in reconsidering the precipitation of September 1 credited to Melbourne, Ravenscraft now believed that that rain had been "chased in here by a cold wave and that Melbourne had nothing to do with the case or the goods." There was widespread disappointment, and some of the faithful strayed. The local committee was not satisfied. "Rainwater Jones" was said to have "come out of his probation pew and gracefully taken a seat on the mourners' bench,"[25] although this lapse was but momentary.

On the other hand, there were many who stood by Melbourne. The *Cheyenne Daily Sun* contended that the mysterious machine had succeeded one time out of two; and even if only 50 percent effective, it was "yet the most marvelous thing the age of mankind has developed." Then in macabre tones, the editor added: "Wouldn't it be intensely romantic and terribly tragic if Melbourne were to be killed by his own lightning and thus die with his secret?" Believers proposed that Wyoming engage the rainmaker's services for a full year, regardless of cost. They suggested that the federal government hire him to combat forest fires. When there was criticism brought against Melbourne, the Cheyenne press, especially, went out of its way to defend him. When a New York newspaper called the "Rain King" "an Australian adventurer," "a rain make-believer" interested only in "the much-talked-of cloud with a silver lining," editor Carroll of the *Daily Leader*, a recent convert, plunged to the rescue. When a Californian named Michael Cahill charged publicly that Melbourne, "the Cheyenne Cloud Cracker," was a "pretender" and had pirated his invention, the *Cheyenne Sun* had a few comments: "Hang the ocean on a clothes line to dry, lasso an avalanche, pin a napkin on the crater of a volcano, skim the milky way with a tea spoon, throw salt on the tail of the noble American eagle, paste 'for rent' on the stars and stripes; do all these but don't, pray don't, question the originality of Melbourne."[26]

In the meantime, Melbourne had been considering several offers in various parts of the West; and on September 9, he left for Salt Lake City, along with his brother and Frank Jones. The Mormon capital was enjoying a wet season, and Melbourne did not demonstrate there. Instead, under the auspices of land agent E. P. Tarpey of the Central Pacific Railroad and C. E. Wentworth of the Union Pacific, he conducted an experiment at Kelton, Utah, a semideserted station on the Central Pacific. Melbourne was to receive five hundred dollars if one-half inch of rain fell by midnight September 17; and it was rumored that, if successful, he would receive a lucrative railroad job. He commenced his operations on the morning of the fourteenth in the Kelton schoolhouse, where with the usual secrecy precautions, he worked day and night, came out only twice for meals, and in the end collected his money, although only .43 inches fell at Kelton.[27]

About this same time, either shortly before or shortly after the Kelton trial, Melbourne attempted to bring rain at the town of Nampa, on the Oregon Short Line in southern Idaho. Here he failed completely and left even before his deadline had expired.[28]

But his reputation had spread, and several groups were bidding for his services. Californians and Coloradans were interested; Reno wanted him for the Nevada state fair; and he acknowledged he had had "two liberal offers" from Texas. Meanwhile the good citizens of Goodland, in drought-ridden western Kansas, were raising funds by public subscription; and Melbourne agreed to produce "a good rain" reaching from 50 to 100 hundred miles in each direction for a flat five hundred dollars. Local committees made the necessary arrangements; the Rock Island Railroad promised half-fare excursions within a radius of 150 miles; and at the county fair late in September, the little borough in western Kansas prepared for an experiment which "will be the means of advertising Sherman county all over the United States, and demonstrate whether or not rain can be produced by artificial means."[29]

Excitement ran high. "He Is Coming!" "Melbourne Is Coming," beamed the local headlines. Handbills carried the picture of this "Ohio Rain Wizard," "the most wonderful Inventor of the Century" who had contracted to bring down rain on the last day of the fair; and hardware proprietor George Hess ran his likeness but misspelled his name in an advertisement: "Rain, Rain: Melborne is coming but, I am here and here to stay. I will sell you Hardware & stores!"[30]

Betting was lively. Many were impressed with what they had heard of the Cheyenne experience, though not all pledged their support. Some called it humbug; one man refused to subscribe because "it was interfering with the Lord's business and harm would come out of it." Another tortured soul professed disbelief and feared that "the first thing we knew we would have a hell of a tornado here that would blow the town from the face of the earth."[31]

When "rain-milker" Melbourne passed through Cheyenne enroute to Goodland late in September, he was "as complacent, confident and sociable as ever." With him were his brother and Frank Jones, who was in charge of the mysterious valise affectionately referred to as "the baby." A hundred people turned out at the station to greet this engaging wonder-worker with a Scotch-Irish brogue and "the appearance of a student." The omen was good: the train arrived in a shower, an occurrence that brought to mind the story of Davy Crockett and the coon. "Don't shoot, Mr. Melbourne, I'll come right down," the rain was supposed to say.[32]

Dampness brought delay, during which the local committee on arrangements paid Melbourne's living expenses and readied the two-story wooden structure built on the fairgrounds, the upper room to be used by the rainmaker and the lower floor by Will Melbourne and Frank Jones to prevent interference by curious interlopers. When the time was right, the wizard began his work: "He entered his den, locked the door from the inside, and a spectator could see no signs of a battle with the elements." He worked steadily for several days, but no rain fell at Goodland by his deadline of October 4. Precipitation did fall in other parts of Kansas, and telegrams received by the town fathers asked that the rainmaker be "shut off." As usual, Melbourne blamed the wind for blowing away the fruits of his labor and claimed the wayward showers as his own; a "misty rain" that fell on October 5 he also requisitioned. Most thought it less than a victory, but the *Chicago Tribune* headlined the story: "Melbourne Causes the Rain to Fall. Complete Success Attends His Latest Experiments at Goodland."[33]

Moving from the fairgrounds to a caboose in the railroad yards, Melbourne conjured up some clouds; but by the time the second effort had ended on October 8, the sun was out and the clouds "nearly all fled like scared sheep." Even this did not entirely deplete the ranks of the loyal. Rain that fell at Kansas City a few days later was attributed to Melbourne operating secretly. Before he left, the rainmaker suggested a seasonal program of producing moisture at ten cents per cultivated acre for some forty counties in western Kansas—a total of about twenty thousand dollars. To make the area "blossom as a rose" for that price was considered cheap by one cynical editor: "If Kansans are gullible enough, and Providence Helps the wizard out with one or two coincident wet spells, this is liable to prove a good thing for Melbourne, who, of course, is not in the business for his health."[34]

Melbourne returned briefly to Canton, then made a journey through the Southwest to Mexico early in 1892. In Texas he gave at least one demonstration of his skill. Kansas observers thought that his technique was to use muriatic acid and zinc to produce hydrogen and oxygen, which, mingled with a little nitrogen, was then "fired" into the air by means of a galvanic battery. Alexander Macfarlane, professor of physics at the University of Texas, believed he must have borrowed his method "from the Bushmen."

> He came to Temple, Texas, hired a shanty on the outskirts of the town, shut himself and an assistant in, and all observers out. All that could be observed from the outside was the issue of some colored gas through a small pipe in the roof. . . . The proceedings of this imposter were gravely discussed by intelligent people; so great is the ignorance of physical nature.[35]

All the while, Melbourne was dickering either personally or through Jones, his manager. He claimed to have declined a contract in Brazil and to have fulfilled one with the government of Mexico, only to be cheated out of his fee of twenty-five hundred dollars. He steadfastly maintained that he would work only on a pay-as-you-go plan, and his stated rates rose. He quoted a figure of five thousand dollars for one inch of rain delivered in Oregon; he hoped to work out an arrangement in Nebraska to supply moisture for two million acres between May 1 and September 1—his price, two hundred thousand dollars, payments to be made monthly, with adjustments if sufficient rain did not fall.[36] With such a proposal, never accepted, he could hardly lose.

Competition forced him to advertise, and he published a brief pamphlet in the spring of 1892, *Rain Production of Frank Melbourne during the Season of 1891*. Its introduction, "To the People of the Arid

Regions," noted that his purpose was to give an account of his "succussful" experiments at Canton, Cheyenne, Kelton, and Goodland and to announce his readiness "to enter into contract to produce sufficient rain for crops, in any part of the United States, on very reasonable terms."[37]

In Cheyenne that same summer he signed an agreement with three counties in eastern Colorado and one in western Nebraska to bring down at least .51 inches of rain within seventy-two hours at Holyoke, Fleming, and Julesburg for six cents per cultivated acre. Again he failed. There was a light shower, hardly enough "to quench the thirst of a grasshopper," according to a contemporary. He did better at O'Neill, Nebraska, but flunked the test a few weeks later at Grand Island, where he had a contract with businessmen and farmers to produce .75 inches within four days for a fee of twenty-five hundred dollars. Such failures and the growing condemnation of Melbourne as a "quack" and "bogus rain-maker" out to fleece the farmers diminished his professional stature.[38]

His reputation was further tarnished when it was later discovered that the dates he selected for producing rain were identical with those for which rainfall was predicted in long-range forecasts in the popular almanac published by Irl R. Hicks of St. Louis. There is some evidence, too, that a barometer was part of Melbourne's heavily guarded "secret" equipment and that he tended to gauge his activities according to its rise or fall.[39]

After 1892 Melbourne dropped from sight. In 1894 his body was found in a shabby Denver hotel room, only the initials F. M. providing identification. His death was listed as suicide.[40]

And so from the scene passed Frank Melbourne, rain doctor, cloud compeller, opportunist extraordinaire. He was a master salesman and practicing psychologist and in that sense was the godfather of a series of would-be rainmakers in the nineties. Scattered amateurs, like John Painter, former county clerk at Broken Bow, Nebraska, and John Crue, cashier of the Madison, Nebraska, State Bank, took crash courses and set up their "weather mills" in various parts of the state. Painter used earthenware crocks, one labeled the "thunder mug" and the other the "lightning mug" by a skeptical editor. In New Mexico "Colonel" William Hopewell, general manager of the Las Animas Cattle Company, and "Professor" Jacob Mitchell were at work on a "new and powerful rain machine" but encountered difficulties due to faulty pipes leading from their chemical tank. But they were newsworthy, and the press believed "that many frauds will bloom out in the rain-making business, but out of the seekers out of notoriety will eventually come forth one Edison, a wizard."[41]

Despite his assertions to the contrary, Melbourne was at least an indirect party to the spate of corporate "pluviculture" ventures that would eclipse him in 1892: entrepreneurs in western Kansas believed they knew a good thing when they saw one. The first competition came in mid-October 1891, not long after Melbourne left Goodland, when the Inter State Artificial Rain Company was chartered "to promote and encourage agriculture and horticulture, and to supply water to the public by producing and increasing the rain fall by artificial means." And just to be sure, the organizers added the buying and selling of real estate as another possibility. Inter State was a Goodland company, registered with a capital stock of one hundred thousand dollars in shares of one thousand dollars each. Its president, E. F. Murphy, was variously described as a lawyer, a doctor, and a railroad agent; its directors included O. H. Smith, a chemist; M. B. Tomblin, head of the Sherman County Bank; and A. B. Montgomery, the secretary of the town company who would also serve as its field manager.[42]

The Inter State Artificial Rain Company used the "Melbourne system," although how they came by it is not clear. Some believed that the firm bought the secret and equipment; others that experimentation by Montgomery led to its accidental discovery; still others were convinced that with a kind of crude industrial espionage the company had stolen the Australian's formula. Melbourne steadfastly denied having sold his process. He intended to retain his secret, he insisted: "There is not enough money in the west to buy it." Be that as it may, the Inter State people had the key to the weather. "They have demonstrated beyond question that they are in possession of the secret of producing rain during the warm season," wrote one newsman. "You can mark up the price of your land and expect an era of prosperity," said another. "Goodland will become the metropolis of western Kansas."[43]

The company contemplated dividing that part of the state into a number of districts and establishing a central rainmaking station, from which rainmaking squads might be sent out as needed. But first it sought to establish itself and its process by a series of "experiments" in Indian Territory (Oklahoma) and Texas. By early November, Murphy and Montgomery were at work with unbridled enthusiasm at Temple, Texas. Of a prospective client, Montgomery wrote: "If he wants the whole Pan Handle of Texas watered we can accommodate him." Murphy was all optimism when he wrote the company treasurer at home: "And I tell you, Marve, we have got the world by the horns with a down hill pull and can all wear diamonds pretty soon. We can water all creation and have some to spare."[44] When he wrote, Murphy had been working day and night and was "pretty well worn out," although there was nothing at the scene to indicate that rain wizards were at work "except suggestive blazes of purple and blue which issued at night from a hole in the roof of the house." Hard labor brought success. It did rain, and Murphy and Montgomery were reported to have sold their secrets for fifty thousand dollars. Except for disgrunted hard-shell Baptists who reserved the rainmaking prerogative to the Almighty, Texans applauded; and the Goodland moisture mixers returned home figuratively to the tune of "See the Conquering Heroes Come," as Murphy had hoped, rather than "The Rogues' March."[45]

Meanwhile, the business was becoming more competitive. Early 1892 saw the chartering of at least two more Goodland rain companies. On January 13 the Swisher Rain Company was registered in Topeka, its nominal capital of one hundred thousand dollars in shares of one hundred dollars each. It was headed by Dr. William B. Swisher, a druggist and county coroner whose chemical experimenting had resulted in a mix so excellent "that when you touch the button the clouds do the rest." Swisher's son-in-law, Calvin Russell, a banker, was a director, as was Frank H. Smith, proprietor of the Metropolitan Drug Store in Goodland.[46]

According to local editors, who believed competition would reduce the cost of rain production, these were men of standing and integrity. Their rainmaking was based strictly on "scientific principles," and this "straightforward business transaction" would operate entirely on a "no rain, no pay" basis. If the "avalanche of proposals" showered upon the new company was any indication, said one sympathetic Goodland editor, there would be plenty of "room for the organization of a number of rain companies to meet the demands of this new and wonderful industry."[47]

This was no idle chatter. Less than a month later the same newspaperman, J. H. "Parson" Stewart of the *Republic*, was announced the president of the new Goodland Artificial Rain Company, chartered "to furnish water for the public by artificial rain fall by scientific methods and to contract for services for the same, and to sell and dispose of the right to use our process in any City, Township, County, State, Territory or Country." Like the other companies, the firm had a capital stock of one hundred thousand dollars divided into one hundred dollar shares. And, like the officers of the other companies, Goodland's president saw a brave new world on the horizon. With rainmaking "reducible to a science," the Great Plains could be transformed "into the very garden and granary of the world."[48]

Thus the sleepy little farm town in northwestern Kansas became the rainmaking capital of the nation—the "Rain Company Town," Stewart called it. There were rumors of a fourth company, the Genuine N. W. Kansas Rain Company, at Ruleton, a few miles to the west; but either it was unincorporated or inactive or perhaps both. On the plains rainmaking was serious business, but back east *Puck* anticipated competition in the cloud-compelling field with tongue in cheek. Its full-page cartoon cover showed two drummers approaching a farmer in his field. Said the first: "I am representing the Thunderbolt Rain-Producing Company—our showers last two hours and twenty minutes, and we make a sample shower free of charge!" Not to be outdone, the second drummer made his sales pitch. "Let me take your order, sir, for the Aquarius Artificial Rain-Making Company—our rain is superior to anything in the market, and we give a silk umbrella and a pair of overshoes with every shower!"[49]

Of the three Kansas companies the Inter State was most active. It ranged as far afield as California, where Murphy and Smith had taken their exclusive gear in its "iron-bound trunk" to fulfill a contract at Pixley in the San Joaquin Valley early in 1892. At first they reported that unusually cool weather had prevented their "rain persuader" from working; but soon they announced brilliant results, although skeptical Californians believed the rainmakers would "have to divide the causes of success with the presiding rain genius of the Pacific Coast, with the honors largely in favor of the latter." Since rain had fallen at the same time over much of California, Nevada, Utah, and Arizona, the chief of the U.S. Weather Bureau in San Francisco labeled the rainmaking efforts "a fizzle," prompting this retort from "Parson" Stewart in Goodland: "He [the chief] is the Goliath of the weather and defies the camp of the rainmakers. Give it to him David." Ranchers at Huron,

north and west of Pixley, also contracted with the Inter State experts to
water sixty thousand acres of wheat land.[50] When Smith and Murphy
returned home by late March, it was to paeans of triumph. Their
western mission had been "Crowned with Success," although newspaper accounts perhaps carried more irony than usual.

> It is a happy hour for Goodland to know that she is not only the Mecca of
> the home seeker; the innermost chamber of these broad plains; the
> morning star among a hundred towns of Western Kansas, but also that she
> holds within her grasp the scepter that even sways the clouds. Its a happy
> hour to know that we have but to smite the rock (a la Moses) and the water
> cometh forth. We are the people.

Even better, Stewart in the *Republic* reported that back in California a
farmer a hundred miles south of Pixley was unhappy because the
Goodland cloud milkers caused so much rain that it interfered with
normal fieldwork.[51]

The history of the Inter State Company in South Dakota is not as
clear as it is intriguing. In the summer of 1892 L. Morris, one of the
directors, was in that state to fill a rain contract. According to the word
reported back, the heavens cooperated and he brought Cheyenne
County "a fine wetting down." Described as "a counterpart of Father
Time, excepting the fact that he carried no scythe," "Old man Morris" was back a year later, doing his rainmaking exercises from an old
creamery building on the edge of Doland, south of Aberdeen. The
exact terms of his agreement are not evident; but likely several counties were involved and had in mind purchasing the Inter State formula
and rights for their area, contingent on Morris's success. What happened next is not certain. One source claims that Morris brought down
rain; that each of the four counties voted bonds of fifteen thousand
dollars, which were then exchanged with the company for the secret
and the right to use it; that subsequently the South Dakotans could not
make the process work; and that in the meantime the Kansan had
legally sold the bonds and left. A second source contends that Morris
did indeed bring rain, but that purchase of the rights depended upon a
second successful trial in the spring, an effort which was not rewarded
and after which the rainmaker went home empty-handed.[52]

The Inter State Company was also operative in eastern Colorado.
Officials met with citizens at Holyoke and again at Akron, indicating
that a series of four "test rains" would cost them twenty-four hundred
dollars. At Holyoke a committee was formed to raise funds, and

several counties made similar efforts. Murphy met with a number of county delegates at Yuma, Colorado, in April 1892 and agreed to conduct four trials in eastern Colorado and Nebraska, all on a "no rain, no pay" basis. It was also reported that a move was underway to create an offshoot company to buy up the process and perpetual rights for an eight-county area of Colorado for a price of twenty-five thousand dollars.[53] Probably there was more talk and dickering than action, but the company did free some of its magical gases into the air of the Centennial State.

Of the other two Kansas companies, the Goodland Artificial Rain Company was strictly local and the Swisher Rain Company primarily so, apart from one effort in Wisconsin and an early "experiment" in Mexico in the spring of 1892. At that time Swisher and two coworkers were in Mexico with a contract to bring two inches of rain near San Pedro for a fee of thirty thousand dollars. The rain experts claimed success—they brought moisture where there had been none for two years, they said—but probably the rain commenced before they had a chance to get their gear into operation.[54]

But the bulk of the rainmaking of all three firms was within the state of Kansas. Even before the registration of the Goodland Artificial Rain Company had been formally completed, Goodland citizens met at the courthouse to select a committee to negotiate for rain. On their part, the companies offered to provide seasonal rainfall for one-half cent per acre when needed or, alternatively, to give the same amount for all cultivated ground for three cents an acre. The first approach would cost $3,456; the second was more imprecise because the amount of cultivated acreage was not known at the time. Acting alone, the Inter State Company offered to furnish precipitation for the growing season for twenty-five hundred dollars; Swisher for two thousand dollars; and the third firm, still organizing and labeled only "Parson's Rain Company," for fifteen hundred dollars. But funding was a problem. Legislative action was needed, but never forthcoming, to permit county commissioners to levy taxes for artificial rainfall. The Kansas attorney general had determined that the irrigation law which allowed county bonding could not be applied to rainmaking.[55]

Thus the bulk of the corporate rainmaking came to be on a fairly short-term, small-scale basis, usually at five hundred dollars or so a throw for success. The spring and summer of 1892 was an especially busy time, with numerous Goodland rainmakers "grinding away on their little coffee mills," as one critic put it. The process was cheap, costing but $50 to $75 per "experiment," and simple—so simple that the wife of the field operator of the Inter State Company could carry on the work when her husband had to leave. There were successes and there were failures, but the companies were blessed with a reasonably moist summer over Kansas, Nebraska, and Missouri. Even at Mankato—where an enterprising merchant advertised "The Rain-maker Is Here! Call early at our store and buy one of our Silk, Serge or Satine Umbrellas"—the Goodlanders finally got rain, though the beginning was less than encouraging: "He commenced Monday when there were a few clouds in the sky, but he got his machine bottom-side up and dispelled the few there were and at present writing it is as clear as a bell."[56]

If editor Stewart is to be believed, it was a remarkable summer. Swisher was making "splendid rain"; the "Parson" himself made "Big Rain" at Council Grove; in August the Inter State Company, which boasted only one failure in twenty-five efforts, declared a small dividend, pointing up Stewart's contention that the "rainmakers are strictly 'in it' and have got a cinch on the weather." But others disagreed. They thought the "rain maker fakes," Stewart included, were "gulling the people in fine shape." All the company activity indicated, said the editor of the *Kansas Farmer*, was that "a drowning man catches at straws."[57]

Often there were complications. In South Dakota the Inter State's "Professor" Morris once found himself in bitter competition with a rival rain manufacturer, one "Captain" Hauser, both with reputations and money at stake and neither willing to halt their machinations, although local citizens worried lest they be washed away. But no problem: rain did not fall. When a number of farmers contributed to making up a pot, company agents could not always collect what they believed due to them. Early in 1893 the Inter State Company contended that recipients of its rainfall still owed about two thousand dollars. Disputes over payment were frequent and occasionally came to court. Before 1892 was over, William Swisher moved to Lincoln, Nebraska. He took his chemical chest along and continued "monkey-ing with the elements." At Lincoln he agreed to bring down rain for a group of farmers for a fee of one thousand dollars, half to be contri-buted by J. H. McMurtry. Rain fell on the third and last day of the deadline, but mainly within the town of Lincoln; then the sun came out "as bright as a new tin pan," to be followed by a general rain all over the state that night. McMurtry refused to pay unless Swisher could prove that the rain was his, and the rainmaker brought suit. During the course of the litigation, Swisher had to display his apparatus in the Lancaster County District Court not only to the judge but also to three chemistry professors acting as witnesses for the defense. "It consisted of two immense mills, jars, a galvanic battery, copper wire, molten zinc, a pair of gigantic funnels, the whole thing connected with small tubes, one of which was supposed to discharge the chemical solution into the outer air." After prolonged debate, during which Swisher swore that he produced the rain in question, the court decided that he need not demonstrate his equipment nor divulge his formula; it also handed down a judgment of fifty dollars on his behalf.[58]

Editor Stewart to the contrary notwithstanding, rainmaking was not always regarded as one of the more genteel professions. One local politician found his association with the Goodland Artificial Rain Company a decided political liability when he ran for the state legislature. More than once, the rainmakers left behind them angry citizens. One of the Goodland Company operators tried his hand in Minden, Nebraska, and after five days of smelly but arid effort decided to leave. "But the citizens first tied him to a telegraph pole, turned the hose of the fire company on him and showed how it could make rain." At Council Grove, Stewart collected only part of his fee on behalf of the same firm; "his" storm left behind broken awnings and windows—and a host of disgruntled citizens. A. B. Montgomery was another who got more than he had bargained for. In the name of the Inter State Company, he took credit for rain around Emporia in the summer of 1892. A cloudburst of the same storm system destroyed James Butler's wheat crop and washed out track of the Santa Fe railroad, causing the death of an engineer. Butler threatened to sue for damages, and the engineer's wife did enter a suit for ten thousand dollars. Apparently neither case was completed, but they posed some interesting questions. If rainmaking were possible, what was the extent of the responsibility of the operator? Could the courts distinguish between natural and man-made rain? How? And some believed that even a substantial judgment for rain-caused damages would be a cheap way of establishing a rainmaking reputation worth millions.[59]

Like the rainmakers who operated on their own, corporate rainmakers were controversial; but informed observers saw them for what they were: opportunists feeding on the farmers' adversity. Company operators could read the almanac predictions as well as anybody, and Hicks's was their favorite, according to several critics. Company rainmakers also had access to Signal Service maps, and barometric changes; and it took no great brilliance to be able to calculate within a day or so when a low pressure area would reach them, with rain a good possibility over a large area. It was noticable that when the weather conditions were unfavorable, the "Swisher Sloppers" and other cloud controllers were conveniently "out of chemicals." Thus farm victims paid for what was natural, and rainmakers "reaped where they did not sow."[60]

The "no rain, no pay" principle was misleading. Rain companies were not called in until drought had prevailed for some time, until people had become desperate and chances were good that rain would come anyway in a few days. It was only a bet, "but a one-sided jug-handled bet," as one onlooker put it. With inexpensive chemicals, intricate but cheap equipment, and several men in the field at different places, the companies could afford to gamble "their gall against several hundred dollars that a dry spell that has already lasted a long time will not last ten days longer. It is a great scheme." Success fed upon success. A general rain like that of July 1892 paid handsomely and paved the way for another cycle: the "dupes" would multiply and the rainmakers "make an excellent livelihood" from their credulity.[61]

But the heyday of the companies was brief. By the autumn of 1894 the big boom was over, and the movement that had taken Kansas by storm had little impact elsewhere. As a Jayhawker poet later summed it up,

> They capitalized the venture,
> And with a corporation
> Sold stock in making rain;
> But, without bias or censure,
> I'll say appeal to the nation
> Appeared to be in vain.[62]

Melbourne and the chartered rain companies originally focused attention on Goodland. A new "rain wizard," backed by the Chicago, Rock Island, and Pacific Railroad Company, would continue to keep the town in the "pluvicultural" limelight. He was Clayton B. Jewell, the young Rock Island dispatcher at Goodland, who supposedly hit upon the rainmaking formula after observing Melbourne in action. In the spring of 1892 Rock Island officials provided $250 worth of chemicals; and Jewell and an assistant, Harry Hutchinson, commenced serious "experiments" from the depot building. The company also allowed him to hook into its line of "2,000 jars electric power"; by May 11 Jewell was taking credit for a "soaking rain" that broke a "long dry spell" and saved crops. These facts, insisted "Parson" Stewart of the *Republic*, should silence "those bare-faced liars" who had been so busy maligning the Goodland rainmakers.[63]

At this time Stewart identified Jewell as a member of one of "our own" rain companies. With Rock Island support Jewell would now embark on a rainmaking career of his own—a career that would see him crisscrossing Kansas and neighboring states by rail, generating and releasing clouds of unnamed gases (along with "a certain perfume which hurt the throat"), and occasionally smiting the clouds with explosive rockets.[64] He even spoke of a grand tour through Iowa and Illinois, ending up at the World's Columbian Exposition in Chicago. Certainly by late 1893, Jewell had eclipsed the three Goodland rain companies.

That the Rock Island was in earnest was indicated when it fitted out a special car for the rainmaker's equipment and use. "When a giant corporation goes at it there surely must be something in it," crowed Stewart, always a champion. Jewell, that "quiet, urbane gentleman" with "unbounded faith in the enterprise," was reported to have tried to induce rain nine times by early June and to have brought down at least one inch each time within forty-eight hours.[65]

Jewell expressed surprise at a certain hostility on the part of the press, especially when the railroad was paying the cost of the work—an estimated four hundred to five hundred dollars per week. The Rock Island commitment was strictly "in the interest of science and in its own interests": good crops meant good freight business. In an effort to promote better public relations, Jewell from time to time opened his special car to observers but was careful not to divulge the nature of his chemicals or the methods used in mixing them.[66]

Jewell toured Kansas and ranged into Nebraska and Oklahoma, exhibiting his prowess at county fairs, "shooting electricity into the heavens," and gaining mixed results. He was reported to be successful 90 percent of the time; and if his luck held, according to a punster, he would become "a Jewell of the first artificial water." At Phillipsburg he tried some chemical-laden rockets set to explode in the atmosphere. The "effect was immediate and wonderful," said an observer. "The light clouds thickened and blackened and soon they witnessed a great storm." But so too, he added, did most of Iowa and Illinois. Despite his excursions into rocketry, Jewell was essentially a smell maker. When a concussionist rainmaker, Captain Redmond, was killed and two of his aides wounded by a premature explosion of his rain cannon at Minneapolis, Kansas, newsmen thought this "a record which Mr. Jewell with his ascending incense idea can not hope to equal."[67]

Although he failed at Liberal, an area "too 'tuff' for any body but the Almighty," Jewell went about his work "as confidently as an angler on his way to a brook he knew was full of hungry trout." It was rumored that an Australian company would pay him one million dollars for his secret, once he demonstrated it to their satisfaction;[68] and from Nebraska, hand-hewn verse extolled the wonders of the new science:

Oh, Jewell, if you have a key to open the heavenly door,
   please turn it just the once for me, and let the water pour;
      precipitate an inch or two of most aquatic rain, and watch
         the good it will do thirsty grass and grain
Insert your patent cork-screw in the bottle of the sky, and
   pull like blazes, won't you, till the wet, wet waters fly?[69]

It was announced in midsummer 1893 that the Jewell rainmaking equipment would be displayed at the World's Fair in Chicago. W. I. Allen, the assistant general manager of the Rock Island stated that the special car was being readied for a tour through Kansas and Iowa and would arrive in the Windy City just in time for "Kansas Week." Indeed, one Canadian bluenose urged Jewell to use his power to bring down rain upon the heads of Sabbath breakers at the fair. But Chicago editors had no use for his "Pluvian influences." "Chicago doesn't believe much in rain making," said the *Times*, "but if Jewell fools around the fair grounds and it should rain it will be a bad job for Jewell, that's all." Jewell went to Oklahoma that fall, deferring the Chicago trip until the summer of 1894, at which time he served as acting deputy marshal during the railroad strikes there.[70]

When he returned from the Cherokee Strip in September 1893, the rainmaker reported having brought down rain thirty-three times from the Rock Island car. Railroad officials were more cautious. In late August the assistant general manager noted that "a couple of employees of this company . . . claim to be able to cause rainfall by artificial means," and that the company had provided materials and transport for experiments "in some eighteen or twenty different locations, and in each case we have had more or less rainfall, which in nearly every instance we can but feel there is something in their claim." Pointing out that from one-half inch to three and one-half inches of precipitation fell over areas from ten to thirty miles wide and from twenty-five to ninety miles long, Allen qualified his statement: "We have been slow to believe there was anything in this business, but at the same time must admit that they are either very fortunate in reaching the different points where they have experimented just in time to have rain storms, or they have certainly hit upon the right thing in the way of rain-making."[71]

But the company renewed its pledge of faith in the spring of 1894 when it expanded the experiments, now fitting out three cars, one managed by Jewell, one by Hutchinson, and one by W. W. La Rue. In April Jewell traveled to South Dakota. According to the press, three counties voted new tax levies in order to purchase his secret formula, and the Kansan was there to instruct them in its application. So much rain fell, according to one story, probably apocryphal, that Jewell was besieged with messages to call a halt. "How much will it cost to stop this rain," one fellow is supposed to have asked; "have a flock of calves in danger of drowning." Jewell, went the account, responded: "Machine wound up for ninety days. Same price for stopping as for starting. Teach the calves to swim."[72]

The Rock Island cloud busters commenced work in Kansas in the second week of May 1894. They planned free demonstrations at Selden, Phillipsburg, and Norcatur, one car near each town; after that, local citizens or municipalities would pay. By May 10 Jewell had contracts with at least five towns and had signed an agreement to bring rain to former senator Farwell's IXL ranch in Texas for fifty thousand dollars if successful. But Jewell and his cohorts did not please everybody; close to home, farmers in Sherman County met and condemned the rainmakers, blaming them for cold weather and high winds and sending a committee "to wait upon these gentlemen and notify them to quit the business." For others the dry spring was a sign of divine displeasure, of reaction to the "impudence of man in trying to take control of the elements out of His hands."[73]

Jewell also displayed his talents at Wichita and Dodge City. "I'll have Douglas avenue in Wichita turned into a canal by to-morrow," he was quoted as saying. There he had at least the moral support of the local rain master, George G. Matthews, another of the chemical school of persuasion. At Dodge City farmers came from miles around to see the Rock Island expert battle nature. Observers later described a "monster mortar" on a flatcar, "a sort of cross between a cannon of exceptionally large caliber and a giant slingshot," which hurled chemical bombs skyward to explode with great streams of yellow smoke.[74]

But rarely did Jewell bombard the heavens, and then only to release chemicals. His standard approach was the generation and dispersal of his "secret" gas. One of the few descriptions of his equipment is from the pen of the Reverend Charles M. Sheldon, Topeka Congregational minister whose book *In His Steps* (1897) became the outstanding tract of the social gospel movement. Sometime in 1894 Sheldon persuaded the Rock Island's division superintendent to allow him to accompany the rainmaker for a time. The car itself was divided into two compartments, one for sleeping and dining, the other for the elaborate mechanical and electrical apparatus that seemed as mysterious to Sheldon "as if they had been the stock in trade of a necromancer." An overhead tank held eight hundred gallons of water, through which gases generated by other equipment were forced, ultimately to be discharged into the outside air. A large twenty-four-cell battery was part of the gear; for, the rainmaker said, "rainmaking is largely an electrical as well as chemical matter." Fifteen hundred feet of gas were released every hour, to ascend sometimes to a height of nearly eight thousand feet. Like other curious onlookers, Sheldon was impressed with the motley display of bottles, pipes, tanks and electrical wires but less awed with the "short and unsatisfactory replies" to his questions. With the machinery working there was little noise, "and the whole thing was very undemonstrative."[75]

Another contemporary description indicated that four gas generators poured gas out of two pipes through the roof, and that Jewell had a wire hookup to the railroad telegraph system so that, in addition to his own battery, he could draw on "the full force of all batteries between Colorado Springs and the Missouri River." Another onlooker noted that the operatives kept their activities hidden, but occasional glimpses gave the impression they were "cooking over a red-hot stove."[76]

While the rain-producing device did its work, Jewell and his guest ate "a hearty supper," "a good bill of fare" supplied by "a colored servant who cooked and did the work." Sheldon's trip was a special one: it coincided with a bitter railroad strike; and during a night of violence, strikers burned smelters and turned over the rainmaking car, smashing bottles, rupturing tanks, and drenching those inside with water. Sheldon was pulled out "bruised and bleeding"; the rainmaker had his face "cut with broken glass and one arm broken", and the cook escaped with bruises but "was nearly killed by fright." Later that night, as Sheldon related it, "a tremendous thunder-storm burst over the two, and drenched the country for miles around." Jewell claimed it, but the Congregational minister remained a skeptic.[77]

While the Rock Island was actively supporting Jewell's experiments, other rainroads were showing a cautious interest. "Parson" Stewart gave the *Topeka Capital* as the source for the rumor that Jewell would fit out twelve rainmaking cars for the Southern Pacific in 1895, a rumor that seemed to be precisely that. During the summer of 1893 B. A. McAllaster, land commissioner for the Union Pacific Railroad, had interviewed E. F. Murphy of the Goodland Inter State Artificial Rain Company; and Murphy agreed to undertake trials on behalf of the line if its top management approved. But he would not permit inspection of his apparatus nor give information on his chemicals. The cautious McAllaster sought cooperation from both the U.S. Department of Agriculture and the Weather Bureau to determine "whether or not there is anything in the rainmaking scheme." The Weather Bureau then asked the University of Texas professor Alexander Macfarlane to act as its observer at the proposed Union Pacific trials; but, in part because of the financial disaster of the summer and fall of 1893, the railroad's officials in Omaha "called a halt to the whole matter."[78]

In the meantime the Rock Island contemplated expanding its own operations by sending three of its rainmakers to the Pecos Valley in west Texas to undertake thirty days of extensive tests. On request the weather Bureau in Washington agreed to furnish trained observers and instruments; but the railroad decided to postpone this southwestern effort indefinitely, proposing, however to "experiment very largely on our own lines in Western Kansas next season, as soon as the dry weather sets in."[79]

Professional railroad journals were "astonished that the manager of the Rock Island should thus attempt to undermine Uncle Jerry Rusk in the affections of the Kansas farmer," but Jewell was news. He was quoted as saying that he had succeeded sixty-six times, and the *New York Engineering News* printed a picture of his special car with its gas pipes projecting through the roof. Despite an unofficial announcement that it planned to add three additional rain cars in 1895, the railroad soon dropped the experiments completely; and its officers were subsequently of the opinion "that they never should have been commenced."[80]

As for Jewell, his reputation and his efforts both moved westward momentarily. His past affiliation with the Rock Island, plus the publicity from California boosters, brought an invitation to try his magic near Los Angeles in the long, dry summer of 1899. Experiments were scheduled for July 18 and 19 but could not proceed until a court injunction and restraining order acquired by a local contractor could be dissolved. That accomplished, Jewell's sixty hours of continuously coaxing the clouds were in vain: the air remained as dry as Carrie Nation's cupboard, and the rainmaker was compelled to return an advance payment of several hundred dollars.[81]

Others, too, were still active in spreading the gospel of rainmaking by the release of chemicals. A Wichita resident, George G. Matthews, in 1896 claimed to have possession of the basic secret and sought to convince the federal government that it should underwrite trials. Several years later Matthews published the "Long Held Secret" formula in the *Wichita Daily Eagle*. It had come to the United States originally, said the newpaper, in the hands of "a foreigner"— presumably Melbourne. It then fell into the possession of Jewell and the Rock Island railroad but somehow was passed along to Matthews and perhaps a few others. From this "original parent recipe" came all other rainmaking gases. The mixture was simple: ten fluid ounces of sulphuric acid, fifty fluid ounces of water, and five ounces of zinc. The gas released was clearly hydrogen, and instructions were explicit:

> Renew every hour and stir every thirty minutes day and night until rain comes. The moment rain begins to fall remove jar or crock. In territory west of Kansas use one-third less; at sea-level double the quantity. In Kansas work only on southerly winds, which are moisture bearing winds. Begin an experiment in a clear sky. One station of the experiment if successful will produce a rain 30 to 50 miles wide in diameter. A better

and more certain result can be secured by having three or more stations 40 to 50 miles apart.[82]

Used on at least two hundred different occasions, Matthews insisted, the recipe had brought rain 90 percent of the time. Such tests had been spread over nearly six years and had consumed over six tons of sulphuric acid. "I think I can prove that the air becomes sensitive to the use of Hydrogen gas in 5 days," he argued, "and in 20 days $^1/_5$ of the quantity will produce full effect of the $^5/_5$ used to start on." But despite Matthews's repeated efforts to interest Washington, the scientific community there rejected both formula and principle. "Of course, you understand that I have no faith whatever in the efficacy of your process of making rain," the Weather Bureau chief wrote him.[83]

But already public belief in the efficacy of cloud milking was on the wane in the wheat and corn belts, although there was always a body of the credulous. Even ardent proponents like "Parson" Stewart had thrown in the towel. "The rain business has passed, it's irrigation now," he acknowledged in September 1894. A few months later both houses of the Kansas legislature rejected measures authorizing county commissioners to levy a special tax in order to finance rainmaking experiments. Perhaps it was symbolic that both bills had been referred to committees concerned with irrigation. About the same time A. B. Montgomery, one of the Goodland corporate enthusiasts, spoke before the Kansas State Board of Agriculture on irrigation, without ever mentioning artificial rainmaking. And late in 1895 Joseph Bristow, editor of *Irrigation Farmer*, published in Salina, summed up the prevailing sentiment when he noted that an era had closed. The rainmaker, he said, was "a thing of the past; he was a fraud; an ingenious tramp who played upon the cupidity and superstitions of the people and who worked them the same as a slight-of-hand performer."[84]

Basically, farmers were beginning to take a more realistic view of the Great Plains as an agricultural region. They were coming to realize that they must adapt their practices to the semiarid climate. Dry-farming techniques, new strains of drought-resistant seed and plants, and the substitution of wheat for corn were all part of this adjustment. So, too, was a corresponding shift toward livestock at the expense of some cash crops. And arching over it all was a new emphasis on irrigation and water conservation. Drought would be intermittent, but soon American farmers in general would be enjoying an era of relatively high farm prices. The conditions that had spawned both Populists and "pluviculturists" on the plains were markedly improved. Bristow had been right where Kansas and Nebraska were concerned: vestiges of the rainmaking boom lingered on, but the real focus would move westward to the Pacific Coast.

# 5. I Will Fill the Moreno Reservoir to Overflowing: Charles M. Hatfield, Miracle Man

Oh, Mr. Hatfield, make 'em hum,
And let that welcome wetness come;
Stir those chemicals up again,
You need money—and we need rain.[1]

Southern California has long been a collector of eccentrics—of faith healers, avant garde artists, or offbeat religious cultists. Thus it was entirely fitting that early in the twentieth century the hub of American rainmaking shifted from northwest Kansas to the Los Angeles–San Diego area. In this transition Clayton Jewell was at least one link, but the soon-to-be-crowned king of the cloud compellers, Charles Mallory Hatfield, would have a being and a following all his own.

Probably another liaison between the Goodland smell makers of the nineties and the new California practitioners was the small-time promoter Frederick A. Binney, a large bewhiskered man who never lost his British accent and who invariably alienated his neighbors by his constant haranguing on the advantages of socialism. In 1899 Binney had a citrus orchard at Helix but lost nearly two-thirds of his crop that year because of the winter drought. At that time he was in touch with one of the Rock Island rainmakers, probably Jewell, and was urging the use of his method around San Diego. "I can furnish the recipes," he promised.[2] Through the newspapers and to the federal government Binney pushed both the sulphuric-acid-and-zinc approach and the use of liquid air to cool the atmosphere. As he subsequently

79

developed the idea, he proposed harnessing windmills to provide electrical power in the California mountains, that power in turn to manufacture the liquid air. Within a few years Binney would be closely allied as an unofficial agent to Charles Hatfield, the man who came to be called "probably the most successful rain maker of modern times."[3]

Hatfield would practice his chemical arts for nearly a quarter of a century. He ranged as far north as the Yukon and as far south as Guatemala. Over the years his fame as a rain producer would far surpass that of Dyrenforth, Melbourne, or Jewell. He was accused of washing out dams and credited with saving millions of dollars worth of crops and defying not only the U.S. Weather Bureau but the elements as well. His work was the theme of poetry and of short stories; his life was the subject of a television program; and ultimately the Native Sons of the Golden West erected a "Hatfield the Rain-maker" historical marker at the site of what was labeled his most flamboyant triumph.

Born in Fort Scott, Kansas, in 1875, Hatfield came with his parents to San Diego during the boom of the middle eighties. His formal education ended with the ninth grade, and the young adult became a salesman for the New Home Sewing Machine Company in Los Angeles. "He was a dandy, too," his younger brother would later assert. Precisely when and how he became interested in artificial rain is not clear. He was exposed to Fred Binney's publicity; and sometime in the late nineties, according to his own account, he first tried his method from an old windmill tower on his father's ranch at Bonsall but never patented it for fear that "rain-producers would spring up like mushrooms all over the country."[4]

His first experiments had been made in his kitchen, he said, when he noticed that certain chemical combinations caused steam from the teakettle to move to them. Hatfield described his secret method as "mainly chemical affinity with the atmosphere. I have nothing to do with bombs, dynamite or explosives of any kind whatever. My methods are original." He concocted his chemicals—twenty-three of them, it was said—in casks, allowing them to age a few days before they were placed in galvanized evaporating pans atop wooden towers twenty or more feet high. In the daytime solar heat speeded vaporization, and at night combustion was added. Only a mild odor was given off, according to Hatfield, although one editor thought otherwise. Nearby farmers might be convinced "a limberger cheese factory has broken loose. . . . These gases smell so bad that it rains in self-defense." Electricity was somehow also an agent in the Hatfield process, with special equipment to provide the required power.[5]

As of 1905 Hatfield claimed to have been "a close student of meteorology" for seven years. Clearly he had no formal training in the field. In 1903 and 1904, to be sure, he had collected from the U.S. Weather Bureau considerable information on weather theory and instruments, not to mention rainfall data for selected California points going back as far as there were records. Included among the Hatfield papers that ultimately found their way to the San Diego Public Library, along with his barometer, rain gauge, and gold-weighing scales, are two well-thumbed and underlined books. One is John Brocklesby's *Elements of Meteorology, with Questions for Examination, Designed for Schools and Academies*, the 1860 edition of a volume originally published in 1848; the other is William Morris Davis's *Elementary Meteorology*, printed in 1902 from an 1894 issue. It seems evident that Hatfield had but limited scientific knowledge of weather or weather theory and that his self-styled "deep and prolonged study of the cause of certain known phenomena in nature" was as much a facade as the vague and elaborate jargon he developed to couch his work.[6]

"I do not make rain," he said. "That would be an absurd claim. I merely attract the clouds and they do the rest. It is a mere matter of cohesive attraction and the conditions that produce rain are drawn by my system just as a magnet draws steel." "My system consists of chemical combinations working in harmony with the very law that makes rain in a natural sense" he explained. "I thought it possible by means of forces of energy potent enough that a condition that actually and naturally exists in a moisture laden atmosphere could be made to bear upon the very influences of that condition, thereby inducing or assisting it in the direction where the demonstrations are going on, and cause it to precipitate its moisture."[7]

From his early efforts near San Diego in 1902 and 1903, Hatfield moved northward to the Los Angeles area, where in February 1904 he erected a twenty-foot evaporating tower in the brush country at La Crescenta. Working with his younger brother Paul, a lad of seventeen, he brewed his fumes for a week, chased off a friendly intruder with a shotgun, and claimed the rain that fell—rain the Weather Bureau said was part of a much larger storm system extending over most of northern California.[8]

He had already experimented with towers in Big Tujunga Canyon
and at Inglewood, where the Hatfield family now resided, and claimed
success in each instance. Early in December 1904 he was operating in
Rubio Canyon near Altadena, apparently financed by a number of Los
Angeles merchants, especially sewing machine dealers. Almost immediately, "Cloud Coaxer" Hatfield found himself in controversy
with George E. Franklin, the official weather forecaster in Los
Angeles, who predicted a general rain farther north but doubted it
would reach the City of the Angels. At first, according to gleeful
newsmen, Hatfield's "chemical affinity highball" made no impact.
Then, while Franklin tacked up more fair-weather bulletins, the rainmaker mixed another "hydrochloric fizz." Indeed, like Melbourne
before him, the new "wizard of the Clouds" went at it night and day
for a week, with only snatches of sleep and food gulped down at work.
Showers did fall on Altadena—about one-third inch—which
"Weather-Guesser" Franklin thought either natural or "a special dis-
pensation of Providence," but certainly not artificial. "Hatfield is
drunk on rainwater," crowed the *Los Angeles Daily Herald*. "When he
becomes sober he will bring his chemicals to the city and ask for Mr.
Franklin's place."[9]

Except to the Weather Bureau, such publicity was encouraging;
and the *Daily Times* reported that "Hatfield's water factory," according to its operator, had proved successful nineteen out of twenty
times—and even the one exception was questionable since rain had
fallen in the mountains nearby. Thus reassured, Hatfield made a
serious proposal to the people of Los Angeles, guaranteeing at least
eighteen inches of rain between mid-December and late April in
exchange for one thousand dollars raised by the chamber of commerce
or through public subscription. "The regular fall rarely exceeds eight
or ten inches," he noted, adding that he would take no pay whatever
should less than eighteen inches fall.[10]

This was no unwarranted gamble on his part. His statement that
Los Angeles's rainfall "rarely exceeds eight or ten inches" is not
borne out by official Weather Bureau records, which indicate that for
the twenty-eight years from 1877 up to but not including 1905, more
than eighteen inches fell in each of fourteen seasons—exactly half the
time. Hatfield bet his reputation against one thousand dollars to be
deposited with the *Examiner*; if he lost, subscribers would receive
their money back, and he would have lost his expenses. But since the

previous ten years had been drier than usual, his chances were en-hanced, a fact at least one editor recognized. "Hatfield, the self-styled 'rain-maker,' certainly has a full amount of nerve," said the *Los Angeles Times*.[11]

Weatherman Franklin scoffed, reiterated the impossibility of creating artificial rain, and pointed out that no scientific society had endorsed Hatfield or his work. But other publicity was more positive. The public was convinced that meteorologists used mainly guesswork anyway and that the slim, young "chemical affinity expert" might well be on the right track. The one thousand dollars was subscribed within three days, with a number of prominent businessmen con-tributing. Hatfield proposed mixing his first batch of chemicals im-mediately and promised the beginning of "an all winter siege" on December 15.[12]

Now George Franklin was really concerned. In a biting letter to his chief in Washington, he described Hatfield's process (based on "what would seem to be a new principle in physics"), lamented the coincidence of natural rain with the Altadena "demonstrations," and suggested that the Weather Bureau publish an official disclaimer of the Hatfield endeavors in its *Monthly Weather Review*. Chief Willis Moore, though sympathetic, believed the "only legal way to check such imposters" was to ignore them until such time as charges might be brought for obtaining money under false pretenses. Thus Franklin was instructed to bide his time and to inform inquirers that Hatfield was a deluder and "that his claims are preposterous."[13]

But as one editor noted, southern California's soil was perfect for get-rich-quick schemers with imagination. "Great head, Mr. Hatfield. The public like guff. Give them and the newpapers plenty of it!"[14]

Hatfield did. Angelenos enjoyed the guff. They laughed and urged the young "rain engineer" not to invoke moisture upon the annual Rose Bowl parade. ("Oh, please, kind sir, don't let it rain on Monday!") New Year's Day was dry; but as 1905 developed, the rains came. When a reporter interviewed Hatfield at his tent in mid-March, he was only one-third inch short of his obligation and yet had a month and a half to go. Newsmen found him quiet and sincere, neither egotistic nor eccentric, despite his small arsenal of knives and pistols. "Censure and ridicule are the first tributes paid to scientific en-lightenment by prejudiced ignorance," he told them.[15]

Press and public alike began to take Hatfield more seriously and to pose the possibility that "he really may be able to produce rain at will." Or might he be "the Frankenstein of the air?" Might he produce "a storm monster that he cannot control?" Some talked about getting an injunction against him; and when eighteen inches had fallen and he proposed to throw in an additional two, the rustic poets rose to the occasion.

> It has drizzled and sprinkled and rained and poured
> The lightnings have flashed and the thunders have roared.
> I've been crossing the streets on a pole or a board,
>    And wading around like a pup.
> You've earned your money, you've done your work well.
> Of your rain-making history surely will tell,
> So now, if you really love us all well,
>    Mr. Hatfield—do—let—up.[16]

Hatfield received one thousand dollars in cash and a great deal more than that in publicity. Press reports reached all corners of the country. A description of his work was preceded by the heading "A Successful Rainmaker" in a Scranton, Pennsylvania, newspaper; the *St. Louis Globe-Democrat*, cagey about the idea of rainmaking in general, admitted that Hatfield had introduced fresh evidence. The *Brooklyn Daily Eagle* carried the headline "Young Wizard of Meteorology Proves His Ability to Fill Orders for Rainstorms"; the accompanying story commented that in the average California mind the much-maligned Hatfield now occupied a place as high as that of Luther Burbank. As far away as London, where English readers read "A Chat with the World's Greatest 'Rain-Maker'" in *Tid-Bits*, Hatfield was newsworthy.[17]

Back home—where merchants were advertising "Genuine 'Hatfield' Umbrellas" at $2.50, $3.50, and $4.50 each, and where the word *raining* was occasionally being replaced by a new one, *Hatfielding*—the rain maestro took to the lecture circuit to discuss "How I Attract Moisture Laden Atmospheres." Tickets for his discourse at Simpson Auditorium on May 12 ranged in price from twenty-five cents to a dollar; and he was scheduled also to appear in Riverside, Redlands, Santa Barbara, San Bernardino, and San Diego before going off to test his chemicals in Arizona and New Mexico.[18]

If some could not decide whether he was "a genius, worthy to be placed with the inventor of X-rays, or merely a toy of Fortune, who, when she is tired of flirting will trump his adrift to be the laughing stock of half the nation," the U.S. Weather Bureau had no doubts. Instead of issuing "a very stiff little statement" on Hatfield, "knocking him out," as a friendly Philadelphia editor suggested, the bureau tried to counter pro-Hatfield stories with a letter to each newspaper that published them. Editors did print these rebuttals, but generally the damage had already been done. Although the *Monthly Weather Review* also carried a detailed critique by Chief Willis Moore, it was hardly on the daily reading list of most Americans.[19]

In California a concerted campaign went forth. Franklin worked overtime in Los Angeles refuting Hatfield's pretensions. Weatherman Alexander McAdie in San Francisco was optimistic, especially when West Coast newspapers began to reprint Moore's warnings with blunt headlines: "Weather Chief Raps Hatfield"; "Hatfield Effort Puny, Says Chief"; and "Rain and Hot Air." McAdie also wrote an article for *Sunset Magazine*, which was reprinted elsewhere, that condemned "rain-making experiments (so-called)" without mentioning Hatfield by name and emphasized that all storms had been predicted by the Weather Bureau and that maps and forecasts had been readily available to all comers, including would-be cloud compellers. Another meteorologist interviewed Hatfield and found him "an attractive psychological study, almost as interesting in his personality as the meteorological wonders that are credited to his wizardly skill." He was a cagey man, this Hatfield, hiding behind a peculiar smile and a host of shibboleths and glittering generalities; he was a sincere man but had deceived himself that rain was his own doing and not mere coincidence.[20]

Hatfield—now "Professor" Charles Hatfield—began to speak in terms of a larger theater. He might, he suggested, be able to rid London of its fogs. "I should like to have the contract for watering the desert of Sahara as soon as the French Government can be made to appreciate that I can really make as much rain as my employers order," he was quoted as saying. He mentioned an agreement with "a big Chicago corporation" to turn western Kansas into grain land for a fee of five thousand dollars on a "no rain, no pay" basis. "From the exposition of the Copernican theory regarding the eath's rotation, every important discovery has been met with ridicule and derision," he said. "I will absolutely convince the world by drenching Kansas this summer."[21]

The Kansas trip never materialized. Hatfield printed up copies of a pledge form soliciting support for a resumption of operations at Altadena, on much the same basis as the previous year. He invited business from around the state and had no difficulty in finding interested parties, including one from Shandon who promised one thousand dollars for fifteen inches of rain—adding that if Hatfield "can demonstrate to some of these 'mud-sills' around here that he has the real thing I can get as much more for him and also repeat the sum paid every year to come."[22]

Whether the rainmaker worked the Shandon area that winter of 1905–1906 is not clear, but he did enhance his reputation with the miners at Grass Valley in November and with the wheat farmers around Newman. After a prolonged dry spell of six months, which lowered the stream level so much that power could not be produced to work the mines, the South Yuba Water Company offered Hatfield $250 to break the drought, with an additional one hundred dollars for each inch of rain up to five inches. Soon "the boy rainmaker of Los Angeles" (he was twenty-nine) had erected his well-publicized black tar-paper tower on the banks of Lake Spaulding and was mixing his brew. Within a few days the press carried the headline "Hatfield Wins Gold and Glory." By his own account he had produced four and one-half inches of rain, filled the reservoirs, and broken one of the greatest droughts in northern California. "Why," said Hatfield, "some of the merchants of Grass Valley were using my name for advertising purposes and I had to look sharp to keep some one from naming a five cent cigar after me." But the money was nothing: he worked to establish a reputation and to prove himself—"to make the world a believer in something that was inevitable. Fifty years from now every State, every city in the Union, will have its rainmaking plants," he predicted.[23]

Soon after this triumph Hatfield moved his gear to Crows Landing, east of Newman and south of Modesto, where by contract he was to boost rainfall in the San Joaquin Valley above the normal six inches. By December 19, 1905, he stopped in Fresno on the way and was interviewed: "He who holds sway over the skies and says clouds come hither and rain fall down, declared last night that there will be a big wet Christmas for the San Joaquin Valley. He is going to have it rain pitch-forks within six days after December 22."[24] Hatfield lived up to his advance billing: Crows Landing had a record season, with thirteen inches. The rainmaker collected a thousand dollars and signed a new

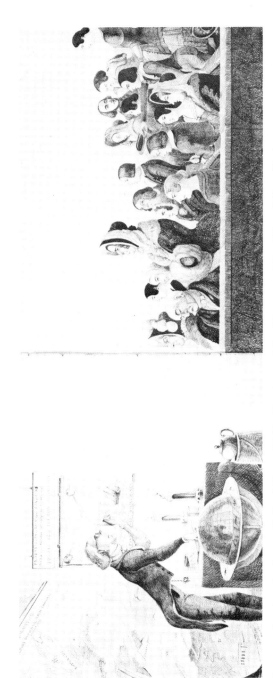

Lyceum Lecture by James Pollard Espy, 1841. Courtesy of the Museum of the City of New York.

From *Scientific American*, November 27, 1880.

1. Lieut. Jno. T. Ellis. 2. ————, Statistician. 3. Paul Draper, Electrician. 4. Gen. R. G. Dyrenforth. 5. Prof. Car Meyer, Balloonist. 6. Prof. G. E. Curtis, Meteorologist. 7. Prof. Rosell, Chemist. 8. J. E. Cæler, Aeronaut. 9. Prof. Powers, Author. The others are cowboys.

The Dyrenforth Rainmaking Expedition. From *Scientific American*, January 2, 1892.

CHAPPIE. "This is great. Maud wants me to take her to the foot-ball game. I'll just buy a thunder-shower and knock out the whole business."

Rainmaking Humor. From *Harper's Weekly*, October 24, 1891.

William F. Wright Rainmaking Funnels. Courtesy of the Nebraska State Historical Society.

**THE NEW COMMERCIAL INDUSTRY.**

FIRST DRUMMER. — I am representing the Thunderbolt Rain-Producing Company — our showers last two hours and twenty minutes, and we make a sample shower free of charge!

SECOND DRUMMER. — Let me take your order, sir, for the Aquarius Artificial Rain-Making Company — our rain is superior to anything in the market, and we give a silk umbrella and a pair of overshoes with every. shower!

From *Puck,* September 9, 1891.

Charles M. Hatfield and Rain Towers, Hemet, California, 1912. Courtesy of the San Diego Public Library.

Making Rain with Electrified Sand. Courtesy of the Cornell University Archives.

contract for the period from November 15, 1906 to April 15, 1907, under which he would receive $500 for the first inch over normal rainfall (now regarded as eight, rather than six, inches); $250 each for the second and third inches beyond eight; and $500 for the fourth. Thus Hatfield completed the first of what would be many "successful seasons among the Crow's Landing wheat farmers."[25]

Around the time of the Grass Valley venture, it was bruited about in the press that Hatfield would soon go off under the auspices of the British government and nine owners of diamond mines and sheep farms "to stab the clouds which float over" South Africa, a venture from which he expected to return "with fresh laurels and bulging pockets." It was also reported that he had signed an agreement to produce rain for Australian placer-mine proprietors.[26] Neither of these opportunities developed, but another— equally spectacular— did. On March 1, 1906, the *Dawson Daily News* announced that Hatfield had been hired to bring down rain for normal mining operations in the Yukon Territory.

Both local mine owners and the Yukon Council, the semi-autonomous governing body of the territory, were involved. If Hatfield produced enough water for hydraulic mining, he was to receive ten thousand dollars, half from the mine operators and half from the council, with his expenses to be paid, rain or shine. The chief astronomer of Canada had already branded the Californian a "Fake Rain Maker" and pointed out the pattern of alternating wet and dry summers in the Yukon. With a prolonged drought each day increasing the chances for moisture and with expense money guaranteed, Hatfield had little to lose.[27]

Local citizens were enthusiastic: one of them suggested that Dawson merchants stock up "on umbrellas, raincoats, rubber boots and canoes." "Hat" might well "make a river out of the Guggenheimer ditch." But when the matter was raised in the Canadian House of Commons, not everyone was so positive. George E. Foster, member from north Toronto, demanded to see the Hatfield contract and questioned the wisdom of expenditures in this fashion. Providence dispensed rains with impartiality, he believed. "But if the Yukon Council, which is by no means impartial in its constitution, is to be installed as the great Rainmaker of this Dominion, it may come to pass that no Conservative will ever get a drop of rain, but it will all be brought down in fruitful showers upon the faithful who stand by the government."[28]

Or might not there be even more catastrophic dangers? the M.P. asked. "Suppose that man Hatfield gets his apparatus at work and tinkers with the vast and delicate atmosphere of the universe, is it not possible that he may pull out a plug, or slip a cog, and this machinery of the universe once started agoing wrong may go on to the complete submersion of this continent." Tongue in cheek, Foster went on to speculate on the international complications and the possibility of a "tremendous bill for damages" should Hatfield interfere "with the vast chain of atmospherical mechanism to which the United States has some claim as well as ourselves." But, as others pointed out, the council was autonomous and might dispose of certain of its funds as it saw fit.[29] Thus the rainmaker was hired.

By mid-June 1906 Dawson had its first look at Hatfield—"a small man, as they run in this northern country, clean shaven and with an office pallor on his face, the student look throughout." Rain appeared to have accompanied him inland from Vancouver, where he bought his chemicals. "He has scared the heavens before starting," sneered M.P. Foster.[30]

The Hatfield brothers worked forty-four days on King Solomon's Dome, some miles to the east of Dawson. Preliminary rain and some hail fell; and the outlook was encouraging, even mystical, to some observers:

> Ye gods of snow, of storm and shower,
> Behind what Hatfield doth this hour;
> His 'lectro chemic vapors rise,
> To wet the world and ease the skies.[31]

In the end, however, the rainmakers failed. The contract was terminated, and Hatfield was paid expenses of something over eleven hundred dollars in full settlement. British observers thought the episode "almost incredible." Hatfield argued that he had not failed, that there had been a basic misunderstanding over the contract. He had brought rain on thirty-six of his forty-four workdays, he insisted, enough to provide adequate water for placer-mining cleanup—his interpretation of what he had agreed to deliver. Mine operators, on the other hand, expected enough water to carry on hydraulic mining, a far more difficult task. Even so, as one onlooker pointed out, the Hatfields "enjoyed a delightful outing in the beautiful arctic summer" at no expense.[32]

Returning to California, Hatfield had a particularly good winter season at Crows Landing, where he was to be paid fifteen hundred dollars if more than twelve inches of rain fell. In the unusually wet winter of 1907, after eleven inches had fallen, farmers urged him to stop so they could get their crops in. Hatfield paid no heed: fourteen inches actually came down before he returned to Inglewood, "his pockets bulging with good Stanislaus County coin."[33]

Skeptical editors often railed at him and other "rain fakirs," but the surplus of rain at Crows Landing made for a remarkably good press. Magazine articles implied acceptance by their very titles: "A Professional Rain-Maker" or "This Man Makes Rain by Wireless Waves." True, the burden of proof was still on this "Fine Appearing and Modest Young Man, with a Scientific Turn of Mind" who gave thoughtful interviews and explained his work. "Great Rainmaker Says He Does Not Force or Frighten Nature, but Gently Assists Her in Providing Showers for Needy Sections." His approach was "by coaxing and wheedling and courting"; and he announced the purchase of new electrical equipment to double the effectiveness of his plant, at the same time expressing the hope that the national government would buy his secret.[34]

His triumphs mounted. To Crows Landing he added Hemet, where he contracted for four inches and "delivered" more than seven. To Hemet he added Sherman County, Oregon, where he brought 2.2 inches to an area between the Blue and the Cascade mountains that normally received .62 inches—so he said. He claimed success in the same region in the following year, 1908, using "Methods Those of Science," according to the Portland press. He continued his annual work in the San Joaquin Valley, where farmers liked "his brand of rain" and found it profitable. "You may laugh if you like," one wheat grower is supposed to have said in 1911, "but I figure that I have made $50,000 by Hatfield's operation." At Crows Landing in 1909, a wet year for all of California, he collected three thousand dollars for thirteen inches, although scoffers denied it was all science and suspected he "used a little planetary conjunction and a little precession of the equinoxes and some other strong stuff." His 1911 contract was his seventh at Crows Landing and reportedly involved farmers representing more than one hundred thousand acres who believed his fees a bargain, especially when a downpour of late January made Hatfield "the hero of the hour."[35]

While U.S. Weather Bureau officials deprecated their efforts, the Hatfield brothers in 1912 filled the lake of the Hemet Land and Water Company, according to Paul, and were successful in bringing down rain for the San Angelo Chamber of Commerce with three towers set up in nearby Carlsbad, Texas. About the same time Hatfield was negotiating with the South African government. In a letter to one of the South African farm organizations, he outlined his qualifications, which included eight years of active experience and sixteen commercial contracts, "all of which have been satisfactory and productive of good results." "Long protracted droughts and dry spells have been broken by my demonstrations time and time again," he said. He expressed a willingness to make rain in the northwest Karoo for a ten-thousand-dollar fee, plus transportation from Los Angeles to South Africa and back for himself and an assistant. As part of a parliamentary inquiry pursuing the matter, the chief meteorologist of the Irrigation Department of Pretoria wrote the Weather Bureau in Washington about "rain inducer" Hatfield and his "remarkable statements, which to say the least, are certainly not lacking in self-confidence." Chief Willis Moore ended Hatfield's African travel plans abruptly, denouncing him as "practicing deception," preying on public credulity, and making "a dire necessity the occasion for the perpetrating of fraud."[36]

Hatfield appears to have been idle in May 1913, when Fred Binney, now acting as his agent, proposed that the federal government underwrite a demonstration at San Diego, paying Hatfield five thousand dollars if he could produce an unprecedented five inches of precipitation there between May and September. When Washington officials turned thumbs down, Binney complained that people had scoffed at Marconi, too, and vowed to ask his representative to raise the matter in Congress.[37]

Earlier—sometime in the first part of 1912—Hatfield had approached the San Diego County Chamber of Commerce, which declined his offer to milk the skies. Binney had written a similar proposition to the San Diego Ctiy Council that same year, without success. But late in 1915, with realtor Binney acting as the intermediary, Hatfield again tried to interest the San Diego city fathers. According to his son who was interviewed later, Binney "was living as usual from hand to mouth" and expected a 5 percent commission. After the whiskery Englishman had provided publicity and access to council-

men, Hatfield appeared before the council in December with an offer
to fill the city reservoir at Moreno Dam. One who was present thought
he had an "impressive presence" but the council's response was at first
skeptical and jocular. Originally, the rainmaker agreed that he would
produce forty inches free but would receive one thousand dollars per
inch for the next ten inches. Then he modified his proposition: "I will
fill the Morena [*sic*] Reservoir to overflowing between now and next
December 20, 1916, for the sum of $10,000, in default of which I ask
no compensation." The drought was already severe, the reservoir only
about one-third full, and the city fathers authorized a contract to be
drawn accordingly, with but one out of the five councilmen dissenting,
calling it "rank foolishness." Whether deliberately or through pro-
crastination, the formal agreement either was never drawn up by the
city attorney or was never signed by the council.[38] However, Hatfield
was willing to begin work on a verbal understanding, and the stage
was set for his most superb moment of glory.

By January 1 he was at work at Moreno, some sixty miles east of
San Diego. With his younger brother Joel, he had hauled in chemicals,
built a tower or perhaps two, and reported a good rain on January 5. A
few days later the official San Diego forecaster discussed an approaching storm, which brought continuing intermittent rain for more
than a week. The month saw record rainfall and soon made Hatfield's
name "more famous locally than that of Yorkville or any of the
handicap winners at the Tijuana racetrack." On January 27 Lower
Otay dam, southeast of the city, gave way, with heavy damage and loss
of life. Rail connections were washed out, streets flooded, and houses
ruined. San Diego had an estimated death toll of fifty.[39]

This was "Hatfield's Flood." A front-page cartoon in the *San
Diego Union* showed an irate farmer chasing the rainmaker into the
bay. It was rumored that armed vigilantes went seeking the Hatfield
brothers and that Charles fled on horseback across the desert toward
Yuma—"and we never heard of him again for many, many years."
This was in error. The two well-armed Hatfields walked the sixty miles
back to San Diego, and on the afternoon of February 4 Charles held a
press conference in Fred Binney's office on Seventh Street. The
"Sky-Milker" came with the demeanor "of the proverbial conquering
hero, home from the fray and awaiting the laurel wreath," said the
*Union*. He announced that he had lived up to his promise to fill Moreno
reservoir and would now formally lay his claim for ten thousand

dollars before the city council. A few days later the council considered it quietly, because some members were "pretty sensitive about it," and referred it to city attorney Terence Cosgrove, a tough, shrewd lawyer on the make.[40]

There was no written, signed legal contract, Cosgrove argued. And until proven otherwise, the deluge had to be considered "an act of God." Hatfield had claimed he was directly responsible for four billion gallons of water in the reservoir and indirectly responsible for another ten billion—whereupon Cosgrove insisted that Moreno could not be filled with Hatfield's mere four billion gallons; hence he had not lived up to his offer. Acting on its attorney's recommendation, the council then rejected Hatfield's claim, although more than one member believed they had an unwritten obligation to the rainmaker.[41]

Threatening to bring suit, Hatfield next proposed a compromise on a pro rata basis, which would also be rejected. Arguing that his reputation was more important than the money, he announced he would settle for four thousand dollars instead of ten thousand dollars. When this was turned down, he did file a suit against the city but did little to press it. Meanwhile, city lawyers promised to recommend payment of every cent of Hatfield's claim if he would sign a statement assuming responsibility for the flood and relieving the city of damages. With some $3.5 million in claims pending, even though most would never be collected, the rainmaker could ill afford to agree. His lawsuit was technically carried on the books until 1938, when it was dismissed as a dead issue.[42]

Some have contended, without real evidence, that Hatfield received under-the-table payments from the city council. This is doubtful, but a case can be made that he was indeed treated unfairly by the city fathers. However that may be, the episode could only enhance the rainmaker's image. The city of San Diego still remembered him in 1948, when it hired a cloud seeder to make it rain and was careful to take out damage insurance. As late as 1961 the 1916 disaster was still known as "Hatfield's Flood"; and California scientists were rearguing the case, holding that rains at that time had nothing to do with chemicals but rather were part of a storm that followed the pattern of other rainy seasons.[43]

Weather Bureau personnel in California had reported the affair in detail to the Washington office. They kept abreast of Hatfield's continuing activities and occasionally published articles designed to reduce his public stature. They complained when the "assistant rain-maker" Paul Hatfield, wearing his uniform of a private first class in the U.S. Infantry, called at the Los Angeles weather office for rainfall data and meteorological summaries for various parts of California. Was it proper for the War Department to permit him "to engage in obtaining money under false pretenses"? Was it proper for the Weather Bureau to furnish him with data "when we know that such data is to be used in fraudulent practices"?[44]

The barrage of favorable publicity became more national in scope. Occasionally a laudatory article could be nipped in the bud, but usually the damage was done before the Weather Bureau could complain. In August 1919, for example, *Everybody's Magazine* carried a highly colored article titled "The Man the Rain Minds," which claimed more than five hundred "demonstrations" for Hatfield—"and his disappointments have been very few." "No magic," the rain wizard was quoted as saying. "It is only scientific." Under fire from Bureau Chief Charles Marvin, *Everybody's* editor lamely apologized, claiming that the general public would now watch Hatfield more closely. "Publicity is the best curative in a democracy for all questionable schemes," he said.[45]

But already much mischief had been done. A piece in *Sunset Magazine* parroted *Everybody's*. The American press borrowed liberally from the article. Newspapers as far away as Australia carried it almost verbatim and prompted Down Under farm and ranch groups to seek further information and Hatfield's address. In Canada a newspaper paraphrasing the article in *Everybody's* helped work up sentiment to bring Hatfield to Canada.[46]

In 1920 Hatfield worked the Crows Landing area as usual and was employed by the Commercial Club of Ephrata, Washington, to make rain on the dry Columbian Plateau. For nearly two months Hatfield operated four towers at nearby Moses Lake before he grew discouraged and dismantled his equipment. Two days later rain fell over a wide area of Washington; and Hatfield, who took the credit, was also credited with a miracle: he had aimed his storm at one county and hit another two hundred miles away![47]

Meanwhile, farmers and ranchers in Alberta were seriously considering importing Hatfield as a drought breaker but were undercut by the Lethbridge Board of Trade, which sought professional advice from both the U.S. Weather Bureau and the Dominion Meteorological

Office in Toronto. Not only did the board publish its adverse replies in local newspapers, it circulated them in pamphlet form, warning that if citizens wished to spend eight or nine thousand dollars, they should invest it in irrigation, not in "a big lumber stand" with "some washing soda on the top." That put an end to the Hatfield boom for 1920, but another dry season reopened it.[48]

Saskatchewan citizens also evidenced an interest, but it was at Medicine Hat in Alberta, some hundred miles east of Lethbridge, that the United Agricultural Association entered into a contract whereby Hatfield agreed to make rain for one thousand dollars per inch to a maximum of four inches between May 1 and August 1, 1921. The rainmaker was there by late April, and the sixty citizens who received him at lunch in the Corona Hotel thought it was a good omen that light showers attended the event.[49]

At Chappice Lake, Hatfield built his tower; it wasn't "as tall as that of Babel," the local editor reported, but it was the largest Hatfield had ever constructed and was designed to withstand winds of ninety miles per hour. Hatfield and his crew lived in "a roomy cook car" and performed their tower duties as many as eight times every twenty-four hours. Sightseers flocked in; and movie-maker William Brennen came to shoot film of the operation, though Hatfield half-believed he was trying to steal his secrets. Within a month old-timers were complaining about unprecedented rainfall, and the United Agricultural Association was forced to postpone its executive meeting because heavy rains had made the roads impassable. When the body did convene, it voted Hatfield his eight thousand dollars in exchange for more than 4.8 inches of precipitation.[50] "Success" begat enthusiasm. As a local wag wrote of "Medicine Hatfield":

> We have the Hat, no doubt about that;
>     We also have the fields.
> Large growth of grains, will follow the rains,
>     With very heavy yields.[51]

Hatfield collected and used the occasion to publicize his "remarkable results" in a special article for a Sheridan, Wyoming, newspaper, in which he pointed out that "Droughts, starvation, famine—they are needless." Despite this and other positive notices, the rainmaker quickly came under fire. Some pointed out that his "success" was merely an awareness of rain cycles and a matter of timing. Others cited weather records for Medicine Hat to show that in only nine of the thirty-seven years since 1884 had the rainfall been below four inches in the three-month contract period and that the average for the entire span was 6.04 inches. Hatfield collected eight thousand dollars for a rainfall that was nearly 1.25 inches below normal.[52]

Back in California Fred Binney was still active. In a long letter published in various western newspapers under the heading "To Get Rain We Must Ask Congress," he charged "3 men in a Washington Bureau" with "blocking the way to this grand result"—namely, the successful use of Hatfield's secret under the auspices of the federal government. No doubt one of the three was Charles Marvin, chief of the U.S. Weather Bureau. Congress, said Binney, should purchase the formula, give Hatfield an annuity of twenty-four thousand dollars, and operate the process throughout the arid West under the supervision of the Division of Forestry.[53]

Early in 1921 Binney proposed that the San Diego city council bring back Hatfield to break the drought; and a local writer, facetiously perhaps, recalled 1916, when the immoderate rainmaker made every river valley in the county "look like the fiords of Norway." Although professional meteorologists demolished Hatfield's "science" and branded him a fraud at every opportunity, they were hard put to keep pace with his spreading fame. A disappointing article appeared in the *London Illustrated News* early in 1922, for example. Hatfield himself had provided the photographs and the information and came on strong. He could increase rainfall by 50 to 300 percent, he said; he predicted that he could readily dispel London's famous fog; and he prophesied that the Canadian and United States governments would soon take over his process.[54]

In the summer of 1922 Hatfield was reported in Naples, invited by the Italian government to break a five-month-old drought. He was anxious, according to the press, to explain his work to Pope Pius and, if the pontiff agreed, to invoke a little secular rain on the Vatican gardens. Tradition has it that when he set up shop near Naples "all Southern Italy was flooded," farmers went "wild with joy," and "Doctor" Hatfield, as the local newspapers called him, became "a bigger hero than Mussolini." But this was a case of myth quickly outgrowing reality. As brother Paul later explained, "We never were in Italy."[55]

In the twenties Hatfield received numerous inquiries, many from abroad. Having seen the article in *Everybody's Magazine*, an officer of a Cuban firm, the Santa Cecilia Corporation, wrote in 1922. Queries came from Australia and South Africa. An olive-oil processor in Tunis was interested; and a wealthy Colombian coffee planter, Guiellermo Gomez, stopped in Los Angeles to confer. A cable from the Anti-Drought Association of Panama asked about the rainmaker in the summer of 1927, but nothing came of any of these feelers from overseas.[56] With a few exceptions Hatfield preferred to work close to home.

One of the exceptions came in 1929, when the brothers traveled to Honduras to save seven hundred thousand acres of drought-stricken banana lands for the Standard Steamship and Fruit Company of New Orleans. Hatfield insisted that the assignment was completed successfully within ten days, although later during divorce proceedings he denied his wife's allegation that he received ten thousand dollars for the job.[57]

At home his reputation continued. The especially dry summer of 1924 brought numerous soundings from Californians: from Ventura farmers, the Colton city fathers, dredge operators, and "one of the largest cattle companies in the San Joaquin Valley." His name was such that an executive engineer of the Southern California Edison Company wrote of him obliquely: "If the party to whom you refer knows what you say he knows and keeps his knowledge to himself in a year such as the present, he is morally guilty of a grave offense against the commonwealth of California." In 1926 while working near Tulare Lake, Hatfield contemplated an agreement to fill Roosevelt Lake in Arizona at a rate of one thousand dollars per billion gallons. "I would come prepared to carry on some of the most powerful tests ever conducted by me," he said. But he never went. For a time, too, it appeared that he might perform his miracles for the American Sugar Cane League, which was prepared to offer eight thousand dollars for two inches of rain in Louisiana. In the end, however, this venture did not materialize, either because moisture came naturally or because of the negative responses Louisianans received when they inquired about Hatfield from the U.S. Weather Bureau.[58]

Although the rainmaker continued his work, it was not always with success. In 1924, while he was under contract with San Bernardino County farmers, natural rain upset his schedule; again, in King County, he was hauling wood for his tower when the rain commenced. In North Dakota a year later, he failed to meet his contract terms.[59] But unless Weather Bureau spokesmen pointed them out, the public heard little of the failures. They warranted no headlines and only slight coverage and did little to tarnish the image of Hatfield as a true bringer of rainfall.

One success for every dozen inquiries or failures kept him in business and brought a kind of amused, tongue-in-cheek publicity that could only be interpreted as positive by the average reader. In mid-March 1924, for example, Hatfield built a tower in the hills west of Coalinga, on the western fringe of the San Joaquin Valley. Coalinga had contributed $1,500; Lemoore, $3,250; and Corcoran, $3,350. Hatfield was to receive two thousand dollars an inch for four inches but nothing for less than one and a half inches. His press was good. He was shown rigging his "Tower of Showers," preparing for this task of "Tickling the Clouds to Tears" and "persuading J. Pluvius to turn on the celestial sprinkling cart." His timing was superb. "Old Jupe was angry," and it "rained little fishes." A cloudburst washed away Hatfield's tent and forced him to spend the night in a tree, an experience well worth the inconvenience in his case. Subsequently this "Ponzi of the Skies" let the world know that he was responsible for the "splendid rainfall" and was pictured in the *Los Angeles Herald*, an umbrella under his arm, "wearing his $8,000 smile."[60]

After he had collected another check for the same amount in the spring of 1925, again operating in the Tulare Lake bottoms, a St. Louis writer was tempted to call him "the Great Hatfield" but settled for "the world's champion guesser." He was credited with flooding an area near Randsburg where rain of any kind was rare, and with washing out three miles of Southern Pacific railroad track in the Mojave Desert.[61]

Rival rainmakers might label him "the bunk": "I can make rain while he is setting up his apparatus," sneered one from Nevada. But there were plenty of believers still scattered among the jealous and the skeptical. The *Los Angeles Sunday Times* probably summed up public attitudes very well in March 1924: "Some think Hatfield is merely a great showman; others something else less complimentary, but some, and always enough for his purposes, think him a man ahead of his time, who can do what the United States Weather Bureau and all modern science say is impossible."[62]

Hatfield's fame was still abroad in the drought-ridden thirties, although the depression knocked the bottom out of the rainmaking market. In 1930, in 1934, and again in 1936, he offered to bring his more than thirty years of experience to bear in combating the devastating dryness of mid-America, asked only expense money. He could do it in a week, he estimated. A number of admiring Californians—firm believers—buttressed his claims and urged President Franklin Roosevelt to utilize his special talents. Six or eight of his towers set up in Kansas or Nebraska would put an end to the dust bowl, they argued.[63]

But for all practical purposes, Hatfield's career was over. This "strange mesmeric personality," this "outstanding rain-doctor of modern times," as the press called him, retired quietly to Glendale to live on past glories until he died in 1958, still a controversial and elusive figure. From time to time the media rehashed the old days, especially 1916, for he was still good copy. Indeed, in 1956 Passing Parade Films Inc. produced "Hatfield, the Rainmaker" for television, focusing on the Moreno Dam episode. Eight years later San Diego engineer Gerald Clarke expressed the opinion that even in the light of modern weather engineering, it was time Hatfield "received deserved acclaim." Another southern Californian, Edmund Jeffrey, commercial pilot, advertising salesman, and bank employee, tried several times to emulate Hatfield's success at Moreno using a tower and the same chemicals, though he admitted he added "a special ingredient which brought on the lightning." Perhaps the supreme recognition would come early in 1973, when the Native Sons of the Golden West dedicated a five-and-one-half-foot red granite column—a "Hatfield the Rainmaker" historical marker—at Lake Moreno.[64]

Had he not been bypassed by technology in the form of modern cloud seeding, perhaps Paul Hatfield would have successfully taken up his brother's mantle. As it was, in the 1960s he proclaimed himself ready to carry on the tradition if the California legislature would waive its law of the previous decade requiring rainmakers to be licensed and to divulge the ingredients they used. Even as late as 1972 Paul Hatfield was using special stationery, the envelopes of which carried a picture of three evaporating towers and the inscription:

> Hatfield Brothers
> Rain Inducing Plant
> Over 500 Demonstrations
> No Failures.[65]

How does one assess the Hatfield saga? Was Charles Hatfield really "a first lieutenant to Jupiter Pluvius himself," as some professed to believe?[66] How correct was his brother in noting that the logbooks for the work had "disappeared," but that "altogether we tried 503 tests. And we never made a failure."[67] Was Hatfield merely a con man, a gambler who—like the racetrack tout—is remembered only when he was right and forgotten when he failed? Of course he was the latter and more. He was a great showman, and he recognized the law of averages when he set to work. Very likely he believed that his chemicals did help bring rain. As was true in the case of so many of the leading "pluviculture" exponents, it was this element of self-delusion, coupled with glib talk and splendid publicity, that made him a professional.

# 6. If We Could Draw Down the Electricity I Think the Water Would Come with It: Rain by Pulling a Switch

Little clouds of vapor
　Sprayed with grains of sand
Make a welcome shower
And a fertile land.[1]

Well-known rainmakers like Jewell and Hatfield had utilized electricity as a practical part of their process. One Kansan, who professed to have done considerable reading on the subject, believed that concussion worked because it electrified the atmosphere.[2] For still others electricity was the very key to unlocking the puzzle of the heavens. As far back as the eighteenth century, scientists, among them Benjamin Franklin, saw electricity as playing a prominent role in the theory of rain. To some of this school electricity explained rainfall and was a medium for the control of rainfall, but there was no universal agreement as to its precise role. Basically, some were "putter-inners," who would charge the atmosphere electrically to bring forth moisture; others were "taker-outers," who would remove current from the air as a sure means of getting rain.

Eighteenth-century French scientists had argued that withdrawing electricity from the air would prevent rain and hail; and in the nineteenth and, indeed, the twentieth centuries, "electric niagaras"—groups of high masts on the hills—were used in Italy and France for this purpose. As early as the 1840s the Englishman George A. Rowell wrote a series of papers in which he held that electricity was the principal agent in evaporation; whether or not rain fell depended mainly on the dryness or dampness of the atmosphere—in other words, on its ability to conduct electricity from the clouds. Mountains naturally caused precipitation by drawing off electricity; volcanoes and fires produced moisture because their smoke increased the air's conductivity. The same could be done artificially, Rowell suggested, by sending a balloon into the clouds, with conducting wires leading from the balloon to the ground to drain off electricity.[3]

This "grounding" concept, using either balloons or kites, was not uncommon. Among its adherents was a Pennsylvania "taker-outer" of 1879, who believed that rain depended upon an equilibrium "of the electrical conditions of the clouds and earth." Establishing a cordon of captive balloons, one every ten or twenty miles, with wires attached to "give communication between the clouds & earth & an electrical equilibrium at once established" would bring down moisture. "If the plan would work it would almost quadruple the crops taking the country through," he predicted.[4]

A dozen years later, when the Department of Agriculture was about to embark on its concussionist experiments, a Colorado rancher tried to convince Secretary Rusk that this was not the most promising approach. Proposing instead that special lightning rods be planted at intervals of one hundred or two hundred feet at government expense around his property, he said, "I think if we could draw down the electricity, I think the water would come with it." These feelings were echoed by a resident of Blue Hill, Maine, in 1901, who contended that "electrical potential" in the air prevented rain particles from coalescing. The cutting of forests, natural conductors of electricity, decreased rainfall, he argued. Rain might be encouraged by establishing a well-grounded network of wires on hilly terrain or by sending up balloons with metallic points linked by wire to the earth in flat country. As it had with other types of "pluviculturists," the Weather Bureau in Washington quietly pointed out the error of the theory—in this instance, that there was no conclusive evidence of a relationship between electricity and rainfall.[5]

Few American rain-by-electricity theorists made any effort to apply their ideas, apart from soliciting aid from the national government. One notable exception was John G. Potts of Denver, a "taker-outer" who did attempt to perfect a balloon device that would work. Near Longmont, Colorado, in the summer of 1912, Potts built a large gas balloon designed to carry a number of grounded metallic points into a thundercloud. But an explosion sprayed sulphuric acid over everyone and destroyed the craft. On the fourth try, however, according to Potts, the balloon was airborne and its action brought down rain. Although seemingly similar to an apparatus patented in Austria in 1874, his invention was patented in 1913, though he never convinced the Weather Bureau of its worth. But he argued in 1917 that with 450 stations employing one thousand persons he could water forty-five thousand square miles of eastern Colorado at twenty-five cents per acre per season and still make a profit of ten cents an acre.[6]

On the opposite side of the ledger were the "putter-inners," those who believed that rain was produced not by removing electricity from the atmosphere, but by putting more in. A few of these believers were uninformed amateurs like J. C. Lyons, genial, garrulous, and at the age of seventy-six, it was said, able to "talk faster and longer than any other man in Montana." In the spring of 1899 Lyons came down to Bozeman from the hills above Livingston to explain his theories to officials of what later became Montana State University. He would use a generator in the center and storage batteries at each corner of a sixty-acre square. Each power source would be wired to a balloon in the air; thus, Lyons argued, electricity would form a circuit from the positive pole in the middle through the atmosphere to the negative points on the corners, cooling and condensing moisture into rainfall. All that was lacking was money to put the idea into practice.[7]

On the other hand, a number of proposals or at least conjectures on making rain by adding electricity to the air came from the scientific community. In 1895 a very reputable professor and organizer and head of the electrical engineering department at Columbia University, Francis Bacon Crocker, thought it not impossible that man could make rain. His idea was to put electricity into the atmosphere by means of a large balloon from which was suspended a ring with many sharp protruding points to be connected by fine wire to a dynamo below. Perhaps because of Crocker's professional stature, at least one editor believed the plan worth testing and expressed the opinion that once the problem of flight were solved, as he thought it would be in a decade or so, an airship that could carry a heavy load of storage batteries would make rainmaking a real possibility.[8]

A few years later another well-known scientist announced that electricity was the cause of rain and that charging the skies could bring it down. Elmer Gates, original thinker, inventor of hundreds of ideas, and a pioneer in experimental psychology, maintained the best-equipped private laboratory in the country at Chevy Chase, Maryland. There he concluded that if a cloud or a section of the atmosphere became positively charged, an adjoining cloud or area must take on a negative charge. Midway between were secondary regions, in which both positive and negative particles commingled and—since opposite charges attract—coalesced to form raindrops. Skeptics strained their imagination and foresaw "immense static machines" charging the breeze to invoke moisture but put this idea in the same general category as concussion, which was used occasionally "to please unsophisticated sons of the soil."[9]

Experiments in Japan and Australia were duly noted by American editors, especially those of J. Graeme Balsillie, who in the half-dozen years after 1914 had at least limited government support in New South Wales for his rainmaking efforts using a metal-coated captive balloon, with a Roentgen-ray tube suspended from it. Convinced that there was no ionization by ultraviolet rays in the atmosphere closer than about fifty thousand feet to the earth, he sought to provide such rays and to electrify minute droplets to set in force mutual attraction and the formation of rain drops. Balsillie applied for a United States patent in 1916; a year later the special rain Precipitation Investigation Committee appointed in New South Wales gave a negative report, and by 1920 the inventor himself admitted defeat. A few years later physicist Charles T. Knipp of the University of Illinois conducted laboratory experiments along the same lines. Knipp, who also saw "a certain element of truth" in rain production by concussion, argued that it was theoretically possible to produce rain by shooting a powerful electric current through water-saturated air when the barometer was falling. But it was a moot point, he contended, since the vastness of nature precluded getting an electrical charge strong enough to do any good.[10]

The early twenties saw the stage set for a more scientific effort in the United States, which—like that of Dyrenforth in an earlier era—caught the public imagination and, momentarily at least, seemed to many finally to have captured the secret of Jupiter Pluvius. This was the set of experiments ranging over half a decade in which scientists from Cornell and Harvard were part of a seeding attempt using electrified sand dropped from airplaines provided by the Army Air Service.

Apparently the driving force in this endeavor was L. Francis Warren, a literate if obscure and often frustrated entrepreneur of uncertain background. Warren claimed to have spent many years in London and to have been with Cecil Rhodes in South Africa before the Boer War. According to his own account, he had once driven cattle from Texas to California, where he had bitter personal experience with drought in the San Joaquin Valley. Often he was addressed as "Doctor"; possibly he was once connected with Columbia University, but he seems not to have been a scientist. By the time of his venture into weather modification, Warren was a man well into his sixties.[11]

How it came about is not clear; but by the summer of 1920 Warren was laying plans with a rotund Cornell University chemist, Wilder D. Bancroft, scion of a distinguished New England family. Since 1895 Bancroft had been at Cornell, where at commencement his University of Leipzig doctoral garb made him "as resplendent as a parrot in a file of crows." A specialist in both electrochemistry and colloids, he was a man of stature and of some means and was very much interested in some of Warren's ideas, especially his simple theory of fog dispersal and rain precipitation.[12] Droplets of water suspended in air were charged either negatively or positively, but a film of condensed air around each prevented their merger when they collided. By spraying a cloud with sand of an opposite electrical charge, droplets could be induced to coalesce and to fall as rain. Bancroft agreed: in his mind there was no doubt of this. "The whole question is one of cost," he said. At one point Warren had also contemplated the use of some "high potentially charged liquid" sprayed into fog from above, but he soon abandoned the idea.[13]

It was obvious that aircraft, either conventional or lighter-than-air, was essential, as well as equipment for electrifying sand just as it was sprayed into the atmosphere. But Warren's means of charging sand particles—probably with a "large static machine" operated from a storage battery—proved unworkable; and in the spring of 1921, possibly on Bancroft's advice, he sought scientific help. He found it in E. Leon Chaffee, a physicist at the Cruft Laboratory at Harvard who agreed to design equipment for this purpose, asking only expenses with further compensation to come later.[14]

Bancroft may also have had some scientific input in the early stages, though never was it suggested that the idea and process of fog dispersal and rainmaking stemmed from anyone but Warren. Still, when Warren in 1920 suggested that Bancroft accept stock for his services, the Ithaca chemist agreed. He took shares in the A R Corporation, a paper firm that existed technically for a number of years but probably never became full-blown.[15]

Meanwhile, in the summer of 1921, Warren was busy in Washington seeking federal backing for fog-busting experiments. Carefully he cultivated important figures in the Army Air Service; then he discovered that the only military money for meteorological research was in the hands of the Signal Corps and felt compelled "to go through the entertainment and visit stunts with a 'new bunch of guys.'" But this was not a serious impediment: he even looked forward to an occasional opportunity "to spend denario and kick up my heels away from home."[16]

Nor did he ignore the Air Service completely. That newly reorganized agency was a flying arm of the government; it was vitally concerned with fog, and artificial rain had great strategic value. Thus Warren explained his process to the chief of the Air Service and begged direct cooperation, specifically in the form of a bombing plane for experimental use. He had also approached the General Electric Company and the Cleveland airplane builder Glenn Martin without avail, but he managed to come up with at least makeshift federal support. "The first attempt at fog and rainmaking in free air, outside of laboratories," he said later, came at McCook Field, near Dayton, in 1921, using electrical equipment "for the most part, drawn from the scrap heap."[17]

Little is known about this effort, but in September Warren was at Dayton, "clearing the decks for action as well as I could." The commanding officer at McCook Field promised to lobby with the secretary of war, and there was obvious cooperation on the part of the Army Air Service. During the following summer, 1922, sand–charging-and-scattering gear that Warren later referred to affectionately as "that throw-together-make-shift pile of junk" had been installed in a French-built Lepere aircraft designated the P-70 by the Air Service. On the last day of June, navy lieutenant John Price flew the craft in an attack on a cloud at McCook, inflicting "great gashes" and causing the cloud to disperse. A second flight destroyed another cloud in an action one observer called "absolutely uncanny," a phrase Warren would use in publicity releases for several years. At least nine different members of the Air Service Engineering Division signed affidavits attesting what they had seen; and Karl Smith, general inspector of naval aircraft for the district, wrote a warm report to the Bureau of Aeronautics. The demonstration, he said, "taught me never to say a thing can't be done. . . . I do not say that Dr. Warren will succeed in precipitating rain, but I do believe he is on the road to at least partial success. . . . His purpose is purely economic and in that, I am not particularly interested, but I do wish to point out to the Bureau the strategical and tactical value that success of this device will lead to." Its great potential for navigation aid and for bombing through cloud cover warranted all possible support, Smith thought.[18]

But the Lepere had limitations: it carried only seventy-five pounds of sand; its equipment was unpredictable in giving a well-defined charge; and soon the apparatus was disassembled so that the plane could participate in races at Selfridge Field. Warren continued the scramble for funds, tapping Bancroft for another five thousand dollars, a full year's salary for the professor.[19]

At the same time Warren was busy applying for a patent on his "new and useful improvements for CONDENSING, COALESCING AND PRECIPITATING ATMOSPHERIC MOISTURE." Filed June 29, 1922, his application specified not only electrified sand but also the alternative possibility of scattering ions from aerial-borne X-rays or from antenna trailed from an aircraft, ideas the Australian Balsillie may have anticipated. But in the spring of 1923, after the *Washington Post* had labeled the approach a "fake," the Patent Office rejected it until it might be sanctioned by the Bureau of Standards or some other official agency. Numerous foreign patents would be granted, but the status of the process at home was in limbo for years while legal appeals went on.[20]

Warren chafed and fumed. Impetuous and sensitive to criticism, he was impatient to "broadcast the development at once." Invariably short of funds and stung by adverse comments, he lashed out at "this cursed army outfit" and protested "the digs and jibes of a raft of pin-headed, skeptical, half-baked nuts," including a Californian named Millikan. "This Millikan I always knew was an ass but thought him harmless, but now I know him for a fakir and dangerous, a disgrace to your profession."[21]

By early 1923 Warren had access to an Air Service Martin aircraft equipped with two sand tanks, one for fine and one for coarse, to give a more selective and controlled seeding. By this time he was using Chaffee's revolving nozzles and charging gear, experimental though they still were. Shortly before beginning a series of flights in February, he released an article to the Associated Press, along with Smith's "absolutely uncanny" report.[22] As described in the news media, these "successful" tests at McCook Field were little short of sensational, although Warren thought the twin-engine Martin less effective than the Lepere of the previous year, with which newsmen often confused it.

Across the land Warren's standard press release, with the invariable modifiers "absolutely uncanny," was topped with positive headlines: "Airmen Make Rain by Dropping Sand"; "Chases Clouds, Brings Rain"; "Scientists Bring Rain, Cause Mist and Clouds to Go"; or "Rain Making Is Now a Success, Declares Cornell Professor"— Wilder D. Bancroft. Warren was particularly confident and spoke of giving London fair weather in the matter of half an hour, of bringing forth blossoms on the desert, and even of using cloudseeding as a military weapon. Editors of newspapers and of popular magazines amplified the belief that the process would "be of great value in the commercial world," that annual precipitation might be doubled in the arid West, and that with electrified sand—"one of the greatest inventions ever made"—the riddle of artificial rain had finally been solved. Old believers like Arthur Brisbane took careful note; even the staid *New York Times* seemed convinced; and the *Washington Post* pointed out that "nature has already in many ways been harnessed to the chariot of man" and expressed the hope "that the experiments at Dayton were as successful as they were at first represented to be." Under the headline "Ordering Rain a la Carte," the *Boston Transcript* saw the McCook successes as the triumph of modern science, one of the "miracles wrought by the airplane," which "promises soon to rank as the only sure manufacturer of rain since the fabled days when Jupiter Pluvius distributed his favors to a world more credulous than scientific."[23]

Friends congratulated Bancroft; queries came from as far away as Melbourne and Pretoria; the "sand baggers" caught the public eye and commentators often let their imagination go in discussing the implications of what had transpired. The *St. Louis Globe-Democrat* was sure that "farming will become more of a joy when the toolhouse back of the windmill has its airplane, and a sandbox transferred from a street-car vestibule is an irrigation plant," but it did foresee some competition among farmers chasing any "unsuspecting little cloud" that ventured into their airspace. Cartoonists flourished, reminiscent of the 1890s. In *Life* the farmer tells the pilot of a sand-dusting plane: "Go up and bust that there cloud over th' ten acre field, Noah—before somebody else gets it; an' fer th' love o' peace, keep off th' ol' woman's washin'!" A cynical correspondent of the *Washington Post* wondered about practical questions of control and predicted that the public, as usual, would be exploited.

> Capital, making its own moisture, can flood the market by properly watering the farmers' crops or can produce a long dry spell to relieve financial drought. . . . The real rain makers will start the usual series of strikes and lockouts and when you go with your little cup to the public utilities company supplying the rain to your section begging for a few drops to save your family, you will receive a frigid stare and be reminded that you haven't ordered that 40 per cent of Pittsburgh rain water which the rain board requires you to buy.[24]

As usual, the United States Weather Bureau took a dim view. As one onlooker put it, meteorologists were "inclined to meet the testimony of eye-witnesses with Hume's celebrated remark about the inadequacy of evidence cited on behalf of miracles." Along with other formulas for rainmaking and "cloud killing" they were consistent in condemning the electrified sand approach. As the bureau chief wrote to a Forest Service supervisor in Montana who inquired about using it to fight forest fires, "sprinkling the cloud with electrified sand, is utterly hopeless." In March 1923, as the swell of publicity developed from the McCook Field tests, the bureau, through the Department of Agriculture Press Service, issued a general release written by William Humphreys under the heading "Rain-Making Not Feasible, Says U.S. Weather Bureau." Concussion, chemicals, forced-air convection, and the Warren-Bancroft approach might be "picturesque and plausible" but were all "entirely futile"—to which Bancroft telegraphed: "No use arguing with the Weather Bureau. Prefer to wait for results and let them do the explaining."[25] The editor of the *New York Times* saw the bureau's criticism as an illustration of the "closed departmental mind." Bancroft's "sin is in telling speciliasts and professionals something new in their own domain." Yet privately Bancroft was roseate but more restrained. He was convinced that the McCook cloud dispersal could be duplicated practically and economically on a larger scale but admitted that believing was "not precisely the same thing as doing so, except in the Mikado."[26]

Warren worked to expand the operation. He planned tests using captive balloons to disperse sand at Moundsville, West Virginia, a series of experiments that were probably never conducted. Through the Army Air Service he sought further funding and urged that efforts be moved to the east coast, where clouds were better and where later rainmaking trials could be made over the Atlantic" in order to avoid any question of damage suits." For his work he needed two balloons, three airplanes, thirty thousand dollars to improve equipment, in particular to acquire generators that would give a charge higher than the ten thousand volts used at McCook and to further develop the centrifugal rotating nozzle apparatus devised by the Chaffees at Harvard.[27]

The Army Air Service, still interested, offered half of the sum requested, with the proviso that all flying arms of the federal government benefit from the results. Both Bancroft and Warren protested that this amounted to a takeover of the process for nothing; but they accepted, even though apparently rejecting a formal contract. "I told them where they could not only get off, but go to," Warren' reported, as he proceeded with the fifteen thousand available.[28]

The new arrangements provided use of the proving ground at Aberdeen, Maryland, a poor site as it turned out, with limited shop and machine facilities and frequent curtailment of flying because of the testing of ground ordnance. Two older DH-4B planes were assigned; and navy personnel and a young scientist named Knight, recommended by Chaffee, commenced outfitting the craft. But the work went slowly, both at Aberdeen and at the Crufts Laboratory, where the Chaffee brothers were attempting to improve the nozzle and charging system. Basic problems included defining precisely the proper size of the sand grain and then imparting the maximum electrical charge to each particle. "The fine stuff when released goes off to Kingdom Come, Tumbucktoo, etc., and does us no good whatever, and the coarse stuff falls like a plummet."[29]

Impatient and critical, Warren grumbled and prodded, ever mindful of the larger picture—as he saw it, the need to have both the DH-4Bs and two larger planes in working order by spring. Then, he said, "we can take our moving pictures and secure much needed funds, otherwise we will all be in the poor house or in the hands of the sheriff." He complained bitterly about his personnel. "What is the use of trying to deal with time when one is dependent upon government action?" he asked. Army officers and professors were very similar, he noted: "They both deal with the affairs of life as though they were sinecures and as though they expected to live forever." He found Knight "slow and lacking pep"; he decided he was "evasive, elusive, secretive, inconsiderate, unappreciative," and fired him. He ranted at the pure scientists; and when E. Leon Chaffee moved too slowly, Warren wondered if they "had backed the wrong horse or ass."[30]

All the while he was "hustling for funds to keep this thing going." Bills invariably diminished his "lubricating medium," as he called it; and he was frequently asking support from Bancroft. "If you have not yet reached the hole in the bottom of your stocking . . . " And Bancroft usually came through with a "life-saver."[31]

Early in 1924 Warren and Bancroft saw a possible breakthrough. Captain C. Christie, British air attaché in Washington, evidenced an interest in the fog dispersal process; and even though the United States government might not agree, Warren believed he ought to be encouraged. After all, with its "miserly $15000" Washington evidently hoped to keep their effort on the financial rocks and to "force us to dance to its music."[32]

In a letter drafted by Warren and edited by Bancroft, the British Air Admiralty was offered an unparalleled opportunity to combat the dense fog that the London Chamber of Commerce estimated sometimes cost city and port losses of five million dollars a day. "Outside of several small interests," Warren wrote, "Prof. Bancroft and myself own and control the whole matter." They were indeed cooperating with the U.S. Army Air Service but had no contract with the government—"in fact refused to sign one"—and had patent applications pending in forty-five countries. Enclosing copies of affidavits and clippings, Warren outlined their technical problems with optimism and sketched out the progress that had been made, including a growing confidence by pilots that they could take off in a fog and get down again. For seventy-five thousand dollars the British government would be permitted to prove the process in England; when convinced of its utility, Whitehall would then become a licensee at a flat fee of two and a half million, plus an annual royalty of five hundred thousand for the life of the patent. "I do not see how they can turn us down," Warren wrote Bancroft; but two months later they did, the Air Admiralty politely indicating that they wished to see results of the Aberdeen trials before giving the proposal serious consideration.[33]

Late in 1923 the two DH-4Bs had been outfitted and intermittent flights made; but the tale was one of constant malfunctioning, either of the planes, which were old, or of the sand-charging apparatus with its interminable sequence of burned-out transformers, defective generators, or poorly designed valves and nozzles. As Warren said, this indifferent gear worked fairly well "until something happens and something happens to one or the other nearly every time we make a flight." Thus the tinkering went on into 1924—and, indeed, beyond. Most trials were unimpressive, though occasionally one "blotted out" its target cloud.[34]

A Warren release to the Associated Press in mid-April of 1924 was as positive as ever but emphasized the McCook Field exploits, not those of Aberdeen. Rational thinkers accepted the Dayton results and the fact that "commercial rain-making now lies within the grasp of men," it noted. Only a few soreheads—"skeptics and shallow thinkers"—disagreed; and they, fortunately "developed little or no following." Meteorologist William Humphreys was one of these and let fly another round of criticism. But he "made an ass of himself," according to Warren, who remarked on the "well-defined quarrel" being waged by the Weather Bureau and the Air Service over the sand experiments.[35]

Grumbling about the "interference of army officers," Warren had both planes sent to Boston for complete modification of the sand valves, the rotating nozzles, and their drive motors. Yet he was both encouraged and suspicious in September, when the Navy Bureau of Aeronautics assigned a Douglas DT-2, a mechanic, and two pilots to help—"and incidently to spy on the work" at Aberdeen, he said. By this time Warren was convinced that "we are being defeated by men of our own selection": scientists, especially the Chaffees, who lacked energy and were prone to practical errors. In September he gave the Chaffees an ultimatum: follow instructions or quit. At the same time he confided to Bancroft, "We must aim to get rid of the Chaffee's if we make a deal with the government." A few weeks later during a test at Aberdeen, one of the nozzles stuck, making Warren "so mad I concluded to fire the whole Chaffee outfit, which we should have done over two years ago." He promptly did so but in such a peremptory fashion as to completely alienate E. Leon Chaffee, who announced he was applying for patents on the sand-charging equipment he had designed. Chaffee believed that the fog dispersal process had "gone far enough to demonstrate that it works," but that in the interest of credibility Warren should put the direction of the operation into the hands of a bona fide engineer or scientist and step out of the limelight.[36]

In early October navy lieutenant H. F. Councill, who had flown the new DT-2 to Aberdeen, reported back on some of the experiments to the chief of the Bureau of Aeronautics. Warren had no funds to equip the DT-2, but Councill had piloted the troublesome old DH-4Ds on a number of occasions and was impressed with the results. Even though the equipment was unreliable and delivered too little sand, he believed that the theory was sound and that the Air Service should make available better aircraft and gear. Councill had seen no precipitation but thought it not beyond the realm of possibility. "To make rain is I am sure the ultimate hope of Dr. Warren and it is no more incredible than was radio twenty years ago."[37]

Councill's flights in September and October were encouraging enough to convince Warren that "a good show in Washington" was in order. First he paved the way with a flowery release to the wire services. Next he visited the presidential secretary, C. Bascom Slemp; for "See Slemp" was the White House byword for accomplishing something in the Coolidge administration. Through Slemp, Warren put pressure on the secretary of war and on Major General Mason M. Patrick of the Air Service to arrange the aerial trials at Bolling Field. (Patrick he characterized as "so stupid & thick he would not see a white goat running over his desk.")[38]

After telephone calls had been made alerting the president, cabinet officials, and members of Congress, on October 30 Warren's DH-4Bs launched an attack on "two large detached blue black cumulous clouds" directly over the nation's capital but "scored a most deplorable failure." Warren believed the equipment had been sabotaged; however, an on-the-spot inspection showed no mechanical shortcomings. (Months later, according to Warren, when the apparatus was being dismantled, it was discovered that one part of the mechanism was bent so that no electrical charge was being given to the sand.) Even so, a feature article in the *New York Times* used the headline "Rain at Man's Will Is Declared Possible," with the subheadings "Wonders at Bolling Field" and "Rains Made to Order."[39]

Then came "several indifferent flights." One plane went out with a need for a new axle; the other required an engine change. Repairs were delayed and commenced only after Warren, in his words, "had a show down with the commanding officer of the District." Lamenting that the Weather Bureau and the Patent Office had been totally uncooperative and that the Air Service had again undercut his work by stripping the planes for racing, Warren once more approached the federal government for renewed funding. In February 1925 he requested that the two Air Service DH-4Bs be overhauled and be made available for another six months, with hangar space assigned at Hartford, Connecticut. In addition, two navy DT-2s should be provided. All personnel and operating costs should be assumed and thirty-five thousand dollars furnished for outfitting. Rather than the Army Air Service alone, Warren proposed that the navy and the Post Office Department –all with an interest in aerial navigation—jointly sponsor the work and all benefit from the results. To date, he noted, the government had spent about seventeen thousand dollars on the project exclusive of personnel and overhead costs, while the input of private time had totaled at least one hundred twenty thousand dollars. He also dropped the not-so-subtle hint that both foreign nations and private corporations were interested but that fog dispersal had a vital and patriotic dimension.[40]

After months of waiting, both the army and navy air arms agreed to provide planes and fifteen thousand dollars for continuing experiments at the civilian field in Hartford. There Warren would supervise the installation of new and improved equipment, much of the work being done by the Hartford Electric Light Company, whose practical electricians pronounced "Chaffee's job as the worst they have ever seen." This only served to convince Warren more firmly that it was the Chaffee-designed equipment that had held them back. "But I am not going to speak more of these grafters who milked us so finely," he promised.[41]

By the end of May 1926, the two army planes were ready for testing, and equipment for two new navy torpedo-carriers was being tried out in the shop. After more modification of the electrical gear, Warren staged trials in June before a number of military officers from Washington and Governor Trumbull of Connecticut. Though no rain fell, clouds were "unmade," and observers and newsmen alike were impressed. Warren exultantly telegraphed Bancroft: "Good luck this afternoon knocked the stuffings out of two small clouds first one in one minute second in two and one half minutes. Am certain we have equipment that will deliver at last."[42]

But generators did continue to burn out, transformers broke down, and the sand was sometimes too damp to flow well. Tests were interrupted momentarily when the sand dusters were ousted from state ground and hangars by the National Guard, who "can't be bothered with us for we are nothing but a d——d nuisance," as one of the navy pilots put it. The same flyer had a few anxious moments on one of his trips when sand blew into the cockpit and blinded one eye. "I dug out about a half a pound of sand but finally had to go to the hospital to get the rest of it out."[43]

But there were good days with impressive results, as on August 23, when Lieutenant (j.g.) DeL. Mills "attacked a cloud" from a height of about thirty-six hundred feet: "Made a trip over it, and on turning around, discovered that it had been cut in half. Made another trip over it and then watched it disappear. Attacked another cloud directly over the field but the sand gave out after one trip over it. Nevertheless that cloud slowly disappeared."[44]

Harvard meteorologist Alexander McAdie had been mildly optimistic about the McCook fog dispersal business in 1923. ("It seems feasible," he said then). In September 1926 he spent two days at Hartford and came away concluding that "with more efficient apparatus, Dr. Warren will be able to get demonstrable results in dispelling clouds and fracturing fog." But rainmaking would require much more work. Still, said McAdie, "the evidence of these two days gives me a belief (which previously was not very strong) that a good beginning has been made, and that the outlook is promising."[45]

Warren apparently lost government support that same year and was unable to gain much private funding, although it was reported in 1927 that, with the backing of several wealthy men, he was contemplating facilities on Long Island to continue his experiments. There is no evidence that he did. Apart from the Air Service, his primary financial contributor was Wilder Bancroft, who by early 1925 had invested at least twenty thousand five hundred dollars of his own and another seven thousand dollars belonging to him and his friends. Other efforts, on his or on Warren's part, to raise funds from private sources came to naught. At various times they had approached important figures (the Lamonts, the Guggenheims, and the Astors); and they had sought to involve General Electric, the Santa Fe Railroad, and the Ford Motor Company—all without avail.[46]

That Warren still hoped to capitalize an enterprise to exploit his process was indicated in 1928, when he published privately a promotional booklet, *Facts and Plans: Rainmaking—Fogs and Radiant Planes*. In it he cited a record of forty-three successes and twenty-six failures over a six-year period, with each failure directly traceable to a malfunction of some part of the equipment. This, in turn, stemmed "from attempting to do a big job with little money." Presumably, Warren was referring to fog dispersal, but he was also thinking in terms of rainmaking. Disagreeing with those who insisted the word tended "to cheapen the work and invites ridicule," he argued that there was abundant moisture even over arid lands and that electrified sand would bring it down, with benefits to society "almost 'beyond the dreams of avarice', not only for our country but for the entire world."[47]

But that was not to be. No more trials were reported, no doubt to the relief of Chief Marvin and his Washington staff. In 1930 the process was still in dispute at the U.S. Patent Office, and apparently nothing came of it. Professional meteorologists denied that it produced rainfall or dispersed more than a negligible amount of fog,[48] but there were many believers. The public was receptive, the press generally kindly disposed or at least not abusive. That bona fide professors from major institutions were involved and that army or navy planes were used gave a cloak of respectability and seemingly the approval of both government and academia.

By contrast, other electrical rainmakers of the same era lacked a scientific base and gave out no information about their work. In the mid-twenties the Weather Bureau felt compelled to rap the knuckles of one named Collonon and another named William Haight of California—the latter having drawn inquiries from Russians— although apart from their use of electricity, the methods of both remain a mystery. Ironically, within a few years the Soviet government would itself be experimenting with methods of precipitating rain and snow, using electrical apparatus attached to World War I sausage-type balloons.[49]

Also vague was the process used by Charles F. Rath, head of several New Jersey chemical companies, who built on discoveries his father made around the turn of the century. Rath claimed to "have discovered the laws of humidity which control the atmospheric electricity and [to] have invented an apparatus which enables me to produce rain wherever and whenever it is needed." Asserting that he had broken the drought in New Jersey, he vainly sought funds from the legislature of the state, from the Farm Federation of New Jersey, and from the U.S. Department of Agriculture, arguing that at stake were prosperity, a lowered cost of living, and broad support for the Republican party. In 1930, in a drought period, he asked President Hoover to appoint a special investigator from the Department of Agriculture— not the Weather Bureau—to inspect his claims. But Rath wanted no money at that point: "The country can make me a national gift after the crop has been saved."[50]

In the 1930s the growing use of the radio was blamed by some for heavy rains and by others for producing drought. Along the latter line, one complainant argued that broadcasting burned the water out of the clouds; unless it were halted, the "whole country will be a desert in another year."[51] Such opinions were hardly rational. Long before, in 1906, Pennsylvanian William A. Scott had insisted that he had "solved the irrigation question": "By means of my wireless telegraphy I think I can bring rain in any section east of the Mississippi River in three days time -- Mo -- Iowa -- Kansas -- &c. 5 days Texas 7 days." Although not ready to divulge his secret to the public he wanted "to try my hand on the dry regions of the West" and was insulted when meteorologist Willis Moore gently pooh-poohed his ideas.[52]

Yet, in theory, rainmaking by radio perhaps was not too far-fetched. In 1926 the distinguished French mathematician and minister of war Paul Painleve suggested that radio waves indeed might aid in bringing rain. Noting that the nuclei around which raindrops collected often were electrified atoms or other particles, known to be affected by radio waves, Painleve asked whether the use of such waves might not influence the weather. At least some scientists were receptive to the idea, but the difficulty was the usual one: too much atmosphere and too few radio waves.[53]

# 7. Sending Up a Soda Water Tank: Rain by Sprinkling the Clouds

When this plan is put in motion
  Then the droughts will cease to be
  And the people of one notion
  Planting orchards broad you'll see.[1]

Melbourne and Hatfield, as well as many of the lesser-known chemical smell makers, worked at ground level or near it. From the late nineteenth century on, others would place their faith in the idea of instilling some chemical substance in the atmosphere to bring about rapid cooling and thus the precipitation of moisture. Some would use rockets; some, balloons or dirigibles; and eventually the airplane would become the medium of experimentation. But however the chemical was put into the air, its action, rather than concussion, was the key to releasing the rain.

One of the earliest of this school of thought, Louis Gathmann of Chicago, was actually one of the most reputable. His approach would have been "based on truly rational principles," according to later observers, were it not for the "ridiculous inadequacy of the means to the end." Born in Germany, Gathmann in 1890 was listed as being in "mill machinery"; in actual practice he was a professional inventor who would make substantial contributions in the development of artillery, improved telescopes, airplanes, and the refining of crude petroleum.[2]

In 1890, while experimenting with liquid carbonic acid gas as a coolant for artillery shells, Gathmann noticed that these shells bursting six hundred feet into the air immediately produced clouds. Further tests convinced him that the evaporation of liquid carbonic acid gas brought rain, and in 1891 he patented the idea of shooting this chemical into the air as a means of creating artificial precipitation.[3]

The method was to "suddenly chill the atmosphere by rapid evaporation," a process that would also clean the air of smoke and fog, if need be. In a little book published to further his invention, Gathmann estimated the cost for "absolute protection of a country against drought for the space of one year" at fifteen cents per acre for ten thousand acres, declining to a mere two cents an acre for a million acres. Since the basic equipment would already have been purchased, costs for the second year would be 75 percent less. Except at first, he scoffed at the concussionists: the key to rainmaking was to "utilize the laws of heat, force and vapor" to lower the temperature of the upper air currents.[4]

Gathmann may have had backing from Senator Farwell, as had Dyrenforth, but he probably did little beyond his early patents. Perhaps he realized, as did scientists like Alexander Macfarlane of the University of Texas, that nature was simply too vast. Macfarlane calculated that if the plan would work at all—which was dubious—it would require more than four hundred thousand dollars worth of liquefied carbonic acid gas to bring down .27 inches of rain over one square mile. Instead of rainmaking, Gathmann turned to his other inventions. In 1901, with congressional appropriations, he built an eighteen-inch gun with special shells and fuses designed to kill by shock. When army ordnance experts rejected the idea, he sold it to German manufacturers, an action that after the eruption of war in 1914 brought heated debate in the halls of Congress.[5]

A rainmaking plan similar to Gathmann's, using the same chemical, was advocated by an Australian nearly a dozen years after Gathmann's proposal. And while Gathmann was patenting his idea, Henry Allen, a civil engineer in India, designed a rocket four inches in diameter and eighteen inches long, capable of rising a mile into the atmosphere. At the proper altitude, ether carried within the rocket would boil furiously, forming spray that lowered temperatures precipitously, while the case descended by parachute trailing a column of cold air and producing rain.[6] About the same time, a Colorado housewife believed that shooting bisulfate of carbon into the clouds would provide the great panacea needed by the arid West.

Why not draw from clouds above us
All the moisture needed here
And make the rolling plains around us
Fields of corn and meadows dear.[7]

As early as 1893 S. P. Gresham, Jr., of the U.S. Signal Corps had commented on the Dyrenforth experiments and had suggested, perhaps facetiously, that the government rainmaker embark on "one of the coming air ships" fitted with refrigeration equipment to pump chilled air into the atmosphere. "Then if nature is agreeable, a tiny shower may be induced to fall." In time the idea of using the "coming air ships" meteorologically would be taken more seriously. For example, Cleveland lawyer, author, and financial agent Henry R. Hudson presented a number of suggestions for airborne rain-producing early in the twentieth century. A graduate of Hiram College, Hudson turned out more than three hundred short stories, in one of which an Arizona rancher kept his acres moist by means of a dirigible equipped with a contraption that sprinkled liquid ammonia over the clouds to bring down rain. Soon he proposed the same idea and variations of it seriously, hoping that they would "prove more efficacious than explosives, profanity or silent prayer." Shortly he discarded the idea of ammonia, toyed with the possibility of salt brine, and then decided that carbon dioxide might work—a suggestion that brought the headline in a Cleveland newspaper "Sending Up a Soda Water Tank." As an alternative, Hudson also considered sand. The means was flexible, he said; what was important was government experimentation, in order eventually that farmers be able to "keep the weather on tap, even as they do cider in the cellar." If not dirigibles, why not heavier-than-air craft? "We have heard much about the aeroplane for war," he said, "why not the aeroplane for peace & large crops?" Willis Moore of the Weather Bureau told him why not, running through the list of rain-making pioneers and concluding bluntly that "the artificial production of rain on a commercial scale is a chimera."[8]

A more familiar name was Arthur Brisbane, son of an eminent social reformer and a highly successful, if sensational, newspaper editor in his own right, who also described himself as belonging "to the great army of would-be-rain-makers" when he laid his thoughts on the subject before President William Howard Taft in the summer of 1910. Brisbane urged government investigations along two lines: the scattering of liquid air into the atmosphere; and the exploding of dust-filled bombs to provide the particles he believed triggered rain formation. Brisbane was a prominent figure; and Taft handled him gingerly and politely, passing his letter on to the army, then to Willis Moore of the Weather Bureau, who responded much more gently than was his wont. Even so, Chief Moore deftly punctured the editor's ideas but did send Brisbane a copy of his new book, *Descriptive Meteorology*, which debunked rainmaking, conferred with him in New York, and offered him the use of the Weather Bureau laboratory at Mount Weather, Virginia, to work out his theories.[9]

At that time Brisbane apparently did nothing more; but over a dozen years later he was back again, suggesting to the secretary of agriculture that "some hydrophilous substance" such as finely powdered lime, with a known affinity for water, might be sprinkled over the clouds to bring down moisture. This might be accomplished, he thought, from a dirigible equipped with a lime container "with a travelling bottom, something perhaps on the order of a manure spreader, with which you are familiar." President Harding thought well of Brisbane and naively told Secretary Henry C. Wallace of the Agriculture Department: "If you have funds available I would be more than glad to see you do it. I find a great deal of pleasure in commending a good many things in which Mr. Brisbane is deeply interested." But the Weather Bureau, to whom the correspondence was passed, was as pessimistic as usual, pointing out that lime would merely dry the atmosphere and was actually used in a number of industrial processes for that specific purpose. Brisbane received these comments gracefully and went off wondering if a vegetable dust, such as that produced by hay, might not be the answer.[10]

Over a period of time a variety of other substances were suggested and a few actually tried for cloud seeding. When it was proposed in 1918 that salt and soda crystals be dropped into cloud formations to produce moisture, Washington officials responded that even were the theory correct—which it was not—113 tons of chemical would be required to produce an inch of rain over one acre, and all ground vegetation, including crops, would be killed in the process. Chlorate of potash or some "hygroscopic dust or spray" such as concentrated crude sulphuric acid were also advocated, with scientists again pointing out the damage a "sulphur acid bath" would do to plant life. A few even more impractical souls would send up ice by balloon to chill the air or would spray water from aircraft over parched fields, both woefully inefficient approaches with much moisture lost by evaporation.[11]

At home and around the world, the possibilities of using liquid air were explored perhaps more fully than those of any other substance during the first quarter or so of the twentieth century. Created under tremendous pressure and kept at temperatures far below zero, liquid air seemed an ideal coolant for weather modification purposes. In his presidential address to the Geographical Section of the Australasian Association for the Advancement of Science in 1904, a Melbourne professor reminisced about central Australia, where drifting clouds seldom brought rain, and "dreamt of the time when kites would spray those clouds with liquid air, and discharge their now wasted contents on to the wasted plains below." A few years later a professor at the Oklahoma State Normal School in Edmond, experimenting with a tower, urged spraying liquid air from a plane; and Canadian fliers made an attempt of their own. In Germany in 1922 the Wegener-Schneider tests were more systematic, even though armament restrictions limited them to antique aircraft with only low-altitude capacity and the trials were unsuccessful. Invariably, however, meteorologists pointed out the usual shortcomings—the hugeness of the atmosphere and prohibitive costs that made desalination of seawater much more attractive as a solution for aridity.[12]

Especially popular in the 1920s was the idea of "powdering the face of the sky" with dust, as one Weather Bureau skeptic called it. As early as 1875 the Frenchman P. J. Coulier had concluded that dust particles were necessary to cloud formation. Five years later the Scotsman John Aitken rediscovered the concept, demonstrating before the Royal Society of Edinburgh that the presence of condensation nuclei, even ordinary dust particles was one of the prerequisites to rainfall. In 1891 a University of Kansas physicist, Lucian I. Blake, had experimented with infusing the air with fine particles to provide such nuclei and had suggested slow-burning "smoke balls," made of turpentine and sawdust or paper pulp, to be suspended from balloons half a mile or more above the ground.[13]

This concept was attractive and would be echoed by others; and occasional experiments were tried in Europe and elsewhere. In London it was suggested that shoveling dust out of a balloon or airplane would dissipate fog. A South African, C. K. Hall, whom one of his countrymen thought "an ignorant gas-bag on meteorological matters," had dropped dust from an aircraft in a series of "cloud control" tests in 1920 and 1921 and had built up a devoted following in the United States and at home, including a Johannesburg poet with more optimism than talent.

> So bang the old Dustpan;
> Do yourself proud;
> Don't worry! The Dustman
> Has vanquished the Cloud.[14]

Hall no doubt helped set the stage for the McCook Field electrified sand experiments, which in a sense used a hybrid approach, with electricity designed to make the nuclei coalesce.

Americans also paid careful attention in 1929, when Royal Air Force planes sprinkled finely powdered kaolin, the pure white clay used for making china, over clouds at Hong Kong in a widely cited experiment that produced more publicity than rain. And in 1934, one of the many entries competing for a prize of five thousand dollars offered by the American Inventor's Congress for an effective mode of making rain was a suggestion to seed clouds with fine dry nitrate. The award remained ungiven. One Brooklynite suggested building large "ascending platforms" about half a mile long, through which the wind might sweep dust upward into the atmosphere to promote precipitation. Another proposed adding nuclei by plane, some smoke to be released directly and some from smudge pots dropped by parachutes.[15]

The airplane had added a new dimension—one that caught the imagination of the average American. A Minnesotan of 1928 recalled the Dayton sand project when he wrote the U.S. Department of Agriculture, "Please send out a bunch of aeroplanes to get the clouds busted up so that we may have some nice clear weather for our threshing." Earlier a New Mexican had urged the establishment of an experimental station somewhere in the Southwest, whence fliers could put cold air, gas, chemicals, or electric current "exactly where it is needed—in or over these loafing clouds." When Chief Charles Marvin pooh-poohed the idea as "little short of foolish" and "an extravagant waste of money," he was simply not as forward-looking as the New Mexican, who saw in the future "a few Flyers herding the summer clouds and milking them even as a few cowboys herd Thousands of cattle and corral them for use."[16]

As it turned out, the cloud seeders were on the right track. But they had not yet hit upon the right substance, nor had they yet found a theoroetical framework to explain the precipitation process. In the twenties and thirties, expecially, knowledge of convective clouds and of the mechanisms of rain formation was proceeding apart from the would-be rainmakers who caught the headlines. Much work was being done with hygroscopic nuclei, and meteorologists were intrigued with the abundance of droplets found in clouds at temperatures well below the freezing point. In 1911 Alfred Wegener had postulated a rapid growth of ice crystals in supercooled clouds, and in keeping with this suggestion the research of a number of scientists laid the foundation for the understanding of cloud formations and the precipitation process. Ultimately, in 1933 the Swede Tor Bergeron set forth a theory that drew together his own findings and those of other scientists: most raindrops originate from ice crystals in clouds at subfreezing temperatures. In 1938 Walter Findeisen, a German, expanded on Bergeron's ideas and presented a clear statement of the thesis, with several new interpretations. It was Findeisen who saw the potential for rainmaking and hail prevention by the introduction of artificial sublimation nuclei; and some, at least, credit him and his Cloud Research Institute with "the first rainmaking effort along modern lines."[17]

But as early as 1930, the Dutchman August W. Veraart had been seeding the clouds over the seaside resort of Scheveningen, financed by his own government and dropping what the press called chipped ice from Fokker trimotors. Early in the following year, a vice president of the Dry Ice Corporation of America suggested to the U.S. Weather Bureau that Veraart would do better to try his produce—solid carbon dioxide—instead. Presumably there was no link between the two men; as a matter of fact Veraart had already been at work using dry ice, with some limited results to which little serious attention was given. But he had only vague ideas about the mechanism of ice-crystal development in supercooled clouds, and unjustifiably sweeping claims discredited his work.[18] It remained for others, notably Bergeron and Findeisen, to formulate a reasonable hypothesis of the physical processes of rain formation.

When the spectacular breakthrough did come, it would be with the work of the Americans Langmuir and Schaefer. Ironically, neither was a meteorologist, and neither seemed aware of Bergeron's 1933 findings or of the advances in the field over the previous quarter of a century. Both on Mount Washington and in the laboratory, they had worked on problems related to cloud physics and had covered some of the same ground independently. As much by chance as by design, Schaefer found that dry ice formed ice crystals from fog particles in a specially cooled freezer unit; and this led to the memorable Schenectady cloud-seeding experiment and the opening of a new phase in the history of weather modification.

# 8. . . . He Could Probably Sell the Brooklyn Bridge without Even Getting Up a Sweat: A Gallery of Rogues

Fakir, seer, man of science
   Farmers in you place reliance
Bring your clouds down from the bay,
   Mix your soup and make 'em pay.
If you fail to bring a squall,
   They'll turn your picture to the wall.[1]

If the exponents of artificial rainmaking included scientists, pseudo-scientists, self-deluders, and sharp psychologists with an eye on the betting odds, they also included a fringe group who ran the gamut from mystics and crackpots to opportunists and pure and simple frauds. Most of these were never taken seriously and were judged for what they were, although apparently some gained enough cash from their efforts to make it worthwhile. A look at a few of these marginal would-be cloud compellers is both fascinating and enlightening.

Throughout the "pluviculture" era a handful of spiritualists hawked their services. Drought, dust storms, and forest fires were "the result of God's Judgment," insisted one; but through his own super-natural power and through his "Susceptibility Judgment Office" in New Orleans, he could induce rain to fall on about two days of each week. Another—Philadelphia dentist, vegetarian, and mystic—cited Oahspe, the new Bible written through John B. Newbrough in 1882, as divine justification for bringing showers by concussion: "*He shall provide explosive gases high up in the air, which shall break the wind currents, establishing vortices from the upper regions downward.*"[2]

Solomon W. Jewett was a seventh son and a New Englander. He advertised himself as "the Magnetic Healer from Vermont," and he

125

promised a natural, sure treatment of all chronic diseases through his special gifts. "Through inspiration," according to his words, he also "received explicit instructions" in 1872 on how to bring down artificial rain. Without divulging any of his secrets, he twice volunteered to demonstrate his abilities to friends in California; at least once he suggested the same to the chief signal officer in Washington, asking only expenses. He was certain of his powers but found it impossible to comply with the government's request for drawings or models. "You will call me visionary," he said; "all great minds like Franklin, & others have been called insane."[3]

Even more of a free spirit was Michael Cahill, "M.D.," who wrote the governor of Kansas from San Francisco in the spring of 1890, presenting an elaborate and far-fetched description of how he believed rain was formed and how rainmaking might be done. Such high-soaring birds as eagles, condors, and "griffins," he said, "open vents for the vapor to ascend and form clouds, like escape valves of steam engines." Other high-flying birds, moving from cloud to cloud and from cloud to earth, in the process bring "jets of vapor" to establish links between the clouds and the ground, thereby causing showers. The federal government, he argued, should protect, feed, and tame the birds and regulate their flight "so as to give timely rain." Four to six pairs of high-altitude birds were needed for each ten to one hundred square miles, to be released whenever moisture was needed.[4]

Cahill also proposed other means of making rain, including a "metalic captive baloon" with wire cables to join clouds and earth. Another alternative was the use of reflectors; still another was "producing vibrations, striking key notes of thunder, by sounding fog horns or running trains with cogged wheels, and other means" apart from explosives, which were too dangerous. Other possibilities were a magnet "powerful enough to deflect the atmospheric electric currents" and "a large Blackman ventilating wheel" to push a column of air from the ground surface into the atmosphere. Cahill invited the national government to put his ideas into practice, with half the profits going to endow homes for orphans and widows. He believed, also, that electric companies and irrigation projects were upsetting the balance of nature and that complete disaster could be averted only by the government purchasing and closing down all such operations.[5]

Without indicating his approach, Cahill claimed to have applied for a patent on a method of artificial rainmaking and blamed Washington ineptness when the patent was never forthcoming. According to him, he sought to explain his ideas to the California legislature in 1886 but received only "fragmentary and informal hearings." He had definite ideas on other "pluviculturists." Edward Powers in *War and the Weather* did "not understand the subject." It was not concussion that jarred down moisture in war, he explained, but 'Electro Magnetism" created by the friction of balls and bullets. Both Melbourne and "the Congressional Dynamiter" Dyrenforth were "poaching on my rights," he charged. Melbourne's patent (which never existed) was "fraudulent and void in law," and he had cautioned the Australian by mail and had complained about him to the governors of Ohio, Wyoming, and Kansas, asking his prosecution as a lawbreaker. Understandably, nobody took Cahill seriously. It was a Kansas editor at the time Melbourne was so popular in 1891 who noted that "a crazy loon in California named Cahill" had charged his ideas had been stolen—"which may prove true as he has no ideas left."[6]

Cahill was too chaotic and unsystematic to be considered an opportunist or a fraud. Not so with Missourian Allen Dorman, a versatile "Inventor, Author and Chemist," as he styled himself early in the twentieth century. Dorman was proprietor of the Dorman Diamond Company, the producer of "the Finest Imitation on the Earth"—at only five dollars for each carat and a half. He also manufactured "Keystone Laxative," sold volumes of his own poetry, and was owner-manager of the "Continental Rain-Making Company" in 1905. Originally, he went into the "pluviculture" business avowedly "for the money there was in it" but subsequently "made some valuable discoveries" and felt justified in offering the public "our scientific methods of rain-making." He used about thirty-five chemicals, he said, after an initial step designed to "mineralize the oxygen of the air" to control electricity. Next, in the evening, "I throw Nucleus above the cloud line, to form rain drops, clouds etc. (the same as in a small receiver) which acts as a body for Negative Electricity, Radiation helps carry the Nucleus upward."

Dorman used a shotgun to "throw up Nucleus" in fifteen successful applications, according to him, but soon sought support from President Theodore Roosevelt (whom he addressed as "Brother Author") and from the Department of Agriculture to buy a small cannon—"about a six pounder." "I will never use it against my flag," he promised. He also urged the establishment of a "Government Rainmaking Station" in Clinton, Missouri, his hometown.[7]

One could enumerate others—optimists like Henry Baker of

Portland, Oregon, self-styled "expert rain producer and weather ad-
juster," who in 1894 sought to promote himself at both state and
national levels, and who promised for three thousand dollars to give
the state of Idaho "all the Rain it would need," and who told Secretary
of Agriculture J. Sterling Morton that the maintenance and travel
expenses and a change of location once a month, "I could cover the
States of California, Arizona, Nevada, New Mexico with rain the year
round."[8] Or what of A. W. Tacke, the twentiety-century cloud cracker
whose approach was the result of "an accident of an over loaded shelf
of Bottles of chemicals falling into a sink" with a stopped-up drain? It
took three years to duplicate the effect, he admitted; but once duplicated, Tacke claimed the ability to milk the clouds at a cost of about a
penny per ten thousand tons of water. Add to the list the Canadian
Frank Clark, who spent fifteen years working on a rainmaking
machine that, when finally perfected in the drought-ridden thirties, not
only produced sprinkles and storms but was equipped to receive music
as well. It was so powerful that only one was needed for all of North
America. And, explained the inventor, "I have made it all by myself in
my spare time."[9]

Yet undoubtedly the most blatant and audacious of all the practicing "pluviculturists" to flash across the American scene was "Dr."
George Ambrosius Immanuel Morrison Sykes, whose complex name
appeared from time to time in New York newspapers and racing sheets
in 1930 and 1931. Slight, bald, and unimposing, with "sad eyes, and a
gentle voice," albeit with a makeup of solid brass, Sykes was no
scientist. He was a flat-earth believer, and he estimated that the sun
was roughly thirty-three hundred miles away. He labeled himself a
"minister of Zoroastrianism" and had once announced the formation
of the "World Order of Zarathustra" to wage war on prohibition,
vivisection, free love, internationalism, meat eating, and other perni-
cious practices. But above all, according to the New York *World*,
Sykes had to be "the champion salesman of the country," capable of
selling the Brooklyn Bridge "without even getting up a sweat."[10]

According to one of his cohorts, Sykes started at the bottom, in
charge of a Gatling gun used by a more experienced California
rainmaker. By the late twenties he was coming into his own. The U.S.
Weather Bureau began to hear of Sykes and his Weather Control
Bureau, which could, spokesmen insisted, either prevent rainfall or
bring it down from the sky. Through the Republican national commit-

tee, Sykes asked to demonstrate his methods to the Department of Agriculture but was ignored.[11]

Soon he circulated a typed statement about his secret equipment and its past successes, a document as brazen and as preposterous as the "Doc" himself. He had developed a new field of weather control— "meteorolurgy." Whereas a meteorologist observed and described the weather, the "meteorolurgist" actually did something about it. Sykes coined words and phrases and strung them together with complete abandon. He spoke of "hydrolurgy" (a radio control service), "thermurgy" (heat and cold control), and "pneumaturgy" (wind control). He also used "ballisturgy" (explosives), noting that "proper angles of fire and barrages for Concussion and sizes of Impellant, Propellant and disruptive (Bursting) Charges are extremely important and must be coordinated to and with the angles of Declination and Inclination on the Meridians and Parallels of the (Magentic) Master Coordinate Projection Charts and Tables." Within these guidelines, he set up his "radio apparatus, antennae, and lightning coordinate grounds, cloud attractors and directors, integrators, and precipitators" and for good measure fired off a four-inch gun loaded with black powder.[12]

The results of this hybrid Rube Goldberg equipment were truly marvelous, according to its promoters. It could produce rain, change snow or hail into rain, check frost, prevent heat waves, and provide sunshine for weeks at a time. From a clear sky, moisture could be drawn in half an hour; from a cloudy one, in fifteen minutes. At the request of an embassy attaché in Washington, Sykes cleared the sky in three hours flat; to Death Valley he provided rain from the roof of a Los Angeles bungalow six hundred miles away. In 1928 he had brought showers to the drought-ridden Columbia Basin in Washington, then moved over to Spokane, where despite Weather Bureau predictions for rain, he kept the Interstate Fairgrounds dry for fair week. Then, he reported, "I got hold of my clouds and took 'em over the mountains down to Los Angeles" and released their moisture.[13]

From Burbank, where he established the Weather Control Bureau, Sykes made contact with the wealthy Mrs. Harriman, who invited him to New York in 1930 to discuss the use of his talents to assure sunny skies over the Belmont Park racetrack. Sykes met Mrs. Harriman in her custom-built Hispano-Suiza at the Turf and Field Club, impressed her with pseudoscientific phrases like "actinic refracting mirrors," "gamma radio ray," and "iodine-silver spray" and was promptly hired to prevent rain by the Westchester Racing Association.[14]

The terms were intriguing. Sykes was to get one thousand dollars a day for six weekdays if no rain fell between 10 A.M. and 4:40 P.M. and twenty-five hundred dollars for Saturday, September 6. But he was to forfeit two thousand dollars for each day it rained. Borrowing two thousand dollars to put up as collateral, Sykes scurried around thirty-six hours in advance to ready his gear. "There are some types of clouds I can dispel with one punch," he is quoted as saying, "but others require a couple of hours of softening up before I shoot it to them."[15]

In the abandoned clubhouse at the Belmont track, Sykes assembled his preposterous contraption, with its "two heavy Vibrator Units and the Chemicalized Repository." The "detonatary compound" was across the way in a small wooden shack. Described in the press as gear "of the sort you might kick up in a good Victorian attic," his machine included batteries, "a battered-looking electric heater," "two outmoded radio sets," "numerous coils of wire," and "a frazzled loop aerial," not to mention an old vase as "part of a sun accumulator" and a toy propeller doubling as "a wind distributer." In addition there were glass jars filled with bright liquid—actually, colored water—and a washtub "full of the most noxious-smelling chemicals outside a slaughterhouse."[16]

The odds were good. On September 6 heavy clouds split at a propitious moment. Lou Gehrig hit his thirty-eighth homer of the season as the Yankees beat the Senators, and Gallant Fox won the Lawrence Realization under blue skies. "Belmont's Joshua Bids Sun Shine," said headlines in the *New York World*. "It Burns $2,500 Dry Hole in Clouds," "Either it was the most amazing coincidence I have ever seen or that fellow has the goods," the head grounds keeper was quoted as saying. And the weather continued to cooperate: over the first week Sykes collected seventy-five hundred dollars and his contract was extended to cover the next Saturday, Futurity Day. But this time the winner, Jamestown, ran in a gentle rain—and it cost Sykes two thousand dollars. Prodded by carping reporters, he promised "as a gesture" to bring rain on September 15, a mistake "like breaking up a full house to draw for four of a kind" a colleague later described it. On the appointed day, according to the press, for awhile "it looked as though his astro-geo-physical spells were working like a dream," but not so. In the end the track remained "as dry as a Southern congressman's vote." Sykes's only comment was, "I guess I let too much rain go on Saturday"; and a Kentucky group dropped a tentative offer to bring him to Churchill Downs.[17]

Although already convinced of the fraud of this "absurd" business, the Weather Bureau saw fit to issue a press warning early in October. Critics of "the fakir Doc Sykes" pointed out that one of the rainmaker's associates was a former prizefighter and another an ex-lawyer "not so long out of the penitentiary." The bureau complined of publicity given Sykes by the *Literary Digest*, even though the sensationalism of the article was tempered with skepticism. Others protested that the bureau itself ought to do more to combat public ignorance in his case and that movies had portrayed Sykes uncritically as if he were a real scientist.[18]

Meanwhile, Sykes went off to work his "skin game" in Virginia, to bring rain in the district around Warrenton. At one point, he boldly visited the Weather Bureau offices in Washington, requesting rain data for that area for the previous month, complaining all the while that government officials like the bureau chief had no right to discredit the activities of private citizens.[19]

Promising that under his system "weather will be made to order," Sykes offered to install his process of full weather control for businessmen in Colombia for one hundred twenty-five thousand dollars a month, over a period of no longer than six months. Early in 1931 he proposed providing the city of New York with twelve inches of rain spread over ninety days, at the rate of twenty-five thousand dollars an inch or a total of at least three hundred thousand dollars. In neither case was his proposition accepted, but the Weather Bureau grew increasingly uneasy. Finally, in the spring of that year, acting on a request of the head of the Department of Geology at the University of Michigan, Charles Marvin turned the matter over to the Post Office Department to determine if Sykes was securing money under false pretenses. The postmaster general responded that Sykes and his associates operated primarily without use of the mails; hence evidence was not sufficient to warrant prosecution. At that point "Dr." George Ambrosius Immanuel Morrison Sykes dropped from public view. In 1934 the Weather Control Bureau was still in business; but its president was Robert Thomas, who was trying to interest the Federal Emergency Relief Administration in its drought-busting process.[20]

## 9. Makin' Rain—It Takes a Lot of Confidence: A Summing Up

There was a young man of Burdett,
Who wanted to get his skin wet
By the rainmaker's art;
But the clouds broke apart
So he sticks to his money, you bet![1]

Taken as a group, the pre-1946 rainmakers were a diverse lot. Though the backgrounds of some are sketchy and their subsequent careers clouded, other—especially the theorists or those not actually selling their services to the public—were men of some stature and attainment. James Espy was a pioneer in meteorology and breathed the spirit of science in his day. Edward Powers was a civil engineer; Louis Gathmann, an inventive genius. The well-educated Robert Dyrenforth blended some science with military efficiency—so it seemed; and Charles Post, though not technically trained, was an eminent businessman and a firm believer in progress through technology. The electrified-sand dusters of the twenties were clad in the respectability of academia: Chaffee at Harvard was a pioneer in electronics and vacuum-tube physics; Bancroft at Cornell would become president of both the American Chemical Society and the American Electrochemical Society; and their use of the modern airplane gave added proof that the old was giving way to the new.

On the other hand, most of the "pluviculture"-for-pay practitioners were bereft of scientific background or inclination. Melbourne was once involved in ranching and real estate in Australia;

apart from that, his past was as veiled as the secrets in his black gripsack. Doc Sykes seemed to have come out of nowhere and would soon disappear in the same direction, lucky to be out of jail. The Kansas company rainmakers were drawn from the ranks of everyday people—lawyers, druggists, and town promoters. Clayton Jewell was a dispatcher for the Rock Island Railroad, and the great Charles Hatfield was a sewing-machine salesman when he found his true calling.

Whatever their past, these men (no women appear) had a good deal in common. Even the scientists among them were practicing salesmen of a sort. Espy, for example, was much in demand and highly effective as a platform speaker in presenting his ideas. Powers, Gathmann, Melbourne, and Warren published books or pamphlets outlining their accomplishments or potential accomplishments. The electrified-sand sowers indeed contemplated making a movie of their operations, to be used to convince the investing public. Like the purveyors of quack medicinal arts, the more spectacular and more deceptive of the rainmakers were men of magnetic personality and profound students of human nature. They knew a strong claim was more convincing than a weak one—especially if neither could be proved. There was little about Melbourne's self-publicity that was subtle: about it lay the aura of the vendor of snake oil or lightning rods. Even stronger, Sykes came across as a supersalesman who could sell shoes to a boa constrictor. Hatfield was effective, but in a softer way. More modest, pragmatic, and down-to-earth, both in appearance and approach, he reminded people of Henry Ford, Everyman's hero. In the makeup of many of the practicing "pluviculturists," indeed, may be seen the general characteristics of the confidence man at large. They were skilled, assured theatricalists and pitchmen who, without the restraints of conventional morality, enjoyed not only their gains but also the sense of power and cleverness that came with their "successes."[2]

Often they operated in a carnival atmosphere with a fanfare that greatly benefited them, although it did nothing for the cause of science. Not uncommonly, spectators crowded to watch, while the practitioners discreetly kept the mysteries of their processes shrouded from view—Hatfield made a great show of protecting his secrecy with shotguns and revolvers. A Sudanese rainmaker imported by a California rancher in 1908 performed before three hundred invited guests.

Charles Post's highly publicized "rain battle" in Michigan became a major attraction for tourists and merrymakers. Long considered "the harvest time for the genial faker," the country fair provided a setting not only for Melbourne but also for lesser-known itinerants like "Professor" M. Smithson Ames, described as a "long-legged, shaggy haired man with tobacco-stained teeth and a huge cannon hitched to his peddler's wagon."[3]

In many instances the press only added to public interest and to the color and drama surrounding the exertions of the cloud milkers. As might be expected, the *Goodland Republic*, edited by "Parson" Stewart, president of one of the town's artificial rain companies, gave at least the local "professionals" favorable coverage. So too did the two Battle Creek newspapers, both owned by Charles Post during his rain-blasting efforts. Rainmakers were always news, the more so when criticism from Washington bureaucrats gave promise of a good donnybrook. Too frequently editors accepted stories without much thought for actual facts, and much of the "success " of "pluvicul-turists" stemmed from favorable publicity in newspapers or magazines. Hatfield's correspondence shows direct links between inquiries by possible clients and articles about him in the national press. Even editors who were critical or skeptical, as were many of Hatfield, unwittingly aided the rainmakers by the very nature of their catchy or alliterative headlines, which were often misleading, or by the persistent and complete coverage they accorded.

Casting aside the mystics and the crackpots and the pure-and-simple frauds, no doubt many of the cloud compellers, Hatfield, Dyrenforth, Warren, and Swisher among them, fully believed that they "had something" and that their labors did change atmospheric conditions. But there had to be a great deal of self-deception. As Starbuck puts it in N. Richard Nash's play *The Rainmaker*, "Makin' rain—it takes a lot of confidence." Believing in oneself was fine, but it also helped to be a practical student of psychology and to be keenly aware of the betting odds. As both Melbourne and Hatfield knew, almanacs and Weather Bureau data were not without utilitarian value. Also useful was an understanding of timing, based on the premise that the chances for success increased as a drought deepened; and it is in this respect that the kinship of the rainmaker and the medical charlatan becomes apparent. In 80 percent of all cases of human ailment, the individual recovers whether he does anything for his infirmity or not;

thus the quack enters the case with an excellent chance of a "cure"[4]—so too the "pluviculturist" called in only after a prolonged dry spell. The successful cloud milker, moreover, was careful to avoid the real desert country, except for grandiose promises to be kept in the distant future. Arizona was never a setting for the "pluviculture" drama, which after all could only be played out where there was a normal and reasonable expectation of precipitation.

The best most of the would-be rainmakers could hope for was that rain would coincide with their manipulations. To the majority, that happened occasionally, not always in a fashion as spectacular as the Otay Dam washout that made Hatfield's name a household word in 1916. "Pluviculturists" would have welcomed a lawsuit in which judge or jury found them responsible for producing rain, but even in more recent times such decisions have not been forthcoming. One case, in which a county court awarded William Swisher fifty dollars, is remarkably vague, and meager records fail to indicate whether the rainmaker was actually credited with bringing down the moisture or not. Certainly this set no precedent. Rainmaking simply was not fitted into the legal framework of the country.

In a functional sense pre-1946 attempts did not work. Not until Tor Bergeron and the early 1930s was there a reasonable hypothesis to explain the growth of moisture particles into drops large enough to fall. By and large, the role of the scientific community tended to be more negative than positive. Professional meteorologists usually were firm in their opposition, which in itself may have discouraged research by other scientists. A few, like Francis Bacon Crocker of Columbia, Charles Knipp of Illinois, and free-lancer Elmer Gates in Maryland, dabbled in the theory of artificial rainfall, largely as a byproduct of other interests, but never sought to apply their ideas on a practical basis. If, as in James Espy's case, the theory was sound, the matter of scale precluded viable results. Comparatively slow advancement in the knowledge of cloud physics coupled with the vastness of the troposphere tended for a time to make artificial precipitation a limited field for serious scholarly inquiry. Even after the breakthrough in 1946, when much scientific work was being done, the same problems had to be recognized. As one scientist testified at Senate hearings in 1951, "There are no hedgerows to define boundaries or streets to guide traffic in the free atmosphere." Because of too little understanding of clouds and rain formation, because of meteorology's continuing layer

of dogma," and because of "grandiose claims" made by postwar
cloud seeders, progress proceeded slowly even then.[5]

It was surprising to many in the "Age of Pluviculture" that people
were willing to pay hard-earned money to fakers and pseudoscientists
claiming to be able to bring down rain for them. To be sure, just as in
the 1950s there would be plenty of Great Plains skeptics even where
modern cloud seeders were concerned, there was an abundance of
scoffers in the late nineteenth century. To tamper with nature violated
the moral precepts of some. Others came with a "wait and see"
attitude and were not impressed with the results. "Old Jules" Sandoz,
for example, rode his pinto down to see Melbourne at work in the
Nebraska Panhandle. When the demonstration was all over, with
thunder, wind, and a few drops of rain and a double rainbow in the
sunshine, "Old Jules" told his neighbors, "I'll keep catching skunks
for a living."[6]

But undoubtedly some kept the faith. Naïveté and gullibility were
part of it, and every society has its share of the unsuspicious. In
general, it is a truism that if there were no "flats" there would be no
"sharps." Beyond that, it must be remembered that most nineteenth-
century Americans were firmly committed to the idea of progress.
They saw it on all sides—in transportation, in farm machinery, and in
the marvels of manufacturing—and might be pardoned for believing
that the practical application of science to control the weather was only
another step or two away. Remember, too, that drought-stricken farmers acted in desperation when they called in a rainmaker. In the best
frontier tradition, sodbusters on the prairies of the Great Plains were
always innovators and gamblers to some extent. A good season or even
the prospects of one were likely to touch off an "irrational optimism,"
just as cumulative years of dryness, as in the early nineties, sent men
grasping at any glimmer of hope, sensible or otherwise. What was
most difficult about the psychology of drought was the feeling of
helplessness in the face of uncontrollable forces.

Again, as the editor of the nation's leading medical journal
pointed out in 1925, human credulity often learns little from experience. In time of stress, pain, or sorrow, science and truth give way
momentarily to less rational approaches, and the sufferer "is ready to
leap at any cure or suggestion that may be offered to him for the
alleviation of his travail, never stopping to inquire as to the motives of
those who would heal him or as to the basis on which their claims may

rest."[7] No doubt people's desperation during a drought fostered the same clutching at faint hopes, however absurd. Unquestionably many people believed that they had little to lose by hiring a rainmaker on a "no rain, no pay" basis, and at least they were doing something. That it might rain anyway, free, did not enter into their thinking; and occasionally, if they entered into contracts on any other basis, the cost might be prohibitive. One old-timer in western Kansas remembered: "Why my folks put every last cent we had into one of those cockeyed deals. I herded cattle for a year to help keep the family alive. And it never did rain."[8]

Most rainmakers never lasted very long; they flashed across the horizon and soon burned themselves out. Occasionally one died on the job. Texan James Boze was killed in 1934 while testing his "moisture bombs" in the air over Waxahachie.[9] Melbourne's career was limited to a few short years; Dyrenforth fell into obscurity immediately after his highly publicized experiment; and Doc Sykes held the headlines for but a few months. William Swisher retired his "black box" and his earthenware crocks early when he "got religion" and began to worry about his intervention with the divine.[10] Charles Hatfield was the notable exception. Of all his genre, he was the most durable: his conduct of the profession spanned a generation, and appeals to Washington during the dust-bowl period of the thirties indicated that even then he was not without dedicated supporters.

Carey McWilliams believes that Hatfield, California's "outstanding water magician," remained active only until Colorado River water was diverted into the Golden State, with no contracts after the passage of the Boulder Dam act in 1928. Certainly the day of the big-name rainmakers was over by that time. Increasingly negative publicity from the scientific community and especially from the U.S. Weather Bureau and the growing emphasis on improved dry farming methods and on irrigation all helped to bring the era of the "pluviculturist" to a close.

But the heritage of the chief players lingered. Indeed, the feats of the best-known rainmakers, Melbourne and Hatfield among them, became part of western folklore. Hatfield was been called "the first popular folk-hero" of the semiarid part of California, and the stories about him came to rival those of Pecos Bill and Paul Bunyon.[11] The words on the "historical marker" erected in 1973 by the Native Sons of the Golden West bear out this contention.

Hatfield the Rainmaker. In January, 1916, Charles M. Hatfield in Agreement with the City of San Diego for $10,000 erected two platforms near Lake Morena releasing chemical vapors into the sky. Rain fell continuously for several days flooding the entire country. When Lower Otay Dam collapsed, a section of Sweetwater Dam was washed out. Damages into the millions resulted along with 15 lives lost. The city called the rain an "act of God" forcing Hatfield to flee the country minus his $10,000.[12]

If the Hatfields and the Dyrenforths and the Melbournes seem to have belonged more to the world of folklore and of mysticism than to science itself, far less than the alchemists and magicians of old were they the precursors of the future. They were not in the mainstream of nineteenth or early twentieth-century science. To be sure, their activities were responses to and reflections of a widely felt need; and indirectly they may have helped call attention to the need, just as primitive rainmakers had done for centuries. But it is likely that little scientific endeavor came as a direct result. Meteorology and a knowledge of cloud physics progressed independently and slowly: only in the mid-twentieth century would they reach a point where theory and technique came together to produce artificial rainmaking that under the best of circumstances could be considered useful.

# Notes

## Chapter 1

1. *Salinas County Democrat* (Salinas, Calif.), March 29, 1899.

2. Quoted in Horace R. Byers, "History of Weather Modification," in *Weather and Climate Modification*, ed. W. N. Hess (New York: John Wiley & Sons, 1974), p. 12.

3. William J. Humphreys, *Rain-Making and Other Weather Vagaries* (Baltimore: William & Wilkins Co., 1926), p. vii; David Starr Jordan, "The Art of Pluviculture," *Science* 62 (July 24, 1925): 81–82; unidentified clipping, Charles and Paul Hatfield Papers, vol. 1, San Diego Public Library. The Jordan article was copied in several other periodicals. *Bulletin of the American Meteorological Society* 6 (August–September 1925): 140; *Monthly Weather Revue and Annual Summary* 53 (June 1925): 261.

4. For ancient and primitive ideas of magical and religious rainmaking, see Humphreys, *Rain-Making*, pp. 5–28; Mark W. Harrington, "Weather Making, Ancient and Modern," *Annual Report of the Board of Regents of the Smithsonian Institution, Showing the Operations, Expenditures, and Conditions of the Institution to July, 1894* (Washington, D.C.: Government Printing Office, 1896), pp. 249–52; *Scientific American* 22 (January 22, 1870): 57; James George Frazer, *The Worship of Nature* (London: Macmillan & Co., 1926), p. 1.

5. J. C. Crowther, *The Social Relations of Science* (New York: Macmillan Co.,1941), pp. 14–15; Louis Pauwels and Jacques Bergier, *Impossible Possibilities,* trans. Andrew White (New York: Stein & Day, 1971), pp. 149–52; V. Gordon Childe, *Magic Craftsmanship and Science* (Liverpool: University Press, 1950), p. 7. See also Charles Singer, *From Magic to Science: Essays on the Scientific Twilight* (New York: Dover, 1958); and Lynn Thorndike, *A History of Magic and Experimental Science,* 8 vols.(New York: Columbia University Press, 1923–58).

6. Richard Harrison Shryock, "American Indifference to Basic Science during the Nineteenth Century," in *The Sociology of Science,* ed. Bernard Barber and Walter Hirsch (New York: Free Press, 1962), pp. 109–10; Nathan Reingold, "American Indifference to Basic Research: A Reappraisal," in *Nineteenth-Century American Science: A Reappraisal,* ed. George H. Daniels (Evanston: Northwestern University Press, 1972), pp. 38–62; Oscar Handlin, "Science and Technology in Popular Culture," in *Science and Culture,* ed. Gerald Holton (Boston: Houghton Mifflin, 1965), pp. 192–93.

7. Stewart H. Holbrook, *The Golden Age of Quackery* (New York: Macmillan Co., 1959), pp. 58, 125–27, 140–41; James Cook, *Remedies and Rackets* (New York: W. W. Norton & Co., 1958), pp. 27–28; T. Swann Harding, *The Popular Practice of Fraud* (New York: Longmans, Green & Co., 1935), pp. 51–52. See also James Harvey Young, *The Toadstool Millionaires: A Social History of Patent Medicines in America before Federal Regulation* (Princeton: Princeton University Press, 1961); and idem, *The Medical Messiahs: A Social History of Health Quackery in Twentieth-Century America* (Princeton: Princeton University Press, 1967).

8. Quoted in Earl W. Hayter, *The Troubled Farmer, 1850–1900* (DeKalb: Northern Illinois University Press, 1968), p. 170; Clifton R. Woolridge, *The Grafters of America* n.p., n.d.), p. 248.

9. H. F. Alciatore to Charles F. Marvin, June 11, 1921, with clipping, *San Diego Union,* June 5, 1921, U.S. Weather Bureau Correspondence (1912–24 Series), box 2454, National Archives and Records Service (cited hereafter as WBC, with series). There are only general or fragmentary treatments of the history of rainmaking. Among them are Jeff Townsend, *Making Rain in America: A History,* International Center for Arid and Semi-Arid Land Studies Publication no. 75–3, (Lubbock, Tex., 1975), which devotes thirty-seven pages to the pre-1946 era; and Daniel S. Halacy, *The Weather Changers* (New York: Harper & Row, 1968), which handles the subject in one of its fourteen chapters. Horace Byers had only a few pages on the topic in his "History of Weather Modification," pp. 4–9. Cited above for their discussion of ancient and primitive rainmaking, Humphreys and Harrington are the most complete sources for the age of "pluviculture" also. Other brief surveys include Clark C. Spence, "A Brief History of Pluviculture," *Pacific North-*

*west Quarterly* 52 (October 1961): 129–38; and Jeanne Schinto, "Rainmakers," *American West* 14 (July/August 1977): 28–33.

10. Harrington, "Weather Making," p. 258. Charles B. Haldeman to Franklin D. Roosevelt, July 19, 1934: Haldeman to C. C. Clark, August 2, 1934; C. C. Clark to Haldeman, July 28, 1934, copy; all in WBC (1931–35 Series), box 2998. Emil Pasotto to "United States Government," August 15, 1925, WBC (1925–30 Series), box 2810.

11. M. F. Rossi to Department of Agriculture, July 12, 1930, WBC (1925–30 Series), box 2810. G. Nordberg to Franklin D. Roosevelt, July 22, 1934; James M. Blackhurst to Roosevelt, June 9, 1934; both in WBC (1931–35 Series), box 2998. Edward Henderson, Jr., to Secretary of Agriculture, October 25, 1930; John Wolfe to Weather Bureau, August 13, 1930; both in WBC (1925–30 Series), box 2810. Albert N. Doerschuk to Henry A. Wallace, July 7, 1936, WBC (1936–42 Series), box 32.

12. *Scientific American* 3 (February 26, 1848): 181; *Symon's Monthly Meteorological Magazine* 5 (March 1870): 32; *Country Gentleman* 38 (September 18, 1873): 596; William H. Obenchain to Chief Signal Officer, March 30, 1882, WBC (Misc. Series), 1882, file 1768, box 388; O. B. M. Powell to Obenchain April 5, 1882, copy, Chief Signal Office, Letters Sent (March 27 to April 25, 1882),15: 183, National Archives and Records Service. Cleveland Abbe to W. B. Warren, December 28, 1882, and January 11, 1883, WBC (Misc. Series), 1883, file 25, box 409; W. B. Warren to Spencer F. Baird, January 2, 1883, copy, Chief Signal Office, Letters Sent (December 27, 1882, to January 26, 1883), 23:82; *Engineering News and American Contract Journal* 18 (September 17, 1887): 197.

13. George Perkins Marsh, *Man and Nature or Physical Geography as Modified by Human Action* (New York: Charles Scribner, 1864), p. 184. For general comments see: Constantin F. Volney, *View of the Climate and Soil of the United States of America*, trans. from the French (London: J. Johnson, 1804), pp. 269–74; Charles W. Janson, *The Stranger in America* (London: for J. Condee, 1807), pp. 63–66; S. P. Hildreth, *Pioneer History: Being an Account of the First Examinations of the Ohio Valley* (Cincinnati: Historical Society of Cincinnati, 1848), pp. 487, 492–93; *American Farmer* 3 (April 6, 1821): 16; Josiah Gregg, *Commerce of the Prairies; or, The Journal of a Santa Fe Trader* (New York: Henry G. Langley; London: Wiley & Putnam, 1844), 2:202–3; Samuel Bowles, *Across the Continent: A Summer's Journey to the Rocky Mountains, the Mormons, and the Pacific States* (Springfield, Mass.: Samuel Bowles, 1865), p. 138: Henry Nash Smith, "Rain Follows the Plow: The Notion of Increased Rainfall for the Great Plains 1844–1880," *Huntington Library Quarterly* 10 (February 1947): 169–93; Henry Nash Smith, *Virgin Land* (New York: Vintage, 1950), pp. 208–13.

14. Samuel Aughey, *Sketches of the Physical Geography and Geology of*

*Nebraska* (Omaha: Daily Republican, 1880), pp. 39–46; Charles Dana Wilber, *The Great Valleys and Prairies of Nebraska and the Northwest* (Omaha: Daily Republican, 1881), pp. 67–70, 143. See Charles R. Kutzleb, "Rain Follows the Plow: The History of an Idea" Ph.D. diss. University of Colorado, 1968).

15. From Mrs. A. D. T. Whitney, "The Rainfall Follows the Plow," *Cheyenne Wells Gazette*, May 19, 1888, quoted in Kutzleb, "Rain Follows the Plow," p. 209.

16. Walter Kollmorgen, "Rainmakers on the Plains," *Scientific Monthly* 40 (February 1935): 152; J. Warren Smith, "Cultivation Does Not Increase Rainfall," *Monthly Weather Review* 47 (December 1919): 858–60.

17. Homer Croy, "The Rainmakers," *Harpers Magazine* 193 (September 1946): 213; Everett Dick, *Conquering the American Desert: Nebraska* (Lincoln: Nebraska State Historical Society, 1975), p. 338.

## Chapter 2

1. F. W. C., "A Tale of the Rain Machine," *Life* 18 (November 5, 1891): 260.

2. *Pathfinder* no. 1709 (October 2, 1926): 3. There is no adequate biography of the man. See L. M. Morehead, *A Few Incidents in the Life of Prof. James P. Espy* (Cincinnati: Robert Clark, 1888); *The National Cyclopaedia of American Biography* (New York: James T. White & Co., 1896), 6:205. Allen Johnson and Dumas Malone, eds., *Dictionary of American Biography* (New York: Scribner's, 1943), 6:185–86; James P. Espy to Alexander Dallas Bache, September 18, 1836, RH 1157, Henry E. Huntington Library, San Marino, Calif.; James P. Espy, "Observations on the Importance of Meteorological Observation," *Journal of the Franklin Institute* 9 (December 1831): 389–406.

3. *National Cyclopaedia of American Biography*, 6:205; *Compte rendu des séances de l'Académie des sciences* 12 (January-June 1841): 454; J. E. McDonald, "James Espy and the Beginnings of Cloud Thermodynamics," *Bulletin of the American Meteorological Society* 44 (October 1963): 634. Arago is referring to Sir Isaac Newton, seventeenth- and eighteenth-century mathematician, and to Baron Georges Leopold Cuvier, the French naturalist whose life also touched both centuries.

4. McDonald, "James Espy," pp. 635, 640–41; Nathan Reingold, "James Pollard Espy," in *Dictionary of Scientific Biography*, ed. Charles G. Gillispie (New York: Charles Scribner's Sons, 1971), 4:410; James P. Espy, "Theory of Rain, Hail, Snow and the Water Spout, Deduced from the Latent Caloric of Vapour and the Specific Caloric of Atmospheric Air," *Transactions of the Geological Society of Pennsylvania* (Philadelphia, 1835), 1, pt. 2:342–43; *Journal of the Franklin Institute* 17 (April 1836): 240–46, 309–16;

*Journal of the Franklin Institute* 18 (August 1836): 100–108; *Proceedings of the American Philosophical Society* 3 (1843): 155; James D. Forbes, "Supplemental Report on Meteorology," in *Report of the Tenth Meeting of the British Association for the Advancement of Science; Held in Glasgow in August, 1840* (London: John Murray, 1841), p. 111; James P. Espy, "On Storms," in *Report of the Tenth Meeting*, p. 39.

5. Espy to Editor (April 2, 1839), *National Gazette and Literary Register* (Philadelphia), April 5, 1839; Espy, "On Storms," p. 39.

6. Thucydides, *History of the Peloponnesian War*, trans. William Smith (New York: H. E. Derby, 1861), bk. 2, p. 81; *London Philosophical Transactions*, quoted in *Scientific American* 76 (April 17, 1897): 243; Martin Dobrizhoffer, *An Account of the Abipones, an Equestrian People of Paraguay* (London: John Murray, 1822), 3:260; *Denver Post*, August 15, 1922; Volney, *View of the Climate*, pp. 269–74; François Arago, *Meteorological Essays*, trans. Colonel Sabine (London: Longman, Brown, Green, & Longman, 1855); 7:213–14; Alexander von Humboldt, *Views of Nature; or, Contemplations on the Sublime Phenomena of Creation; with Scientific Illustrastions*, trans. E. C. Otte and R. H. Whitlocke (London: n.p., 1850), p. 366; Titus Smith, "Natural History of Nova Scotia," *Magazine of Natural History* 8 (December 1835): 648; *Proceedings of the American Philosophical Society* 2 (November and December 1841): 116.

7. James P. Espy, *To the Friends of Science* (n.p., 1845), pp. 4–5; James P. Espy, *Second Report on Meteorology to the Secretary of the Navy*, Senate Exec. Doc. no. 39, 31st Cong., 1st sess., 1850, pp. 20–21; James P. Espy, *Fourth Meteorological Report*, Senate Exec. Doc. no. 54, 34th Cong., 3rd sess., 1856–57, p. 37.

8. Espy, *Fourth Meteorological Report*, pp. 37–38.

9. *Popular Science Monthly* 34 (April 1889): 840; *Bangor Advertiser*, quoted in *Niles' Register* 61 (October 23, 1841): 116.

10. Quoted in *Niles' Register* 56 (June 22, 1839): 269; *Niles' Register* 57 (October 12, 1839): 100; *Hunt's Merchant Magazine* 2 (February 1840): 136–41, 241–46; *Hunt's Merchant Magazine* 5 (October 1841): 338–55; *Hunt's Merchant Magazine* 13 (December 1845): 534–46; *The Hesperian, or Western Monthly Magazine* 2 (January 1839): 239–41; Robert Hare, *Queries and Strictures, by Dr. Hare, Respecting Espy's Meteorological Report to the Naval Department* (Philadelphia: R. W. Barnard & Sons, 1852), pp. 6–7; *Journal of the Franklin Institute* 23 (January-May 1839): 38–50, 80, 149–58, 217–31, 289–98; T. B. Butler, *The Philosophy of the Weather* (New York: D. Appleton & Co., 1856), pp. 245–46; Olmsted lecture to New York Mercantile Library Association, quoted in *Hunt's Merchant Magazine* 1 (December 1839): 522.

11. Quoted in *Niles' Register* 56 (June 22, 1839): 268.

12. Gregg, *Commerce of the Prairies*, 2:iii, 30.

13. Espy, *To the Friends of Science*, pp. 1–4; *Niles' Register* 58 (June 27,

1840): 272; Espy, *Second Report*, pp. 14–17; Espy, *Fourth Meteorological Report*, pp. 30–36; *Cincinnati Gazette*, October 30, 1856.

14. Espy, *Fourth Meteorological Report*, pp. 32–33.

15. *Sangamo Journal* (Springfield, Ill.), December 24, 1846. Espy also invented a ventilator for ships and large buildings and hoped that the federal government would purchase his rights for its own use. Apart from an appropriation of $250 to install one ventilator in the U.S. Senate chamber, Congress apparently never acted. See *Niles' Register* 62 (May 2, 1842): 148; *House Reports* no. 531, 29th Cong., 1st sess., 1856, pp. 1–4; *Senate Documents* no. 91, 29th Cong., 2d sess., 1846–47, pp. 1–5; *House Reports* no. 54, 31st Cong., 1st sess., 1850, pp. 1–6; *Congressional Globe*, 29th Cong., 1st sess., 1845–46, 15:562, 580, 587, 696; *Congressional Globe*, 29th Cong., 2d sess., 1846–47, 16:246, 450, 468, 502.

16. *Niles' Register* 68 (April 12, 1845): 96; *Illinois Farmer* 5 (November 1, 1860): 189; Henry F. French, *Farm Drainage* (New York: A. O. Moore & Co., 1859), pp. 281, 282–85. See also *Mining and Scientific Press* (San Francisco), 28 (February 28, 1874): 136.

17. See entries for December 10 and 14, 1838, and January 16, 1839, *Journal of the Senate of the Commonwealth of Pennsylvania, Session of 1838–39, Which Commenced at Harrisburg on the Fourth Day of December, 1838* (Harrisburg: E. Guyer, 1838–39), 1:20, 56, 243; entry for March 18, 1840, *Journal of the Fiftieth House of Representatives of the Commonwealth of Pennsylvania: Commenced at Harrisburg, Tuesday, the Seventh Day of January, in the Year of Our Lord One Thousand Eight Hundred and Forty, and of the Commonwealth the Sixty-Fourth* (Harrisburg: Holbrook, Hemlock & Bratton, 1840), 2, pt. 2:273, 274–75; entries for April 4, April 13, and May 22, 1840, *Journal of Fiftieth House*, 1:802, 911–12, 1112.

18. Entry for December 18, 1838, *Congressional Globe*, 25th Cong., 3d sess., 1838–39, 7: 41, 42.

19. Adams warned Espy that a petition to the House would do no good but grudgingly promised to support any action that passed the Senate. Entry for January 6, 1842, Diary of John Quincy Adams, Adams Family Papers, microfilm reel no. 46, Massachusetts Historical Society, Boston. Hans Carvel and his wife were obviously characters from an early folk or fairy tale, but the author has been unable to identify them further.

20. Espy wanted all military posts and lighthouses equipped with standardized meteorological instruments and trained observers, himself to oversee the work. He asked that Congress provide funds for this and for the purchase of a hundred additional sets of instruments to be distributed to volunteers. He also requested the franking privilege for himself. Memorandum, "Mr. Espy's wishes of Jan, 1842," Letters Received and Other Loose Papers, Adams Family Papers, microfilm reel no. 520.

21. Entries for January 19, 1842, and February 8, 1844, Diary of John

Quincy Adams, Adams Family Papers, microfilm reels no. 46 and 47. See also *Hunt's Merchant Magazine* 6 (March 1842): 272.

22. James Shaw, "The Great Tornado of 1860," *Transactions of the Illinois State Agricultural Society* 4 (1859–60): 578; *Pacific Rural Press* 43 (February 13, 1892): 153.

23. *Mining and Scientific Press* 6 (September 7, 1863): 2; I. A. Lapham, "The Great Fires of 1871 in the Northwest," *Journal of the Franklin Institute* 64 (July 1872): 46–47; *Nature* 4 (October 19, 1871): 494; Edward Powers, *War and the Weather* (Delavan, Wis.: privately published, 1890), p. 86.

24. John Trowbridge, "Great Fires and Rain Storms," *Popular Science Monthly* 2 (December 1872): 211; Henry quoted in Robert De C. Ward, "Artificial Rain: A Review of the Subject to the Close of 1889," *American Meteorological Journal* 8 (March 1892): 492; *Nature* 3 (February 16 and April 6, 1871): 307, 448. See also *Nature* 6 (June 13, 1872): 121; *Science* 3 (March 7, 1884): 276.

25. Ward, "Artificial Rain," pp. 484, 485.

26. As disproof of the theory, this official cited a survey of forty-two major fires over a twenty-one-year period in Australia, after which no rain fell within the following forty-eight-hour-period. Henry Chamberlain Russell, *Anniversary Address* (To the Royal Society of New South Wales, May 3, 1882) (Sidney: Thomas Richards, 1883), pp. 12, 17–19, 27.

27. Joseph G. Konvalinka, *Memoirs of an Inventor and Scientist A Mine of Original Ingenious Ideas, Published in a Series of Pamphlets, No. IIII, Clouds and Rain, How to Produce Rain and How to Improve and Colonize Arid Countries* (Long Island: privately published, 1891), pp. 1, 3–8, 10–15, 17–21, supps. 5–7.

28. Ford A. Carpenter, "Convectional Clouds Induced by Forest Fires," *Monthly Weather Review* 47 (March 1919): 143–46; Aladar Rovo and Henry Gorog, "On a Scientific Method of Rain Making," transcript of translation, WBC (1936–42 Series), box 32; W. R. Gregg to A. De Balasy, May 10, 1937, WBC (1936–42 Series), box 32; Louis J. Battan, *Harvesting the Clouds* (Garden City, N.Y.: Doubleday & Co., 1969), pp. 53–55. For other twentieth-century scientists receptive at least to the Espy principle but not its practicality, see *Literary Digest* 35 (December 7, 1907): 867; *Scientific American* 151 (October 1934): 218; *Scientific Monthly* 30 (January 1930): 13.

29. *Illinois Farmer* 5 (November 1, 1860): 189; *Daily Chicago Democrat*, September 5, 1860; *Scientific American* 43 (August 21, 1880): 113; Alexander Macfarlane, "On Rainmaking," *Transactions for the Texas Academy of Science* 1 (November 1893): 78, 79–80; *National Cyclopaedia of American Biography*, 8:107; J. M. Matthews to J. Sterling Morton, January 21, 1896; Head, Forestry Division to Matthews, January 30, 1896, draft; both in WBC (Misc. Series), 1896, file 650, box 1131.

30. Charles F. Marvin to W. E. Beard, November 18, 1925, copy: Beard

to Joseph W. Byrns, November 16, 1925; both in WBC (1925–30 Series), box 2810. *New York Times*, May 4, 1935. John Coop to the Smithsonian Institute, October 5, 1931; Coop to Secretary of Agriculture, September 17, 1934; Willis Gregg to Coop, September 27, 1934, copy; Jake L. Walters to Franklin D. Roosevelt, August 10, 1934; all in WBC (1931–35 Series), box 2998. See also Marion Powers to Chief of the Weather Bureau, March 26, 1904, WBC (1904), box 1795.

31. E. N. Lildegran to Henry A. Wallace, August 14, 1934, WBC (1931–35 Series), box 2998; *Denver Post*, May 8 and September 18, 1935; *Science News Letter* 66 (September 4, 1954): 157.

32. George O. Davis to Secretary of Agriculture, January 5, 1940, WBC (1936–42 Series), box 32.

33. In a ten-mile-per-hour wind, such a device would deflect upward over four billion feet of air per hour, Pitkin insisted. What he ignored was that the frail structure would be subject to the equivalent of one hundred thousand tons of pressure under these circumstances. Macfarlane, "On Rainmaking," pp. 78–79; Cleveland Abbe, "On the Production of Rain," *Agricultural Science* 6 (July 1892): 302; Humphreys, *Rain-Making*, pp. 40–41. On the other hand, a big-thinking Omaha lawyer in 1934 decided that the addition of moveable metal planes five hundred to one thousand feet high along the highest points of the Continental Divide from Mexico to Canada would deflect the moisture-laden westerlies to the Great Plains, where they would lose their rain. At the same time a Nebraska legislator suggested a scheme described by the head of the Weather Bureau as "certainly heroic." Certain peaks of the Rockies might be "decapitated," said the solon, so they would not obstruct the westerly winds, leaving the winds free to bring their moisture to the plains. Anson H. Bigelow to the Weather Bureau, August 11, 1934; Laurie J. Quinby to Eleanor Roosevelt, February 6, 1935; Willis R. Gregg to Laurie Quinby, May 21, 1935; all in WBC (1931–1935 Series), box 2998.

34. *Oklahoma State Register* (Guthrie), July 7, 1921; *Cyclorain Trust* (brochure, 1921), pp. 1, 8; Ira N. Terrill to Secretary of Agriculture, September 15, 1921, WBC (1912–24 Series), box 2454.

35. See *The Cyclorain* (brochure, 1918), pp. 1; 3–4, 8; *The Cyclorain* (brochure, 1921), pp. 1–4, 8; Charles Marvin to Robert Ward, January 15, 1919; Marvin to J. B. Newton, November 7, 1919; Marvin to Terrill, March 5, 1920; Marvin to Jump, August 8, 1921, copy; Marvin to Rush D. Simmons, September 20, 1921, copy; Terrill to Marvin, December 6, 1918, and April 12, 1920, and March 8, 1920; Terrill to Secretary of Agriculture, February 27, 1920, and July 29, 1921, and September 15, 1921; all in WBC (1912–24 Series), box 2454.

36. *Popular Science Monthly* 34 (April 1889): 840; *Annual Report of the Board of Regents of the Smithsonian Institution Showing the Operations, Expenditures, and Condition of the Institution for the Year 1859* (Washington,

D.C.: Thomas H. Ford, 1860) p. 110; W. E. Knowles Middleton, *A History of the Theories of Rain and Other Forms of Precipitation* (New York: Franklin Watts, 1966), p. 160.

## Chapter 3

1. From "Me and Uncle Jerry," *New York Sun*, September 6, 1891.
2. Plutarch. *The Lives of the Noble Grecians and Romans* (New York: Modern Library, 1949), p. 507. Part of this chapter was originally published in *Arizona and the West* 3 (Autumn 1961): 205–32.
3. *Boston Globe*, quoted in *Wood River Times* (Hailey, Idaho), December 1, 1893; Humphreys, *Rain-Making*, p. 30.
4. Charles Darwin, *Journal of Researches into the Natural History and Geology of the Countries Visited during the Voyage of H. M. S. Beagle Round the World* (New York: Harper & Brothers, 1859), 1:111.
5. *The Life of Benvenuto Cellini*, trans. J. A. Symonds (New York: n.p., 1930), p. 271; *Memoirs of the Count de Forbin* (London: J. Pemberton, 1731), 1:27; Abbe, "On the Production of Rain," pp. 298–99; Arago, *Meteorological Essays*, pp. 214–15, 218, 221; Humphreys, *Rain-Making*, p. 82; Ward, "Artificial Rain," pp. 484–86; Sir Napier Shaw, *The Air and Its Ways* (Cambridge: University Press, 1923), p. 220; C. E. P. Brooks, *Climate in Everyday Life* (New York: Philosophical Library, 1951), p. 261.
6. *American Journal of Science and Arts* 32 (September 1861): 296.
7. John Evarts to editor (October 29, 1891), *Scientific American* 65 (November 21, 1891): 325; *Mining and Scientific Press* 6 (September 7, 1863): 2.
8. See Charles Le Maout, *Exposé de la doctrine des condensations* (Saint-Brieuc: privately published, 1856), pp. 1–17; *Météorologie effets du canon & du son des cloches sur l'atmosphère* (Saint-Brieuc: privately published, 1861), pp. 1–15; Andrew Steinmetz, *Sunshine and Showers: Their Influence throughout Creation* (London: Reeve & Co., 1867), pp. 332–36; *Symons's Monthly Meteorological Magazine* 26 (July 1891): 82.
9. Edward Powers, *War and the Weather; or, The Artificial Production of Rain* (Chicago: S. C. Griggs & Co., 1871), pp. 9–74, 75–76.
10. Ibid., pp. 4, 87–88; entry for February 28, 1874, *Congressional Record*, 43d Cong., 1st sess., 1873–74, p. 1882; *American Agriculturist* 31 (February 1872): 46; *Production of Rain by Artillery-Firing*, House Report no. 786, 43d Cong., 1st sess., 1873–74, p. 1; Powers to General Albert Myer (October 30, 1870), WBC (Misc. Series), 1870, file P–24, box 294.
11. *Scientific American* 24 (January 1, 1871): 4; *Scientific American* 25 (September 2, 1871): 153; William H. Allee to General Albert Myer, September 14, 1874, WBC (Misc. Series), 1874, box 325. Myer responded that

without congressional appropriations, his office had no funds for such tests. Garrick Mallery to Allee, September 29, 1874, copy, Office of Chief Signal Officer, Meteorological Division, Letters Sent (Misc. Series), vol. 8 (June 1–December 31, 1874.

12. Fred H. Hart, *The Sazerac Lying Club* (San Francisco: Henry Keller & Co., 1878), pp. 69–70; *Scientific American* 23 (September 10, 1870): 167; *Mining and Scientific Press* 27 (February 28, 1874): 136; *Mining and Scientific Press* 34 (March 10, 1877): 152; John Tice, "Do Battles Cause Storms?" *American Meteorologist* 1 (June 1876): 138–45; Allee to Myer (September 14, 1874), WBC (Misc. Series), 1874, box 325; *Scientific American Supplement* (April 14, 1877): 1070.

13. *Pacific Rural Press* 42 (September 26, 1891): 259; U.S. Patent Office, *Specifications & Drawings of Patents for July, 1880* (Washington, D.C.: Government Printing Office, 1880), 1:179, 642–43; *Scientific American* 43 (August 14 and November 27, 1880): 106, 342; Francis B. Heitman, comp., *Historical Register and Dictionary of the United States Army* (Washington, D.C.: Government Printing Office, 1903), 1:851. Sources, both American and German, charged that Ruggles had "borrowed" his idea from Ferdinand Hatterman of New Zealand. John T. Ellis, "Making Rain," *Californian* 1 (October 1891–May 1892): 106; *American Monthly Review of Reviews* 32 (December 1905): 746.

14. *Daily Democratic Statesman* (Austin, Tex.), April 16, 1879.

15. Ruggles to Secretary of the Navy, April 16, 1879, WBC (Misc. Series), 1879, file 1073, box 348; Ruggles to Secretary of War, November 17, 1879, WBC (Misc. Series), 1879, file 2119, box 351; General W. B. Hazen to Ruggles, March 1, 1884, copy, Chief Signal Officer, Letters Sent, vol. 34 (February 20–March 22, 1884); entries for January 15 and March 2, 1880, *Congressional Record*, 46th Cong., 2d sess., 1879–80, pp. 362, 1268; *Memorial of Daniel Ruggles, Asking for an Appropriation to Be Expended in Developing His System of Producting Rainfall*, Senate Misc. Doc. no. 39, 46th Cong., 2d sess., 1879–80, pp. 7, 12–13, 17–18.

16. Ruggles to Editor (December 16, 1891), *New York Tribune*, January 3, 1892; Henry Pomeroy to Charles B. Farwell, August 1, 1890, Division of Forestry Correspondence, Letters Received, tray 46, tier 11, National Archives and Records Service (cited hereafter as DFC).

17. *Helena Daily Herald*, February 4 and 6, 1882. For foreign inventions see *Scientific American* 51 (October 25, 1884): 258; *Scientific American* 56 (March 19, 1887): 181; *Engineering News and American Contract Journal* 13 (January 3, 1885): 15. The western agents for James Pain and Sons, "Pyrotechnists" of London, New York, Chicago, and Melbourne, approached the governor of Kansas to this end in 1889. Thearie and Cooper to Lyman U. Humphrey, Chicago, May 14, 1889, Governor Lyman U. Humphrey MSS, Correspondence Received, box 10, Kansas Historical Society, Topeka.

18. F. B. Jones to Norman J. Coleman, August 26, 1886, copy, Chief
Signal Officer, Letters Sent (Misc. Series), vol. 18 (July 20–August 26, 1886);
E. O. Wiener to W. B. Hazen, January/no other date/1883, WBC (Misc.
Series), 1883, file 250, box 409; H. H. C. Dunwoody to Secretary of War,
August 9, 1887, copy, WBC (Signal Series), 1887, file 5088, box 206; George
H. Chase to Norman J. Coleman, August 7, 1886, WBC (Signal Series),
1886, box 166; Thomas J. Brown to Secretary of War Endicott, August 1,
1887, WBC (Signal Series), 1887, file 5088, box 206.

19. Powers, *War and the Weather* (1890 ed.) pp. 200–201.

20. Ibid., pp. 3–4, 132, 135, 201–2. For some of Powers' earlier promotional efforts see *National Republican* (Washington, D.C.), February 24,
1874; *Golden Age* (New York), May 11, 1872.

21. Anti-Powers arguments are found in *Symon's Monthly Meteorological Magazine* 26 (July 1891): 81–82; *Scientific American* 63 (December 20,
1890): 385; Harrington, "Weather Making," p. 264; Macfarlane, "On Rainmaking," p. 76; William Morris Davis, "The Theories of Artificial and
Natural Rainfall," *American Meteorological Journal* 8 (March 1892):
494–95, 499. For Powers' rebuttal, see Edward Powers, "Artificial Rain,"
*American Meteorological Journal* 9 (August 1892): 178–84.

22. *United States Statutes at Large*, vol. 26 (1890), p. 286; *American
Meteorological Journal* 8 (June 1891): 84. The head of the Division of
Forestry gave Farwell credit for pushing the bill through but thought that
"Senator Jones of Nevada was also interested." Bernhard E. Fernow to Henry
L. Penfield, April 30, 1891, copy, DFC, Letters Sent, book G; Allen Johnson
et al., eds., *Dictionary of American Biography* (New York: Scribner's
1943–73), 6:494–95 (cited hereafter as *DAB*); Fernow, "Artificial Rain," in
*Report of the Secretary of Agriculture . . . 1890*, p. 227.

23. Fernow to Jeremiah Rusk, August 8, 1890; Laurice L. Brown to
Rusk, August 26, 1890; J. W. Gregory to Fernow, March 14, 1891; G. Edward
Turner to Sir Julian Pauncefote, February 10, 1891, copy; Hazen to Fernow,
September 18 and 25, 1890; Harrington to Fernow, September 30, 1890; all in
DFC, Letters Received, tray 46, tier 11. Fernow to Edwin Willets, September
29, 1890, copy; Fernow to Harrington, October 16, 1890, copy; both in DFC,
Letters Sent, book G.

24. Quoted in *Electrical Review* 18 (May 23, 1891): 174; *Engineering
and Mining Journal* 51 (May 2, 1891): 522–23. For Fernow's preliminary
work on the project, see *Report of the Secretary of Agriculture . . . 1891*, p.
194; *New York Sun*, August 9, 1891; Fernow to Chief of Army Ordnance,
November 18, 1890, copy; Fernow to A. W. Greely, November 18, 1890, copy;
Fernow to President, Du Pont Powder Works, November 20, 1890, copy; all in
DFC, Letters Sent, book G; D. A. Hammond to Fernow, January 23, 1891,
DFC, Letters Received, tray 46, tier 11.

25. Depositions in R. G. Dyrenforth Service Record, National Archives

and Records Service; *Who Was Who in America (1897–1942)* (Chicago: Marquis, 1943), 1:353; *Who's Who in America (1901–2)* (Chicago: Marquis, 1910), p. 332; *New York Sun*, August 9, 1891; *Washington Post*, July 9, 1910.

26. Fernow to J. W. Gregory, March 18, 1891, copy, DFC, Letters Sent, book H; Hazen to Fernow, August 12, 1891, DFC, Letters Received, tray 45, tier 11.

27. Dyrenforth to Edwin Willets, February 25, 1891, DFC, Letters Received, tray 45, tier 11. Fernow once implied that Ruggles and Dyrenforth were to share leadership of the experiments—"two gentlemen," he said, "who have a special desire to make them successful." Fernow to J. W. Gregory, March 18, 1891, copy; Fernow to Alfred Miller, April 8, 1891, copy; both in DFC, Letters Sent, book H. *New York Tribune*, March 15, 1891.

28. Carl E. Myers to Dyrenforth, February 19, 1891, copy, DFC, Letters Received, tray 46, tier 11; *Experiments in Production of Rainfall*, Senate Exec. Doc. no. 45, 52d Cong., 1st sess., 1891–92, pp. 5–8; *Engineering News and American Contract Journal* 13 (June 20, 1885): 391; *Scientific American Supplement* (March 30, 1895), p. 16051.

29. Dyrenforth's original appointment stipulated that the expenses of Ruggles in Washington should be paid for a limited time. *Experiments in Production of Rainfall*, p. 59; William J. Rhees to Rusk, June 23, 1891, in *Experiments in Production of Rainfall*, p. 9.

30. *Experiments in Production of Rainfall*, pp. 9–10, 11–12.

31. *Wichita Daily Eagle*, August 1, 1890; *New York Tribune*, July 29, 1890, and March 15, 1891; *Chicago Daily Tribune*, July 15, 1891; *United States Statutes at Large*, 26 (1891), p. 1040; *Report of the Secretary of Agriculture . . . 1891*, p. 58; *Experiments in Production of Rainfall*, p. 59.

32. Hazen to Fernow, August 12, 1891, DFC, Letters Received, tray 46, tier 11.

33. *Washington Post*, August 16, 1891; *Experiments in Production of Rainfall*, pp. 11–12.

34. *Experiments in Production of Rainfall*, pp. 13–14; Macfarlane, "On Rainmaking," p. 77.

35. *Chicago Daily Tribune*, August 12, 1891; *Rocky Mountain News* (Denver), August 12, 1891; *Washington Post*, August 13, 1891; *New York Sun*, August 13, 1891; *Chicago Times*, August 13, 1891. See also *New York World*, August 13, 1891; *Cheyenne Daily Leader*, August 12, 1891; *Kansas Weekly Capital* (Topeka), August 13, 1891.

36. *Experiments in Production of Rainfall*, pp. 20–21, 23.

37. *Washington Post*, August 20 and 21, 1891; *Chicago Daily Tribune*, August 20 and 22, 1891; *New York Sun*, August 20, 1891. See also *Brooklyn* (N.Y.) *Daily Eagle*, August 20 and 22, 1891.

38. *Experiments in Production of Rainfall*, pp. 16, 23, 25–26.

39. *New York Sun*, September 6, 1891; *Washington Post*, August 28,

1891; *Rocky Mountain News*, August 28, 1891.

40. *Experiments in Production of Rainfall*, p. 26; *Washington Post*, August 31, 1891; *Chicago Daily Tribune*, August 22, 1891; *New York World*, September 2, 1891.

41. *Puck* 30 (September 30, 1891): 87; *Experiments in Production of Rainfall*, pp. 27–32, 40. For newspaper accounts of this phase, see *Rocky Mountain News*, September 20, 1891; *Cheyenne Daily Sun*, September 20, 1891; *Minneapolis Tribune*, September 20, 1891; *Salt Lake Tribune*, September 16, 1891; *Washington Post*, October 2, 1891.

42. *Minneapolis Tribune*, September 28, 1891.

43. *Experiments in Production of Rainfall*, pp. 34, 37–41; *Washington Post*, October 2, 17, and 19, 1891. A brief account of the San Diego experiment is also found in John C. Rayburn, "The Rainmakers in Duval," *Southwestern Historical Quarterly* 61 (July 1957): 101–14. The same author treats the Midland trials in "Cannonading the Clouds at Midland, 1891," *West Texas Historical Association Year Book* 34 (October 1958), 50–66.

44. *Experiments in Production of Rainfall*, pp. 53, 55.

45. Ibid., pp. 57–59.

46. *Rocky Mountain News*, September 6, 1891; *New York Tribune*, September 25, 1891; *Washington Post*, September 4, 1891. See also *New York Sun*, August 24, 1891; *Kansas Weekly Capital*, October 1, 1891.

47. *Puck* 30 (September 23 and October 28, 1891): 75, 155; *Life* 18 (November 12, 1891): 274–75.

48. From W. F. C., "Tale of the Rain Machine," *Life* 18 (November 5, 1891): 260.

49. *Nation* 53 (October 1 and 22, 1891): 253–54, 310; *North American Review* 153 (October 1891): 385–404. A typical example of how local editors tended to devote much space to Dyrenforth's views in the *North American Review* and to ignore Newcomb's is seen in the Hailey, Idaho, newspaper, the weekly *Wood River Times*, September 30 and October 7, 1891.

50. *Farm Implement News* 12 (September 1891): 72; *Farm Implement News* 13 (October 1891): 25.

51. Curtis to Fernow, February 9, 1892; Fernow to Harrington, February 10, 1892, both in WBC (1892), file 1791, box 840; *Report of the Secretary of Agriculture . . . 1891*, p. 58. For Curtis's published comments, see "The Facts about Rain-Making," *Engineering Magazine* 3 (July 1892): 548–51; "Rain-Making in Texas," *Nature* 44 (October 22, 1891): 594; *Inventive Age* 3 (December 29, 1891): 2; *Western Christian Advocate*, September 24, 1891.

52. Entry for June 8, 1892, *Congressional Record*, 52d Cong., 1st sess., 1891–92, p. 5153.

53. Ibid., pp. 5155–56; *United States Statutes at Large*, 27 (1892), p. 76.

54. *Washington Post*, October 30 and November 4, 1892; *Evening Star* (Washington, D.C.), November 3, 1892, Harrington to Hazen, November 4,

1892; Harrington to Rusk, November 4, 1892, with unidentified clipping; all in WBC (1892), file 1791, box 840. *Washington Post*, November 2, 1892; *San Antonio Daily Express,* December 4, 1892.

55. *Washington Post*, November 6, 1892. Harrington to L. F. Passailaigue, November 7, 1892, copy; Acting Secretary of the Weather Bureau to Harrington, November 7, 1892; both in WBC (1892), file 1791, box 840. *Dallas Morning News*, November 22, 1892; *San Antonio Daily Express*, December 4, 1892; *Kansas Weekly Capital*, November 17, 1892.

56. Chart and remarks for November 22, 25 and 26, 1892, compiled by L. F. Passailaigue, WBC (1892), file 1791, box 840; *San Antonio Daily Express*, November 30 and December 4, 1892; *New York World*, December 4, 1892; *Chicago Daily Tribune*, December 11, 1892; *San Antonio Daily News*, November 28, 1892.

57. *San Antonio Daily Express*, December 2, 1892; *San Antonio Evening Star*, December 2, 1892; *New York Tribune*, November 21, 1892; *Detroit Tribune*, November 24, 1892; *Report of the Secretary of Agriculture . . . 1892*, p. 55. Clippings from other newspapers are also found in WBC (1892), file 1791, box 840.

58. *Washington Post*, December 5 and 7, 1892; *Chicago Times*, December 3, 1892.

59. J. Sterling Morton to Dyrenforth, May 16, 1893, copy; Harrington to Morton, May 16, 1893, copy; both in WBC (1893), file 7192, box 869. Morton to Harrington, May 13, 1893, WBC (1893), file 7813, box 873.

60. *Washington Post*, July 9, 1910; *Sunday Star* (Washington, D.C.), July 10, 1910.

61. Entry for January 23, 1899, *Congressional Record*, 55th Cong., 3d sess., 1898–99, p. 919. Willis L. Moore to Secretary of Agriculture James Wilson, April 11, 1899, copy; Department of Agriculture memorandum, April 13, 1899; both in WBC (1899), file 3771, box 1368. Secretary of Agriculture, undated form letter, stereotyped copy, U.S. Weather Bureau Library, Suitland, Md.; *Pacific Rural Press* 42 (November 7, 1891): 397; *Engineering Magazine* 2 (October 1891): 124.

62. *San Antonio Daily Express*, December 4, 1892; *Globe-Republican* (Dodge City), February 3, 1893.

63. F. L. Darrow, "The Problem of Making Rain to Order," *Saint Nicholas Magazine* 57 (May 1930): 540; Robert De C. Ward, "How Far Can Man Control His Climate?" *Scientific Monthly* 30 (January 1930): 12–13.

64. *Scientific American* 68 (April 22, 1893): 242; *Scientific American* 69 (September 23, 1893): 200; *New York Tribune*, August 20, 1893; *Goodland News*, August 24, 1893; *American Meteorological Journal* 10 (December 1893): 357; *Goodland Republic*, June 16, 1893; *Pacific Rural Press* 45 (June 3, 1893): 485.

65. Dick, *Conquering the American Desert*, p. 341; *Minneapolis* (Kans.)

*Messenger*, June 8, 1893; William F. Wright, *The Universe As It Is* (Lincoln: Woodruff Printing Co., 1898), pp. 14, 193–98; 325–36; G. A. Loveland to Willis Moore, August 23, 1901, WBC (1901), file 8013, box 1556; *Chicago Daily News*, August 13, 1901; *Annual Report of the Commissioner of Patents* (Washington, D.C.: Government Printing Office, 1902), p. 776.

66. Henry S. Lehman to Secretary of Agriculture, December 11, 1899; Lehman to Willis Moore, December 27, 1899; both in WBC (1899), file 11227, box 1414.

67. *New York Times*, October 23, 1901; George E. Franklin, "The Work of the Rainmakers in the Arid Regions," *The Official Proceedings of the Twelfth National Irrigation Congress Held at El Paso, Texas, Nov. 15–16–17–18, 1904* (Galveston: Clarke & Curtis, 1905), pp. 426–27; Willis Moore to John C. Cooper, August 7, 1901, WBC (1901), file 7196, box 1552; Moore to Editor, *New York Times*, November 4, 1901, copy, Chief Clerk, U.S. Weather Bureau, Letters Sent (October 13–November 21, 1901), 62:279, National Archives and Records Service; Moore to T. C. Ford, June 5, 1901, WBC (1901), file 4943, box 1539; *New York Tribune*, June 6 and 11, 1903.

68. Willis Moore to James S. Whipple, October 23 and 25, 1908, copies; Whipple to Moore, October 24 and 28, 1908; all in WBC (1908), file 5815, box 2162. *New York Evening Post*, September 2, 1910; *New York Times*, August 27, 1910.

69. *DAB*, 15:112–13; Charles Dudley Eaves, "Charles William Post, the Rainmaker," *Southwestern Historical Quarterly* 43 (April 1940): 425. Much of the material on Post's Texas experiments has been taken from this article. I am also indebted to R. Sylvan Dunn of the Southwest Collection at Texas Tech University for copies of letters from the Double U Company papers on the subject.

70. Eaves, "Charles William Post," pp. 426–27; Post to Double U Co., June 8, 1911; Post to Double U Co., June 4, 1911, telegram; Double U Co. to Post, July 8, 1911; A. D. Marhoff to Double U Co. Board of Managers, June 9, 1911; all in Double U Co. MSS.

71. *Harper's Weekly* 55 (February 24, 1912): 8. The *Illustrated London News* 141 (September 28, 1912): 473, ran the piece virtually intact. Eaves, "Charles William Post," pp. 427–34, 435, 436; Marhoff to Double U Co., August 5 and 8, 1912, Double U Co. MSS.

72. H. W. Johnson to Moore, July 11, 1912; Moore to Charles F. Schneider, July 17 and 19, 1912, copies; Moore to Johnson, July, 19, 1912, copy; leaflet, July 21, 1912; all in WBC (1912–24 Series), box 2454.

73. Moore to Weather Bureau observers at Detroit, Alpena, Grand Haven, Lansing, Chicago, Toledo, and Grand Rapids, July 23, 1912, WBC (1912–24 Series), box 2454; *Battle Creek Daily Journal*, July 22, 1912; *Battle Creek Enquirer*, July 24, 1912; Battle Creek Industrial Association et al. to Moore, July 24, 1912, telegram, WBC (1912–24 Series), box 2454.

74. Moore to Battle Creek Industrial Association et al., July 25, 1912, telegram, copy; Schneider to Moore, July 25 and 27, 1912; all in WBC (1912–24 Series), box 2454. *Rural New-Yorker* 71 (October 19, 1912): 1066.

75. *Battle Creek Enquirer*, July 24, 1912; *Evening News* (Battle Creek), July 24, 1912.

76. *Adrian* (Mich.) *Telegram*, July 24, 1912, quoted in *Battle Creek Daily Moon*, July 26, 1912. For examples of how the story appeared, see *Detroit News*, July 24, 1912; *Sandusky* (Ohio) *Register*, August 2, 1912; *Peoria Evening Star*, August 3, 1912; *Indianapolis Star*, August 11, 1912; *Austin Statesman* August 13 and September 13, 1912; *Scientific American* 107 (August 10, 1912): *Rural New-Yorker* 71 (October 19, 1912): 1066; *Literary Digest* 45 (November 2, 1912): 784–85.

77. *St. Louis Post Dispatch*, July 7, 1912; *Mining and Scientific Press* 78 (March 4, 1899): 230; Leo H. Fisher to Lawrence Richey, August 11, 1930, WBC (1925–30 Series), box 2810; *Rain-Making Experiments at Oamaru* (Wellington: John Mackay, 1908), pp. 5–6; *Scientific American* 100 (March 27, 1909): 238; entry for March 7, 1911, *Parliamentary Debates* (Commons), 5th ser., 22:1177; *Washington Post*, March 26, 1911.

78. The 1914 article was in *Pearson's Weekly*. *Scientific American* 111 (October 24, 1914): 330; *Literary Digest* 44 (November 14, 1914): 953; *Monthly Weather Review* 45 (September 1917): 450–51; *Monthly Weather Review* 47 (March 1919): 166.

79. Edward Baines to General Billy Mitchell, June 16, 1921; Charles Marvin to Baines, July 29, 1921, copy; Marvin to David Dudgeon, July 11, 1924, copy; all in WBC (1912–24 Series), box 2454. Andrew A. Manning to J. J. McSwain, August 14, 1925, photostat; McSwain to Dwight F. Davis, August 18, 1925; Davis to McSwain, August 24, 1925, copy; all in WBC (1925–30 Series), box 2810. *Denver Post*, April 9, May 4, and August 4, 1935.

80. E. L. Torrance to Franklin D. Roosevelt, June 7, 1935, telegram, WBC (1930–35 Series), box 2998. Gordon Mull to Henry A. Wallace, August 18, 1936; Benjamin M. Powers to Wallace, July 7, 1936; W. R. Gregg to Powers, July 10, 1936, copy; all in WBC (1936–42 Series), box 32. *Science News Letter* 32 (September 19, 1942): 190–91.

81. *Scientific American Supplement* (August 11 and 18, 1894), pp. 15525–56, 15539–40; *North American Review* 153 (October 1891): 398–404; Davis, "The Theories," pp. 494–95; Ward, "Artificial Rain," p. 493; *Industrialist* (Manhattan, Kans.) 18 (October 1, 1892): 26.

## Chapter 4

1. From "Romance of the Rainmaker," Lincoln Phifer, *The Dramas of Kansas* (Chicago: privately published, 1915), p. 161.

2. *Rocky Mountain News*, September 6, 1891. A portion of this chapter has previously appeared as "Melbourne, the Australian Rain Wizard," in *Annals of Wyoming* 30 (April 1961): 5–18.

3. For a sound treatment of the Kansas "pluviculturists" of the 1890s, see Martha B. Caldwell, "Some Kansas Rain Makers," *Kansas Historical Quarterly* 7 (August 1938): 306–24. For a study that focuses on Melbourne and Sherman County, see Paul Dee Travis, "Myths and Panaceas: A Study of the Attempts to Create Rain Artificially in the Semiarid Regions of Kansas" (M.A. thesis, Wichita State University, 1966).

4. Homer Croy, *Corn Country* (New York: Duell, Sloan & Pearce, 1947), p. 136.

5. *Rocky Mountain News*, August 2, 1891; *Cheyenne Daily Sun*, August 28, 1891.

6. *Rocky Mountain News*, July 28 and August 2, 1891; *Cheyenne Daily Sun*, August 13, 1891; *Globe-Republican*, August 5, 1891.

7. *Cheyenne Daily Sun*, August 13, 1891; *Rocky Mountain News*, August 2 and 13, 1891; Melbourne to George W. Baxter (Ohio, June 11, 1891), *Cheyenne Daily Leader*, June 19, 1891.

8. *Salt Lake Tribune*, September 19, 1891; *Rocky Mountain News*, August 3 and September 6, 1891; *Cheyenne Daily Sun*, August 13 and September 5, 1891.

9. *Globe-Republican*, August 5, 1891.

10. *New York Tribune*, August 6, 1891.

11. *Rocky Mountain News*, August 2, 1891; Melbourne to George W. Baxter (June 11, 1891), *Cheyenne Daily Leader*, June 19, 1891; *Cheyenne Daily Sun*, August 23, 1891; *Chicago Daily Tribune*, August 24, 1891.

12. *Rocky Mountain News*, August 28, 1891; *Cheyenne Daily Sun*, August 28, 1891.

13. *Cheyenne Daily Sun*, August 28, 1891; *Cheyenne Daily Leader*, September 1, 1891.

14. *Cheyenne Daily Sun*, August 28, 1891.

15. *Cheyenne Daily Leader*, August 29, 1891.

16. Ibid.; *Cheyenne Daily Sun*, August 30, 1891.

17. *Cheyenne Daily Leader*, August 30 and September 1, 1891; *Cheyenne Daily Sun*, August 28 and 30, and September 1, 1891.

18. *Cheyenne Daily Sun*, September 2, 1891; *Cheyenne Daily Leader*, September 4, 1891; *Rocky Mountain News*, September 2, 1891.

19. *Cheyenne Daily Sun*, September 2, 1891; *Cheyenne Daily Leader*, September 2, 1891; *Rocky Mountain News*, September 2, 1891; *Salt Lake Tribune*, September 2, 1891; *Minneapolis Tribune*, September 2, 1891.

20. Quoted in the *Cheyenne Daily Leader*, September 8, 1891.

21. *Salt Lake Tribune*, September 3, 1892; *Washington Evening Star*, September 2, 1891; *Chicago Daily Tribune*, September 19 and 20, 1891; *Rocky*

*Mountain News*, September 6 and 8, 1891. See also the *New York Tribune*, September 20, 1891. "Truly, we live in the nineteenth century, but will wonders never cease?" asked the editor of an Idaho weekly newspaper. *Wood River Times*, September 9, 1891.

22. *Cheyenne Daily Leader*, September 2, 1891; *Cheyenne Daily Sun*, September 2, 1891.

23. *Cheyenne Daily Sun*, September 3, 4, and 5, 1891.

24. Ibid., September 6 and 8, 1891.

25. Ibid., September 8, 1891.

26. Ibid., September 8, 11, and 15, 1891; *Cheyenne Daily Leader*, October 1 and 8, 1891.

27. *Cheyenne Daily Sun*, September 5, 9, and 10, 1891; *Rocky Mountain News*, September 3, 1891. Melbourne insisted that he did not guarantee ½ inch for Kelton itself, but ½ inch on the average for a sixty-mile radius. *Salt Lake Tribune*, September 15, 18, and 19, 1891; *Cheyenne Daily Leader*, September 17, 1891.

28. *Cheyenne Daily Sun*, September 15 and 26, 1891.

29. *Salt Lake Tribune*, September 18, 1891; *Goodland News*, September 10, 1891; *Rocky Mountain News*, September 20, 1891; *Sherman County Farmer* (Goodland), September 10, 1891; Caldwell, "Some Kansas Rain Makers," p. 309.

30. *Sherman County Farmer*, September 17 and 24, 1891; *Goodland News*, September 10, 1891.

31. *Goodland News*, September 24, 1891.

32. *Cheyenne Daily Sun*, September 26, 1891; *Goodland News*, October 1, 1891; *Sherman County Farmer*, October 1, 1891; *Minneapolis Tribune*, September 26, 1891.

33. *Kansas Weekly Capital*, October 1, 1891; *Goodland News*, October 1, 1891; *Sherman County Farmer*, October 1, 1891; *Cheyenne Daily Sun*, October 7 and 11, 1891; *Kansas Weekly Vapital*, October 8 and 15, 1891; Federal Writers' Project, *Kansas* (New York: Viking Press, 1949), p. 335; *Chicago Daily Tribune*, October 6, 1891.

34. *Kansas Weekly Capital*, October 15, 1891; *Goodland News*, October 8, 1891; *Sherman County Farmer*, October 8, 1891; *Brooklyn Daily Eagle*, October 18, 1891; *Cheyenne Daily Sun*, October 11, 1891; *Globe-Republican*, October 22 and December 10, 1891.

35. *Sherman County Farmer*, October 15, 1891; Macfarlane, "On Rainmaking," p. 75.

36. *Cheyenne Daily Sun*, October 30, 1891; *Goodland Republic*, April 1, 1892. Melbourne to Jones, February 13, 1892, and January 2, 1892; W. M. Burnett to Melbourne, May 21, 1892; all in Agnes Wright Spring, "Rainmakers of the 'Nineties," *Colorado Magazine* 32 (October 1955): 296–98.

37. The introduction of this pamphlet is quoted in full in Spring, "Rain-

makers of the 'Nineties," p. 294.

38. Quoted in Alvin T. Steinel, *History of Agriculture in Colorado* (Fort Collins: State Agricultural College, 1926), p. 261; Dick, *Conquering the Great American Desert*, pp. 341–42; *Oberlin* (Kans.) *Opinion*, quoted in *Goodland News*, December 10, 1891; *Industrialist* 18 (October 1, 1892): 26.

39. Steinel, *History*, p. 261; *Cheyenne Daily Sun*, September 8, 1891.

40. Steinel, *History*, p. 261.

41. Dick, *Conquering the Great American Desert*, pp. 242–43; *Rocky Mountain News*, September 3 and 12, 1891.

42. Kansas Secretary of State, Corporations Book 46 (1891–92), p. 46, Kansas Historical Society, Topeka; *Sherman County Farmer*, January 7, 1892; *Rocky Mountain News*, July 10, 1892; W.P.A., *Kansas*, p. 335.

43. W.P.A., *Kansas*, p. 335; *Goodland News*, October 22, November 5, and December 24, 1891; *Rocky Mountain News*, July 10, 1892; *Cheyenne Daily Sun*, October 30, 1891; *Sherman County Farmer*, January 7, 1892.

44. *Goodland News*, October 22 and November 5, 1891.

45. *Sherman County Farmer*, November 12, 1891; *Goodland News*, November 5, 12, and 19, 1891.

46. Kansas Secretary of State, Corporations Book 44 (1891–92), p. 209; *Goodland News*, January 7, 1892; *Goodland Republic*, January 15 and 22, 1892.

47. *Goodland Republic*, January 8, 1892; *Sherman County Farmer*, January 14, 1892.

48. Kansas Secretary of State, Corporations Book 44 (1891–92), p. 254; *Goodland Republic*, January 8, 1892.

49. *Goodland Republic*, May 12, 1893; *Sherman County Farmer*, March 3, 1892; *Puck* 30 (September 9, 1891): 33.

50. *Goodland News*, January 28, February 11, and 18, 1892; *Pacific Rural Press* 43 (February 6, 13, and 27, 1892): 116, 153, 190; *Goodland Republic*, February 19, 1892.

51. *Goodland News*, March 24, 1892; *Goodland Republic*, March 11, 1892.

52. *Goodland Republic*, July 15, 1892, and July 7, 1893; *Goodland News*, November 5, 1891, and May 1894; *Topeka Daily Capital*, January 27, 1906; Edwin C. Torrey, *Early Days in Dakota* (Glendale, Calif.: Arthur H. Clark Co., 1925), pp. 273–74.

53. *Goodland News*, January 7 and April 21, 1892; *Goodland Republic*, January 8 and February 12, 1892.

54. *Goodland News*, May 12 and 19, 1892; *Goodland Republic*, April 1, 1892; *Rocky Mountain News*, July 10, 1892.

55. *Goodland News*, December 24, 1891, and January 28, 1892; *Goodland Republic*, February 5, 1892.

56. Quoted in *Goodland News*, April 20 and May 11, 1893; *Goodland*

*Republic*, June 30, 1893; *Jewell County Monitor* (Mankato, Kans.), June 29 and July 6, 1892.

57. *Goodland Republic*, June 24, July 29, and August 5, 1892, and April 21, 1893; *Goodland News*, August 6, 1892; *Jewell County Republican* (Jewell, Kans.), August 5, 1892.

58. Croy, *Corn Country*, p. 140; *Goodland News*, August 4, 1892, and January 12, 1893; *Homestead* 38 (November 4, 1892): 1029; *Lincoln Daily Call*, January 7, 1893; *Lincoln Alliance Independent*, January 19, 1893; copy, transcript of Lancaster County Court, Record 21, p. 275, courtesy of the district court, Lancaster County, Lincoln, Nebraska.

59. *Goodland Republic*, October 7, 1892, and July 28, 1893; *Jewell County Republican*, August 19 and 26, 1892; *Goodland News*, July 20 and November 30, 1893; *Homestead* 34 (July 28, 1893): 687.

60. *Britton* (S. Dak.) *Sentinel*, quoted in *Goodland News*, May 17, 1894, and 1892; *Council Grove* (Kans.) *Republican*, August 12, 1892; H. R. Hilton to Editor, July 29, 1892, *Topeka Daily Capital*, August 3, 1892.

61. *Homestead* 38 (November 4, 1892): 1029; *Jewell Country Republican*, July 29, 1892; *Topeka Daily Capital*, July 30, 1892.

62. From "Romance of the Rainmaker," Phifer, *The Dramas of Kansas*, p. 162.

63. *Goodland News*, May 4 and May 11, 1893; *Goodland Republic*, May 11, 1893.

64. *Globe-Republican*, June 9, 1893.

65. *Goodland Republic*, June 2 and 16, 1893; *Globe-Republican*, June 2, 1893; *Meade County Globe* (Meade, Kans.), June 8, 1893.

66. *Goodland Republic*, June 2, 16, and 23, 1893; *Globe-Republican*, June 9, 1893.

67. *Goodland News*, June 29, 1893; *Phillipsburg* (Kans.) *Dispatch*, June 29, 1893; *Kansas City Times*, quoted in *Goodland News*, June 15, 1893; *Goodland Republic*, June 30, 1893; *Topeka Daily Capital*, quoted in *Jewell County Monitor*, July 12, 1893; *Kansas City Times*, quoted in *Goodland News*, June 29, 1893.

68. *Liberal* (Kans.) *News*, July 6 and 13, 1893; *Goodland Republic*, July 14 and 21, 1893.

69. Quoted in *Goodland Republic*, August 4, 1893.

70. *Goodland Republic*, July 21 and September 29, 1893, and July 27, 1894; *Chicago Times*, June 22, 1893.

71. *Goodland Republic*, September 29, 1893; W. I. Allen to Mark Harrington, August 22, 1893, WBC (1893), file 7192, box 869.

72. *Goodland News*, April 26 and May 10, 1894; *Goodland Republic*, April 27, 1894.

73. *Goodland News*, May 10, 1894.

74. *Wichita Eagle*, quoted in *Goodland News*, June 14, 1894; clipping,

*Kansas City Times*, February 19, 1938, in Rain and Rainfall Clippings, vol. 2, pt. 2, Kansas Historical Society, clippings, *Kansas City Times*, August 26, 1930, in Rock Island Railroad Clippings, vol. 1, Kansas Historical Society.

75. Charles M. Sheldon, "A Trip with a Professional Rain-Maker," *Saint Nicholas Magazine* 27 (August 1900): 900–901, 901–2.

76. *Goodland Republic*, July 7, 1893; Harrington, "Weather Making," p. 268.

77. Sheldon, "A Trip," pp. 902, 904.

78. *Goodland Republic*, July 27, 1894; B. A. McAllaster to Howard Miller, August 7, 1893; Alexander Macfarlane to Mark Harrington, August 16, 1893, telegram; Howard Miller to Alexander McAdie, August 18, 1893; all in WBC (1893), file 7192, box 869.

79. W. J. Allen to Mark Harrington, October 2, 1893; Allen to Harrington, September 21, 1893; Harrington to J. Sterling Morton, September 27, 1893; all in ibid.; Harrington to Allen, September 20, 1893, copy, Chief of the Weather Bureau, Letters Sent, book 3 (May 19–November 11, 1893), National Archives and Records Service.

80. *Railroad Gazette* 26 (September 21, 1894): 652; *Engineering News* 33 (February 14, 1895): 109; *Engineering News* 45 (January 10, 1901): 32; *New York Tribune*, April 7, 1895.

81. Franklin, "Work of the Rainmakers," p. 426. There is no indication that Jewell continued his rainmaking activity. He died in Coffeyville, Kansas, in 1906 at the age of forty-four, having served for the last seven years of his life as chief dispatcher of the Missouri Pacific Railroad there. Clipping, *Topeka Daily Capital*, April 12, 1906, in Kansas Scrapbook, Biography, vol. 2, Kansas Historical Society.

82. George G. Matthews to A. W. Greeley, October 20, 1896, WBC (1896), file 8418, box 1185; *Daily Eagle*, July 30, 1899.

83. Matthews to Directors, Smithsonian Institution, April 21, 1900; Willis Moore to Matthews, May 9, 1900, copy; both in WBC (1900), file 3597, box 1448. See also Victor Murdock to Whom It May Concern, November 23, 1908, copy; H. G. Ruggles to Secretary of War Jacob M. Dickinson, December 9, 1909; James Wilson to H. G. Ruggles, December 18, 1909; all in WBC (1909), file 7692, box 2246.

84. *Goodland Republic*, September 21, 1894; *Proceedings of the House of Representatives of the State of Kansas, Ninth Biennial Session, Begun at Topeka, January 8, 1895* (Topeka: Hamilton Printing Co., 1895), pp. 872, 874, 985; *Proceedings of the Senate of the State of Kansas, Ninth Biennial Session, Begun at Topeka, January 8, 1895* (Topeka: Hamilton Printing Co.,1895), pp. 255, 264, 314; *Ninth Biennial Report of the Kansas State Board of Agriculture* (Topeka: Hamilton Printing Co., 1895), pp. 334–37; A. Bower Sageser, *Joseph L. Bristow: Kansas Progressive* (Lawrence and London: University Press of Kansas, 1968), p. 20.

**Chapter 5**

1. By H. J. R., unidentified clipping, Hatfield Scrapbook, vol. 1, Los Angeles Public Library.

2. Fred A. Binney to U.S. Weather Bureau, December 30, 1899, WBC (1900), file 198, box 1425; Eric A. Binney, "The Twins Story," pp. 37, 39 (Typescript reminiscences), San Diego Historical Society; Thomas W. Patterson, "Hatfield the Rainmaker," *Journal of San Diego History* 16 (Winter 1970): 13. The Patterson article is the standard work on Hatfield.

3. *San Diego Union*, January 26 and 30, and February 9, 12, and 22, 1900; *San Diego Evening Tribune*, February 5, 1900. Fred A. Binney to Willis Moore, January 15 and February 4, 1900; Ford Carpenter to Moore, February 13, 1900; all in WBC (1900), file 198, box 1425. Binney to Secretary of Agriculture, June 20, 1903; Moore to Binney, June 27, 1903, copy; both in WBC (1903), file 7750, box 1718. Victor Rubin, "Rain Made to Order," *Popular Mechanics* 51 (March 1929): 390.

4. Paul A. Hatfield, "The Hatfield Brothers, Rainmakers," p. 6, interview, U.C.L.A. Oral History Program 1972, U.C.L.A. Library; *Los Angeles Examiner*, March 19, 1905.

5. *San Francisco Examiner*, May 14, 1905; Franklin, "Work of the Rainmakers," p. 428; unidentified clippings (2), Hatfield Scrapbook 1; *Stockton Daily Evening Record*, February 15, 1907.

6. *Tid-Bits* (London), June 17, 1905, clipping in Hatfield Scrapbook 1, Hatfield to Willis Moore, October 6, 1903; Moore to Hatfield, October 12, 1903, copy; both in WBC (1903), file 10490, box 1742. Hatfield to Moore, June 1, 1904, WBC (1904), file 6634, box 1812; *San Diego Evening Tribune*, January 18, 1972; Charles M. Hatfield, "Artificial Attraction of Moisture," *Bob Taylor's Magazine*, n.d., clipping in Hatfield Scrapbook 1.

7. Unidentified clipping, n.d.; clipping, *Fresno Morning Republican*, December 20, 1905; Hatfield, "Artificial Attraction of Moisture"; all in Hatfield Scrapbook 1. *Sunday Oregonian* (Portland), June 7, 1908.

8. *Los Angeles Times*, February 2, 1904; Franklin, "Work of the Rainmakers," p. 428; Patterson, "Hatfield," pp. 4–6.

9. Patterson, "Hatfield," p. 9; unidentified clipping, n.d., Hatfield Scrapbook 1; *Los Angeles Examiner*, December 1 and 3, 1904; *Los Angeles Daily Herald*, December 2 and 3, 1904; *Los Angeles Evening Express*, December 2 and 3, 1904.

10. *Los Angeles Daily Times*, December 3 and 6, 1904.

11. Los Angeles Rainfall Chart, 1877–1905, in WBC (1904), file 14425, box 1860; *Los Angeles Examiner*, December 7, 1904; *Los Angeles Daily Times*, December 7, 1904.

12. *Los Angeles Daily Herald*, December 8 and 11, 1904; *Los Angeles*

*Examiner*, December 8, 1904; *Riverside Daily Press*, December 9, 1904; Hatfield to J. A. Willson, December 12, 1904, unidentified clipping, Hatfield Scrapbook 1.

13. Franklin to Moore, December 12, 1904; Moore to Franklin, December 29, 1904, copy; both in WBC (1904), file 14425, box 1860.

14. *Los Angeles Graphic*, December 25, 1904.

15. Unidentified clipping, n.d., Hatfield Scrapbook 1; *Los Angeles Examiner*, March 19, 1905.

16. *Los Angeles Examiner*, March 20, 1905; J. N., "To the Rain-Maker," clipping, *Los Angeles Express*, n.d., Hatfield Scrapbook 1.

17. *Scranton* (Pa.) *Republican*, May 6, 1905; *St. Louis Daily Globe-Democrat*, May 27, 1905; *Brooklyn Daily Eagle*, May 21, 1905; "A Chat with the World's Greatest 'Rain-Maker'" *Tid-Bits*, June 17, 1905, in Hatfield Scrapbook 1.

18. See a copy of admission ticket and unidentified clippings, Hatfield Scrapbook 1.

19. *Arkansas Traveler*, n.d., clipping, ibid. H. M. Watts to Moore, May 9, 1905; Moore to Watts, May 10, 1905, copy; both in WBC (1904), file 14425, box 1860. See also Moore to Editor, *Scranton Republican*, May 22, 1905, copy; Moore to Editor, *St. Louis Daily Globe-Democrat*, May 29, 1905, copy; Moore to Editor, *New York Tribune*, May 9, 1905, copy; all in Chief Clerks Weather Bureau, Letters Sent, book C (May 9–June 15, 1905); vol. 98 (March 16–April 11, 1905); *Monthly Weather Review* 33 (April 1905): 152–53.

20. Franklin to Moore, April 12 and May 9, 1905; McAdie to Moore, May 16, 1905; both in WBC (1904), file 14425, box 1860. *Los Angeles Daily Herald*, May 7, 1905; *Los Angeles Examiner*, May 7, 1905; *Los Angeles Daily Times*, May 7, 1905; McAdie, "The Los Angeles Rain-Making," *Sunset Magazine* 15 (October 1905): 575–77; *San Francisco Examiner*, May 14, 1905.

21. *San Francisco Examiner*, May 14, 1905. Unidentified clipping, Hatfield Scrapbook 1. This is probably William Everett Wing, "Coaxing Rain from Unwilling Clouds," in *Human Life, a Magazine of To-day* (Boston).

22. Copy, pledge form and unidentified clipping, n.d., Hatfield Scrapbook 1; Lloyd H. Brubaker to S. E. Hatfield, November 25, 1905, Charles and Paul Hatfield Papers, vol. 2.

23. Clipping, *Los Angeles Examiner*, n.d.; unidentified clipping, n.d.; clipping, *Nevada City Daily Miner-Transcript*, n.d.; clipping, *San Francisco Examiner*, n.d.; all in Hatfield Scrapbook 1.

24. *Fresno Morning Republican*, December 20, 1905.

25. *South Pasadenan*, April 19, 1906; clipping, *West Side Index*, n.d., Hatfield Scrapbook 1.

26. Clipping, *Los Angeles Herald*, n.d., Hatfield Scrapbook 1; *Fresno Morning Republican*, December 20, 1905.

27. Clipping, *Los Angeles Express*, n.d., Hatfield Scrapbook 1; remarks of George E. Foster (March 26, 1906), *Official Report of the Debates of the House of Commons of the Dominion of Canada*, 10th Parliament, 2d sess. (1906), 74:560–61; *Monthly Weather Review* 34 (February 1906): 84–85; *Toronto News*, March 3, 1906.

28. Clipping, *Dawson Weekly News*, April 13, 1906, Hatfield Scrapbook 1; remarks of George E. Foster (March 26, 1906), *Official Report of Debates*, 10th Parliament, 2d sess. (1906), 74:561.

29. Remarks of George E. Foster (March 26, 1906), *Official Report of Debates*, 10th Parliament, 2d sess. (1906), 74:561.

30. Clipping, *Yukon World*, n.d., Hatfield Scrapbook 1; Hatfield, "The Hatfield Brothers," pp. 46–47; remarks of George E. Foster (March 26, 1906), *Official Report of Debates*, 10th Parliament, 2d sess. (1906), 76:5934.

31. From Philip Holloway, "Rain, Rain, Come Again," clipping *Dawson Daily News*, n.d., Hatfield Scrapbook 1.

32. Hatfield implied that he received twenty-five hundred dollars, but other sources set the figure considerably lower. Clipping, *Fresno Morning Republican*, n.d., Hatfield Scrapbook 1; *London Times*, February 11, 1907; *Quarterly Journal of the Royal Meteorological Society* 33 (July 1907); 199–200; *Symons's Monthly Meteorological Magazine* 41 (July 1906): 115. Clipping, *Fresno Morning Republican*, n.d.; clipping, *Pasadena Daily News*, October 24, 1906; both in Hatfield Scrapbook 1. *Los Angeles Examiner*, August 14, 1906; *Seattle Post-Intelligencer*, August 5, 1906; *Western Magazine* 1 (September 1906): 80, 81; *Engineering and Mining Journal* 82 (September 8, 1906): 455.

33. Unidentified clipping, n.d.; clipping, *Los Angeles Evening News*, March 11, 1907; both in Hatfield Scrapbook 1. *Fresno Morning Republican*, March 7, 1907.

34. As opposed to a negative commentary like *Pacific Rural Press* 73 (February 2, 1907): 66, see for example *San Francisco Chronicle*, August 3, 1907; *Stockton Daily Evening Record*, February 15, 1907; "This Man Makes Rain by Wireless Waves," *World Magazine* (July 21, 1907), in Hatfield Scrapbook 1. For a mildly skeptical article, which implied acceptance by its very title, see "A Professional Rain-Maker," *Delineator* 70 (November 1907), in Hatfield Scrapbook 1. *Stockton Daily Evening Record*, January 23 and February 15, 1907; *San Francisco Examiner*, August 3, 1907.

35. *Morning Oregonian*, July 30, 1907; *Sunday Oregonian*, June 7, 1908. Clipping, *Hemet News*, n.d.; unidentified clippings (2); all in Hatfield Scrapbook 1. *Pacific Rural Press* 77 (February 20 and May 8, 1909): 142, 350; *Inglewood Times*, June 26, 1909; *Los Angeles Examiner*, November 14, 1910; *Modesto Morning Herald*, January 29, 1911.

36. Unidentified clipping, June 14, 1912, loose with Hatfield Scrapbooks; Hatfield, "The Hatfield Brothers," pp. 114, 116; Ford Carpenter to

Moore, October 1, 1912; Hatfield to F. Walsh, October 22, 1912, in *Cape Times*, January 14, 1913, copy; C. Stewart to Moore, February 1913/no other date/; Moore to Stewart, March 19, 1913, copy; all in WBC (1912–24 Series), box 2454.

37. Binney to Secretary of Agriculture, May 6, 1913, and n.d./received May 24, 1913/; Alger Fast to Binney, May 1, 1913, copy; H. E. Williams to Binney, May 14, 1913, copy; all in WBC (1912–24 Series), box 2454.

38. Clipping, *San Diego Survey and Exposition News* 2 (December 1912), n.p., in Walter Bellon MSS, San Diego Historical Society; Patterson, "Hatfield," p. 14; Binney to Editor, *San Diego Union*, n.d., clipping, Hatfield Scrapbook 2; *San Diego Union*, December 10 and 14, 1915; Shelley J. Higgins, *This Fantastic City San Diego* (San Diego: City of San Diego, 1956), p. 176, 181, 183; "The Inside Story of Hatfield—the Rainmaker," typescript, pp. 1–2, Walter Bellon MSS.

39. Patterson, "Hatfield," p. 16; *San Diego Union*, January 18 and February 10, 1916. On January 17, a teen-age lad commented on Hatfield's tower, "For the last three days we have had very much rain, but it is said that the City Council won't pay him until he has proved that he has made it rain!" Staffan Kronberg, "Life at the Raja Yoga School from a Growing Boy's Point of View," p. 27, handwritten collection of translated excerpts from letters, in San Diego Historical Society.

40. *San Diego Union*, January 26 and February 5, 1916; Charles S. Moore, interview, May 17, 1960, p. 11, typescript, San Diego Historical Society; H. F. Alciatore to Charles Marvin, March 30, 1918, WBC (1912–24 Series), box 2454.

41. Patterson, "Hatfield," p. 25; "The Inside Story of Hatfield—the Rainmaker," p. 8, Walter Bellon MSS; *San Diego Union*, February 10 and 18, 1916.

42. *San Diego Union*, February 20 and 22, 1916; Higgins, *This Fantastic City*, p. 183.

43. Edgar F. Hastings, "Memory Stories," p. 49, typescript, San Diego Historical Society; Patterson, "Hatfield," pp. 26–27; *Business Week*, no vol., no. 991 (August 28, 1948): 36; *San Diego Union*, January 1, 1961; unidentified clipping (1960) in "Rainmakers" clipping file, San Diego Historical Society.

44. *Los Angeles Herald*, January 25, 1919. H. F. Alciatore to Marvin, March 30, 1918; Ford Carpenter to Cleveland Abbe, May 8, 1918; Carpenter to Marvin, August 21, 1918, and February 1, 1919; E. A. Beales to Carpenter, August 20, 1918; all in WBC (1912–24 Series), box 2454.

45. Charles Alma Byers, "The Man the Rain Minds," *Everybody's Magazine* 41 (August 1919): 112. Chief Marvin's negative comments apparently killed a pro-Hatfield story scheduled for *American Magazine* in 1919. Marvin to John M. Siddall, March 18, 1919, copy; Marvin to Editor, *Everybody's Magazine*, August 8, 1919, copy; V. Jordan to Marvin, August 23,

1919; all in WBC (1912–24 Series), box 2454. *True Stories* had also portrayed Hatfield favorably. "Does He Make Rain?," *True Stories* (June 1919): 68–69, in Hatfield Papers 5. Several years earlier, a short story in *Scribner's* had featured a rainmaker who must have been drawn from Hatfield in real life. He was a smell maker who used towers and exhibited tremendous faith in himself and his process. He died of snakebite, a tragic figure on the desert, just as "his" rain began to fall. Margaret Adelaide Wilson, "The Rain-Makers," *Scribner's Magazine* 61 (April 1917): 503–9.

46. *Sunset Magazine* 43 (December 1919): 48; *Chicago Saturday Blade*, October 11, 1919; *Brisbane Sun*, December 7, 1919, in Hatfield Scrapbook 2. John T. Dale to Secretary of Agriculture, November 4, 1919; J. S. Rose to Marvin, February 4, 1920; Deputy Minister of Saskatchewan to Marvin, March 31, 1921; all in WBC (1912–24 Series), box 2454. Hatfield was also receiving acclaim from South Africa, but a direct connection with *Everybody's* is not clear. Clippings, *Farmer's Weekly*, October 29, 1919, and January 14, 1920, U.S. Weather Bureau Library, Suitland, Md.

47. Clipping, *Sierra Madre* (Calif.) *News*, April 23, 1920, Hatfield Scrapbook 2; *Seattle Star*, July 9 and 14, 1920; *Seattle Post-Intelligencer*, July 17, 1920.

48. J. S. Rose to Marvin, February 4, 1920; E. C. Cranstoun to Director of Reclamation, February 23, 1920; Marvin to Rose, February 17, 1920, copy: Marvin to Cranstoun, March 18, 1920, copy; G. R. Marnoch to Marvin, January 25, 1921; clippings, *Lethbridge Daily Herald*, January 31 and February 27, 1920; *Vulcan Advocate* (n.d.); all in WBC (1912–24 Series), box 2454. *Rainmaking or Irrigation?* (Lethbridge: n.p., 1920), p. 3

49. Deputy Minister of Saskatchewan to Marvin, March 31, 1921; Marvin to Marnoch, February 5, 1921, copy; both in WBC (1912–24 Series), box 2454. *Washington Post*, February 1, 1921; *New York Times*, February 1, 1921; clipping, *Medicine Hat Daily News*, April 21, 1921, Hatfield Scrapbook 2.

50. Clippings, *Medicine Hat Daily News*, May 10 and 20, 1921, and *Chicago Tribune*, July 26, 1921, in Hatfield Scrapbook 2; unidentified clipping (n.d.), Hatfield Papers 1.

51. Unidentified clipping (n.d., 1921), Hatfield Scrapbook 2.

52. *Sheridan* (Wyo.) *Post*, August 17, 1921, in ibid.; *Monthly Weather Review* 49 (November 1921): 614; *Literary Digest* 71 (December 10, 1921: 19–20; *Review of Reviews* 65 (January 1922): 104–5; *Engineering News-Record* 86 (June 23, 1921): 1090.

53. Unidentified clipping in letter, H. J. Hanson to Leon M. Eastabrook, December 29, 1920, WBC (1912-24 Series), box 2454.

54. *San Diego Sun*, April 30, 1921. Of course, added the *Sun* writer, the drenching touched every part of the country except southern Texas, Louisiana, Florida, and the Carolinas. *San Diego Union*, June 5, 1921. H. F. Alciatore to Marvin, May 3, 1921; Marvin to Alciatore, May 13, 1921, copy; Editor,

*Oxnard* (Calif.) *Daily Courier* to Marvin, December 15, 1921; Marvin to Editor, *Oxnard Daily Courier*, December 15, 1921, telegram, copy; Henry C. Wallace to Marvin, July 27, 1921; *Oxnard Daily Courier*, December 15, 1921; all in WBC (1912–24 Series), box 2454. *Illustrated London News* 160 (February 5, 1922): 145.

55. *New York Times*, August 22, 1922; *Los Angeles Sunday Times*, March 30, 1924; *San Antonio Express*, July 20, 1924; unidentified clipping (n.d.), Hatfield Scrapbook 2; Hatfield, "The Hatfield Brothers," p. 135.

56. Robert L. Dean to Hatfield, June 23, 1920, in Hatfield Papers 2. Arthur J. Reynolds to U.S. Weather Bureau, October 24, 1922; Secretary for Agriculture, Union of South Africa, to U.S. Secretary of Agriculture, n.d., received August 1, 1924; both in WBC (1912–24 Series), box 2454. Hatfield, "The Hatfield Brothers," p. 144; unidentified clippings (n.d.), Hatfield Scrapbook 2; *New York Times*, November 4, 1924; *Los Angeles Daily Times*, September 25, 1924; *Los Angeles Evening Express*, September 25, 1924; *Los Angeles Illustrated Daily News*, July 29, 1927.

57. Hatfield, "The Hatfield Brothers," p. 112; Mrs. Walter E. Lyon to Franklin D. Roosevelt, May 8, 1934, WBC (1931–35 Series), box 2998; *San Diego Union*, February 24, 1931.

58. *Los Angeles Daily Times*, February 29, 1924; *San Bernardino Daily Sun*, February 28, 1924. Russell A. Elliget to Hatfield, September 24, 1924; Edward G. Cummings to Hatfield, October 27, 1924; H. A. Barre to W. W. Elliott, August 16, 1924; Hatfield to J. W. Tapp, March 30, 1926; all in Hatfield Papers 2. *New Orleans States*, April 28, 1925; unidentified clipping (n.d.); both in Hatfield Scrapbook 2. Stephen Munson to Marvin, April 29, 1925, telegram; Marvin to Munson, April 29, 1925, telegram, copy; both in WBC (1912–24 Series), box 2454.

59. Clipping, Napoleon, N.Dak., *Homestead*, April 24, 1925, in WBC (1912–24 Series), box 2454; *Bulletin of the American Meteorological Society* 5 (April 1924): 56.

60. *San Francisco Call and Post*, March 15, 1924; *San Francisco Examiner*, March 17 and 18, 1924; *Los Angeles Sunday Times*, March 30, 1924; *Los Angeles Evening Herald*, March 27 and April 23, 1924; *Fresno Bee*, April 2, 1924.

61. *New York Evening Post*, April 18, 1924; *St. Louis Post-Dispatch*, May 3, 1925; *San Diego Sun*, July 18, 1936.

62. Unidentified clipping, February 24, 1926, Hatfield Papers 1; *Los Angeles Sunday Times*, March 30, 1924.

63. *Los Angeles Evening Herald*, August 6, 1930; *Glendale News-Press*, August 9, 1934; *San Diego Sun*, July 18, 1936. Mrs. Walter E. Lyon to Franklin D. Roosevelt, May 8, 1934; Frederick A. Johnson to Roosevelt, August 19, 1934; both in WBC (1931–35 Series), box 2810. Mary Bavicky to Roosevelt, July 2, 1936; Daniel Ballmer to Roosevelt, August 6, 1936; both in

WBC (1936–42 Series), box 32.

64. *Kansas City Star*, August 12, 1934. *San Diego Union*, October 28, 1956; April 15, 1958; December 2, 9, and 10, 1960; April 5, 1964; August 8, 9, and 27, 1966; January 6, 1973. *Boulder* (Colo.) *Daily Camera*, August 8, 1966; Donald S. Stanford, "Hatfield, the Rainmaker," revised script, mimeographed (August 30, 1956), Hatfield Papers 6. For typical spectacular modern treatments of Hatfield, see Jack E. Branstetter, "Charles M. Hatfield Rainmaker," *Hi-Desert Speculator* 4 (September 1965): 4–16; John Olson, "The Conscientious Rainmaker," *San Diego Magazine* (January–February 1950), pp. 20–23, 32; Walter Wagner, "Hatfield the Rainmaker," *Kiwanis Magazine* (Summer 1970), pp. 29–33; Hatfield Papers 3; Brad Williams & Choral Pepper, *Lost Legends of the West* (New York: Holt, Rinehart & Winston, 1970), pp. 147–56; and William C. Miller, "When the Rainmaker Came to San Diego," *Westways* 57 (March 1965): 2–4.

65. See envelopes postmarked Pearblossom, Calif., January 1971 and July 1972, Hatfield Papers 5.

66. *San Antonio Express*, July 20, 1924.

67. Hatfield, "The Hatfield Brothers," pp. 133, 134.


**Chapter 6**

---

1. Quoted in *Pathfinder*, no. 1709 (October 2, 1926), p. 3.

2. Laurice L. Brown to Jeremiah Rusk, August 26, 1890. WBC, Gen. Corres., box 12, "Rainmaking" file.

3. Abbe, "On the Production of Rain," p. 299; Charles F. Talman, "Can We Control the Weather?," *Outlook* 133 (March 14, 1923): 495; Brooks, *Climate in Everyday Life*, p. 262; USDA *Experiment Station Record* 30 (1914): 511; George Augustus Rowell, *Papers on the Cause of Rain, Storms, the Aurora, and Terrestrial Magnetism* (London and Edinbourgh: Williams & Norgate, 1871), pp. 1–2, 15.

4. *Scientific American* 65 (November 21, 1891): 326; Harrington, "Weather Making," p. 260; D. A. Compton to Commissioner of Agriculture, April 1879, no other date, copy, WBC (Misc. Series), 1879, file 724, box 347.

5. Henry Holdes to Jeremiash Rusk, n.d., after December 30, 1890, WBC, Gen. Corres., box 12, "Rainmaking" file. F. A. Fisher to Weather Bureau, August 24, 1901; Willis Moore to Fisher, October 21, 1901, copy; both in WBC (1901), file 8036, box 1556.

6. *Science* 72 (August 15, 1930): supp. xii; *Rocky Mountain News*, July 21, 1912; *Denver Post*, May 10, 1914. John G. Potts to D. F. Houston, September 25, 1917; Potts to Charles Marvin, October 15, 1917; Marvin to Potts, September 29, 1917, copy; all in WBC (1912–24 Series), box 2425.

7. *New York Tribune*, April 16, 1899; *Mining and Scientific Press* 78

(March 4, 1899): 230; J. C. Lyons to Secretary of Agriculture, January 15, 1900, WBC (1900), file 783, box 1431.

8. *National Cyclopaedia of American Biography*, 12:424; *Pacific Rural Press* (May 4, 1895): 286.

9. *National Cyclopaedia of American Biography*, 10:354–55; *Electricity* 18 (January 10, 1900): 210.

10. J. Graeme Balsillie to William C. Magelssen, February 12, 1918, WBC (1912–24 Series), box 2454; Shaw, *The Air and Its Ways*, p. 222; *Electricity* 21 (December 11, 1901): 329; *Science* 72 (August 15, 1930): supps. x, xii; *Experiment Station Record* 14 (February 1903): 618–19; *Electrical Review* 74 (May 22, 1914): 872; *Electrical Review* 77 (July 30, 1915): 145; *Electrical Review* 78 (February 4, 1916): 150; *Electrical Review* 81 (September 28, November 2 and 30, 1917): 295, 447, 521; *Electrical Review* 87 (July 2, 1920): 32; *Popular Mechanics* 51 (March 1929): 386, 388.

11. *New York Herald*, February 15, 1923; L. Francis Warren to Wilder D. Bancroft, October 18, 1924, Wilder D. Bancroft MSS, box 16, Department of Manuscripts and University Archives, John M. Olin Library, Cornell University.

12. Bancroft was the grandson of historian-statesman George Bancroft. A voracious reader who never lost his Boston accent, he became president of both the American Chemical Society and the American Electrochemical Society. In addition he was a cofounder and a financial supporter of the *Journal of Physical Chemistry*. Gillispie, *Dictionary of Scientific Biography* (New York: Scribner's, 1971), 1:431; Emile M. Chamot and Fred H. Rhodes, "The Development of the Department of Chemistry and of the School of Chemical Engineering at Cornell," typescript (n.d.), pp. 71–72, Department of Manuscripts and University Archives, John M. Olin Library, Cornell University.

13. Bancroft to Warren, August 23, 1920, copy, Bancroft MSS, box 16; *American Fertilizer* 68 (April 21, 1923): 27–28; Donovan McClure, "A New Kind of Rain-maker, " *Saint Nicholas Magazine* 50 (August 1923): 1077–78; "Fog Removal and Rain Making," *Science* 57 (March 2, 1923): supp. ix; Warren to Chief of the Air Service, May 27, 1921, copy, Bancroft MSS, box 16.

14. For Chaffee, see *Who Was Who in America* (Chicago: Marquis, 1976), 6:73–74.

15. Bancroft to Warren, August 23, 1920, copy; Clayton J. Heermance to Bancroft, March 3, 1926; both in Bancroft MSS, box 16.

16. Warren to Bancroft, May 21, 1921, in ibid.

17. Warren to Chief of the Air Service, May 27, 1921, copy; Warren to Bancroft, September 19, 1921; L. Francis Warren, *Facts and Plans: Rainmaking–Fogs and Radiant Planes* (n. p., January 2, 1928), p. 1, copy; all in ibid.

18. Warren to Bancroft, September 19, 1921, and September 10, 1924; Karl F. Smith to Bureau of Aeronautics, July 1, 1922, copy; affidavits (all June 30, 1922), copies; all in ibid.

19. Warren, *Facts and Plans*, p. 2; Warren to Bancroft, July 11, 1922, Bancroft MSS, box 16. Bancroft's salary at Cornell went to five thousand dollars in 1921, but inherited wealth and consulting fees (four thousand dollars annually from one company alone) permitted money for such investments. Charles D. Bostwick to Bancroft, June 21, 1921; L. E. Sanders to Bancroft, July 25, 1921; both in Bancroft MSS, box 32.

20. Luke Francis Warren, Application for Patent, typescript copy; Maxwell Barus to Bancroft, May 29, 1923; Bancroft to Barus, December 18 and 31, 1923, copies; affidavit of Wilder D. Bancroft (n.d.), copy; all in Bancroft MSS, box 16.

21. Warren to Bancroft, January 25, 1923, in ibid. Probably this was Robert A. Millikan, dustinguished physicist and 1923 Nobel Laureate at the California Institute of Technology.

22. Ibid.

23. See clippings, *New Haven Register*, February 12, 1923; *Boston Herald*, February 12, 1922; *Providence Bulletin*, February 12, 1923; *Binghamton Press*, February 12, 1923; all in Romeyn Berry Papers, Department of Manuscripts and University Archives, John M. Olin Library, Cornell University. *New York Times*, February 12, 15, 16, and 18 and March 23, 1923; *American Fertilizer* 58 (April 21, 1923): 28; *Aviation* 14 (February 19, 1923: 223; unidentified clipping (1923), Bancroft MSS, box 16; *Washington Post*, February 14, 1923; *Boston Transcript*, quoted in *Washington Post*, February 17, 1923.

24. Snodgrass to Bancroft, May 4, 1923; C. Stewart to Bancroft, May 17, 1923; clipping, *Life* (n.d.), p. 24; all in Bancroft MSS, box 16. Robert T. Morris to Bancroft, March 21, 1923, Bancroft MSS, box 33; *Globe-Democrat*, quoted in "Rainmaking by Airplane," *Literary Digest* 76 (March 17, 1923): 25; J. F. Skogland to Editor, February 14, 1923, *Washington Post*, February 16, 1923.

25. Talman, "Can We Control," p. 494. Marvin to H. T. Gisborne, March 12, 1923, copy; Gisborne to W. J. Humphreys, March 5, 1923; press release, mimeographed (March 21, 1923); all in WBC (1912–24 Series), box 2454. New York Times, March 22, 1923; clipping, *New York Post*, February 23, 1923, in Berry Papers; clipping, *New York Sun*, March 21, 1923, in Bancroft MSS, box 16.

26. *New York Times*, March 23, 1923; Bancroft to C. Christie, March 14, 1923, copy, Bancroft MSS, box 16.

27. Warren to General M. M. Patrick, February 24, 1923, copy, Bancroft MSS, box 16.

28. W. H. Frank to Warren, March 6, 1923, copy; Bancroft to M. M.

Patrick, March 12, 1923, copy; Warren to Bancroft, August 10, 1923; all in ibid.

29. Warren, *Facts and Plans*, p. 3. Warren to Bancroft, October 1, 1923; Warren to George Thomson, December 18, 1923, copy; both in Bancroft MSS, Box 16.

30. Warren to Bancroft, October 1 and November 13, 1923, and March 10, 1924; Warren to E. Leon Chaffee, December 1, 1923, and January 18 and February 2, 1924, copies; all in Bancroft MSS, box 16.

31. Warren to Bancroft, February 13, March 10 and 28, May 1 and 12, 1924, April 15 and May 23, 1924, all in ibid.

32. C. Christie to Warren, March 4, 1924; Warren to Bancroft, March 10, 1924; both in ibid.

33. In earlier draft, reworked by Bancroft, Warren had asked a flat two million dollars and royalties of only three hundred fifty thousand dollars a year. Warren to Christie, March 15, 1924, copy; Warren to Bancroft, March 28, 1924, and May 23, 1924; Christie to Warren, March 21, 1924, copy; all in ibid.

34. Warren to George Thomson, December 18, 1923, copy; Warren to Bancroft, May 1, August 4, and September 10, 1924, and April 15, 1924; all in ibid.

35. Press release, April 15, 1924, copy; Warren to Bancroft, August 4 and September 10, 1924; all in ibid.

36. Warren to Bancroft, April 15, May 1 and 23, September 10, October 4, 1924; E. A. Lehman to Raymond O. Chaffee, September 27, 1924, copy; E. Leon Chaffee to Warren, November 13, 1924, copy; E. Leon Chaffee to Bancroft, November 25, 1924; all in ibid.

37. H. F. Councill to Chief of Bureau of Aeronautics, n.d., copy, ibid.

38. Warren to Bancroft, October 4, 1924, and October 18, 1924; both in ibid.; *DAB*, Supp. 3, pp. 714–15.

39. Warren, *Facts and Plans,* pp. 4–5; *New York Times*, November 9, 1924.

40. Warren to Bancroft, December 4, 1924, February 5 and 8, 1925; Warren "To the United States Government—Plan and Offer," February 13, 1925, copy; all in Bancroft MSS, box 16.

41. Warren to Bancroft, August 21, 1925; Hartford, March 27, 1926; both in ibid.; Warren, *Facts and Plans*, p. 6.

42. Warren to Bancroft, May 31 and June 18, 1926, Bancroft MSS, box 16; *New York Times*, June 19 and 20, 1926.

43. DeL. Mills, August 29, September 4 and 11, 1926, in *Weekly News Letter,* copies, Bancroft MSS, box 16.

44. DeL. Mills, August 29, 1926, *Weekly News Letter*, copy, in ibid.

45. Alexander McAdie, "Dispelling Clouds," notes on Dr. L. Francis Warren Experiments at Hartford, September 27–29, 1926, typescript copy, in

ibid.; Alexander McAdie, *Making the Weather* (New York: Macmillan Co., 1923), p. 33.

46. *New York Times*, May 4, 1927. According to Bancroft's statement early in 1925, four years earlier "we pooled things"—he put in nine thousand dollars and Warren contributed his invention—with each sharing equally in stock and control. In 1922 Bancroft invested another five thousand dollars; and in 1924, with friends, he subscribed an additional seven thousand dollars. Beyond that, he advanced sixty-five hundred dollars more to sustain Warren and to cover patent expenses. Bancroft to Warren, January 31, 1925, copy, Bancroft MSS, box 16. How much of Bancroft's investment was in scientific advice is not clear; probably some but not much. Nor is there any firm indication of who his friends were, apart from Sam Stone, president of the Colt Firearms Company. Warren spoke of "our corporation," and clearly he and Bancroft were the controlling owners. Warren to Bancroft, February 5 and 25, 1925; Bancroft to /Corliss?/ Lamont, February 27, no year given, draft. Warren to Bancroft, January 15, 1923; May 21, 1921; May 16, July 13, and August 22, 1925; April 12, 1926. Warren to Harry Guggenheim, June 14, 1926, copy; Guggenheim to Warren, June 18, 1926, copy; W. Cameron Forbes to Bancroft, January 4, 1923; all in Bancroft MSS, box 16.

47. Warren, *Facts and Plans,* pp. 8, 13, 15, 16.

48. *New York Times*, August 8, 1930; *Popular Mechanics* 51 (March 1929): 390; Edgar W. Woolard, Memorandum to Chief, July 8, 1936, WBC (1936–42 Series), box 32.

49. *San Francisco Examiner*, April 18, 1924, clipping in Hatfield Papers 1. A. Dmitrieff to Weather Bureau, May 28, 1928; C. C. Clark to Dmitrieff, May 31, 1928, copy; both in WBC (1925–30 Series), box 2810. *New York Times*, April 10 and 12, 1932.

50. Charles F. Rath to Henry C. Wallace, January 18, 1922; Charles Marvin to Rath, February 2, 1922, copy; both in WBC (1912–24 Series), box 2454. Rath to Herbert Hoover, August 6, 1930, WBC (1925–30 Series), box 2810; Rath to Henry A. Wallace, July 7, 1933, WBC (1931–35 Series), box 2998.

51. Edward Henderson, Jr., to Secretary of Agriculture, October 25, 1930, WBC (1925–30 Series), box 2810. For other comments on the role of radio in producing either rain or drought, see Virginia Arledge to Marvin, August 6, 1930; Marvin to Arledge, August 8, 1930, copy; both in WBC (1925–30 Series), box 2810. R. E. Spencer to Earl Godwin, October 9, 1941, WBC (1936–42 Series), box 32; *Scientific American* 151 (October 1934): 217; *Scientific Monthly* 30 (January 1930): 5.

52. William A. Scott to Secretary of Agriculture, January 8, 1906; Willis Moore to Scott, January 11, 1906, copy; both in WBC (1906), file 194, box 1970. Scott had the last word. "I happen to be the man who first succeeded in transmitting wireless telegraph messages & think I know more about electric-

ity than the combined world besides." Scott to Secretary of Agriculture, January 13, 1906, WBC (1906), file 194, box 1970.

53. E. E. Free and Travis Hoke, *Weather* (New York: Robert M. McBride & Co., 1928), p. 325.

## Chapter 7

1. Included in Ella Sibley to Henry A. Wallace, August 1, 1936, WBC (1936–42 Series), box 32.

2. Frederick Collins, "The Art of Rainmaking," *New York Herald* clipping, c. August 1905, in Hatfield Scrapbook 1; *New York Tribune*, December 12, 1891; *Who Was Who in America* (Chicago: Marquis Co., 1969), 4:349; Reuben H. Donnelley, comp., *The Lakeside Annual Directory of the City of Chicago, 1890* (Chicago: Chicago Directory Co., 1890), p. 821.

3. Louis Gathmann, *Rain Produced at Will* (Chicago: n.p., 1891), pp. 13, 38; Specifications, Patent no. 462,795 (November 10, 1891), in U.S. Weather Bureau Library, Suitland, Md.

4. Specifications, Patent no. 462,795 (November 10, 1891); Harrington, "Weather Making," p. 263; Gathmann, *Rain Produced at Will*, p. 11; *Kansas Farmer*, February 10, 1892.

5. *Scientific American Supplement* (November 4, 1893), p. 14881; *New York Times*, June 4, 1917.

6. W. D. C. Worcester, *Rain Making by Concussion and Reduction of Temperature* (Sidney: John Sands, 1901), p. 9; *Scientific American Supplement* (May 7, 1892), p. 13632.

7. Ella Sibley to Henry A. Wallace, August 1, 1936, WBC (1936–42 Series), box 32.

8. S. P. Gresham, Jr., in undated clipping (prior to May 17, 1893), in WBC (1893), file 7192, box 840; *Cleveland Leader*, March 19, 1911; *Cleveland Plain Dealer*, March 7, 1911. Henry Hudson to Secretary of Agriculture James Wilson, March 23, 1911; Hudson to Willis Moore, March 22 and 29, 1911; William Gordon to Moore, March 8 and 20, 1811; Moore to Gordon, March 24, 1911, copy; Moore to Hudson, April 5, 1911, copy; all in WBC (1911), file 1801, box 2344.

9. *DAB*, 22:62–64. Arthur Brisbane to William Howard Taft, August 16, 1910; Charles D. Norton to Leonard Wood, August 18, 1910; Wood to Moore, August 23, 1910; Moore to Wood, August 25, 1910, copy; all in WBC (1910), file 5430, box 2311. Moore to Chief Clerk, Weather Bureau, September 6, 1910, copy, WBC (1910), file 5615, box 2312.

10. Brisbane to Henry C. Wallace, February 14, 1923; Warren G. Harding to Wallace, February 17, 1923, copy; Wallace to Harding, March 2, 1923, copy; Wallace to Brisbane, March 5, 1923, copy; Brisbane to Wallace, March

7, 1923; all in WBC (1912–24 Series), box 2454.

11. Frank C. Snodgrass to Department of Agriculture, July 8, 1918; Snodgrass to President Calvin Coolidge, September 13, 1918; Charles Marvin to Snodgrass, August 16, 1918, copy; all in WBC (1912–24 Series), box 2454. Humphreys, *Rain-Making*, pp. 53–54, 56–57, 56–57, 69–70; "The Case against 'Rain-Making,'" *American Review of Reviews* 65 (January 1922): 105; *Popular Science Monthly* 129 (July 1936): 35.

12. J. W. Gregory, *The Climate of Australasia in Reference to Its Control by the Southern Ocean* (Melbourne: Whitcomb & Tombs, 1904), p. 88; *New York Times*, January 26, 1912; F. Loewe, "Some Forerunners of Rainmaking by Seeding of Clouds," *Weather* 8 (February 1953): 36; Shaw, *The Weather and Its Ways*, p. 221.

13. Middleton, *A History of the Theories of Rain*, pp. 172–74. Aitken's work originally appeared in the *Transactions* of the Royal Society of Edinburgh in 1880 and is conveniently found in Cargill G. Knott, ed., *Collected Scientific Papers of John Aitken, LL.D., F.R.S.* (Cambridge: University Press, 1923), pp. 34–67; Lucian I. Blake, "Can We Make It Rain?" *Science* 18 (November 27, 1891): 296–97; *Scientific American* 67 (December 31, 1892): 420.

14. Shaw, *The Air and Its Ways*, p. 221; S. E. Gladding to Weather Bureau, June 8, 1898, WBC (1898), file 4746, box 1296; *Calgary Herald*, March 11, 1920, clipping, in WBC (1912–24 Series), box 2454. From S. H. Boyle, "Hymn of the Cloud Controller," unidentified clipping, with Edgar H. R. Evans to Charles Marvin, September 1, 1923; see also Evans to Marvin, February 25, 1923; Marvin to Evans, April 18, 1923, copy; all in WBC (1912–24 Series), box 2454.

15. C. W. Jeffries, "Attempts to Induce Rainfall," *Nature* 124 (September 28, 1929): 482; Ward, "How Far Can Man Control His Climate?," p. 14; F. L. Darrow, "The Problem of Making Rain to Order," *Saint Nicholas Magazine* 57 (May 1930): 539; *Bulletin of the American Meteorological Society* 15 (December 1934): 305; unidentified clipping, Hatfield Papers 1; Simon Zuchtmann to Franklin D. Roosevelt, August 28, 1934, WBC (1931–35 Series), box 2998; Raymond R. Gregg to Henry A. Wallace, July 29, 1939, WBC (1936–42 Series), box 32.

16. Andrew Hallum to Department of Agriculture, September 1, 1926, WBC (1925–30 Series), box 2810; Paul Cheney to Secretary of Agriculture, February 24, 1924; Cheney to Charles Marvin, March 16, 1924; Marvin to Cheney, March 4 and 22, 1924, copies; all in WBC (1912–24 Series), box 2454.

17. Byers, "History of Weather Modification," pp. 7–9; Townsend, *Making Rain in America*, p. 40; Loewe, "Some Forerunners," p. 35; B. J. Mason, *Clouds, Rain and Rainmaking* (Cambridge: Cambridge University Press, 1975), pp. 124–25.

18. *New York Times*, August 11, 1930, and April 1, 1931; C. L. Jones to Weather Bureau, April 8, 1931, WBC (1931–35 Series), box 2998; Battan, *Harvesting the Clouds*, p. 64.

## Chapter 8

1. *Fresno Bee*, February 14, 1926.

2. George Bazile to Secretary of Agriculture, April 16, 1935; Bazile to Willis Gregg, April 26, 1935; Gregg to Bazile, April 20, 1935, copy; all in WBC (1931–35 Series), box 2998. John C. Cooper to Secretary of Agriculture, August 2, 1901, WBC (1901), file 7196, box 1552.

3. For Jewett, see printed handbill (n.d.); Solomon W. Jewett to Chief Signa Officer, March 21 and 27, 1874; all in WBC (Misc. Series), 1874, box 322. Garrick Mallery to Jewett, March 25 and 30, 1874, copies, both in Chief Signal Officer, Letters Sent, Misc. Series (September 16, 1873–May 30, 1874), vol. 7.

4. Michael Cahill to Lyman U. Humphrey, May 12, 1890, and March 2, 1891, both in Lyman U. Humphrey MSS, Correspondence Received, Subject File, box 10, Kansas Historical Society, Topeka.

5. Cahill to Humphrey, March 2 and 29, 1891; Cahill to Humphrey, May 12, 1890; all in ibid.

6. Cahill to Humphrey, March 29, October 11, November 8, and December 26, 1891, in ibid.; *Cheyenne Daily Sun*, September 15, 1891; *Oberlin Opinion*, quoted in *Goodland News*, December 10, 1891.

7. "A Card, Continental Rain-Making Company," (Clinton, Mo., 1905); Allen Dorman to Theodore Roosevelt, September 20, 1904; Dorman to "Experiment Stations Irrigation, Drainage Investigations, etc:—Washington," April 3, 1905; all in WBC (1904), file 11125, box 1841.

8. Henry Baker to Governor William J. McConnell, August 29, 1894, from McConnell Papers, Idaho State Archives, published in *Idaho Yesterdays* 6 (Fall 1962): 25; Baker to J. Sterling Morton, September 22, 1894, WBC (Misc. Series), 1894, box 1016.

9. A. W. Tacke to Arthur M. Hyde, December 12, 1929; Tacke to Charles Marvin, September 10, October 21, and November 18, 1929; R. W. Dunlap to Tacke, December 27, 1929, copy; memorandum, J. B. Kincer to Marvin, December 19, 1929; J. B. Wall to Fred W. Pope, January 13, 1930, copy; Wall to Walter J. Bennett, January 14, 1930, copy; Bennett to Marvin, January 15, 1930; all in WBC (1925–30 Series), box 2810. *New York Times*, August 2, 1934.

10. Quoted in "Sykes Sells Sunshine, Say Shrewd Sport Satraps," *Literary Digest* 106 (September 27, 1930): 38; *New York World*, September 15 and 16, 1930.

11. Jimmy McDonald, who for years wrote a column in New York under the pen name Colonel John R. Stingo, says that Sykes was "Director of Ordnance" for a well-known California rainmaker, "Joseph Canfield Hatfield," *New Yorker* 28 (September 13, 1952): 54. Whether this was meant to be Charles Hatfield or not is unclear; certainly, Hatfield was not a concussionist. For the approach to the Department of Agriculture through several politicians, see Semour L. Rau to William Jardine, July 21, 1927, copy; E. E. Free to C. F. Talman, November 9, 1928; Free to G. W. Alexander, November 9, 1928, copy; Talman to Free, November 14, 1928; all in WBC (1912–24 Series), box 2454.

12. Weather Control Bureau, typed statement, "First Issue, July 7, 1929", WBC (1921–25 Series), box 2998.

13. G. A. I. M. Sykes to Herbert Hoover, August 7, 1930; clipping, *Washington Star*, October 23, 1930; both in WBC (1925–30 Series), box 2810. "Sykes Sells Sunshine," p. 42.

14. *New Yorker* 28 (September 20, 1952): 60–61.

15. Ibid., p. 62; *New York Times*, September 10, 1930.

16. *New York Times*, September 10, 1930; *New Yorker* 28 (September 20, 1952): 63–64; "Sykes Sells Sunshine," p. 40; *New York World*, September 16, 1930.

17. *New York World*, September 14, 16, and 17, 1930; *New York Times*, September 14 and 16, 1930; *New Yorker* 28 (September 13, 1952): 65–66.

18. *New York Times*, October 7, 1930. Charles Marvin to A. H. Grebe and Co., August 13, 1930, telegram, copy; "One of Their Former Friends Who Got Stuck" to Weather Bureau, October 15, 1930; Harvey M. Watts to Marvin, October 15, 1930; all in WBC (1925–30 Series), box 2810.

19. Memorandum, Chief Clerk of Weather Bureau, October 23, 1930; Marvin to Chief Clerk, October 25, 1930; both in WBC (1925–30 Series), box 2810.

20. *New York Times*, February 8, 1931. Sykes to Rafael Del Castillo and Co., April 2, 1931; Willam H. Hobbs to Marvin, April 13, 1931; Marvin to Hobbs, April 17, 1931, copy; Elton Marshall to Marvin, April 28 and June 24, 1931; Robert Tomas to Perry A. Fellows, July 1, 1934; all in WBC (1931–35 Series), box 2998.

## Chapter 9

1. *Lethbridge Herald*, July 6, 1920, quoted in *Rainmaking or Irrigation?*, p. 2.

2. Morris Fishbein, *The Medical Follies* (New York: Boni & Liveright, 1925), pp. 14–15; Richard H. Blum, *Deceivers and Deceived* (Springfield, Ill.: Charles C. Thomas, 1972), pp. 13–15.

3. Woolridge, *The Grafters of America*, p. 248; Wagner, "Hatfield the Rainmaker," p. 30.

4. N. Richard Nash, *The Rainmaker* (New York: Random House, 1955), p. 71; Cook, *Remedies and Rackets*, p. 8.

5. Statement of W. F. McDonald, March 14, 1951, copy WBC (1951–54 Series), box 8; William Gilman, *Science: U.S.A.* (New York: Viking Press, 1965), p. 450.

6. J. Eugene Haas, "Sociological Aspects of Weather Modification," in Hess, ed., *Weather and Climate Modification,* pp. 797–800; clipping, *Topeka Journal*, May 11, 1951, Rain and Rainfall Clippings 2; Mari Sandoz, *Old Jules* (Lincoln: University of Nebraska Press, 1962), p. 149.

7. Allen D. Edwards, "The Sociology of Drought," *Rural Sociology* 4 (1939): 200–201; Fishbein, *The Medical Follies*, p. 13.

8. Clipping, *Topeka Journal*, April 5, 1951, Rain and Rainfall Clippings 2.

9. S. C. H. Grent to Franklin D. Roosevelt, August 12, 1934, unidentified clipping in WBC (1931–35 Series), box 2998; *New York Times*, August 26 and 30, and September 1, 1934; *Lubbock Morning Avalanche*, August 29 and September 2, 1934.

10. Louise Pound, "Nebraska Rain Lore and Rain Making," *California Folklore Quarterly* 5 (April 1946): 141.

11. Carey McWilliams, *Southern California Country* (New York: Duell, Sloan & Pearce, 1946), pp. 196, 197, 198, 199. See also Pound, "Nebraska Rain Lore," pp. 129–42.

12. *San Diego Union*, January 6, 1973.

# Index

177